New World Orderings

SINOTHEORY A series edited by
Carlos Rojas and Eileen Cheng-yin Chow

Lisa Rofel and Carlos Rojas, editors

China and the Global South

NEW
WORLD
   ORDERINGS

Duke University Press Durham and London 2022

Designed by Aimee C. Harrison
Typeset in Untitled Serif and Degular by Westchester Publishing
Services

Library of Congress Cataloging-in-Publication Data
Names: Rofel, Lisa, [date] editor. | Rojas, Carlos, [date] editor.
Title: New world orderings : China and the Global South / Lisa Rofel and
Carlos Rojas, editors.
Other titles: Sinotheory.
Description: Durham : Duke University Press, 2023. | Series: Sinotheory |
Includes bibliographical references and index.
Identifiers: LCCN 2022020087 (print)
LCCN 2022020088 (ebook)
ISBN 9781478016373 (hardcover)
ISBN 9781478019015 (paperback)
ISBN 9781478023647 (ebook)
Subjects: LCSH: Geopolitics—China. | China—Foreign relations—21st
century. | China—Foreign economic relations—21st century. | China—
Foreign relations—Southeast Asia. | China—Foreign relations—Africa. |
China—Foreign relations—Latin America. | Southeast Asia—Foreign
relations—China. | Africa—Foreign relations—China. | Latin America—
Foreign relations—China. | BISAC: SOCIAL SCIENCE / Anthropology /
Cultural & Social | HISTORY / Asia / China
Classification: LCC DS779.47 .N49 2023 (print)
LCC DS779.47 (ebook)
DDC 327.51—dc23/eng/20220713
LC record available at https://lccn.loc.gov/2022020087
LC ebook record available at https://lccn.loc.gov/2022020088

Cover art: Gao Rong, *Return*, 2015. Courtesy of the artist and Eli Klein
Gallery © Gao Rong.

CONTENTS

ACKNOWLEDGMENTS

An important goal of any edited volume is to create intellectual community. We would first of all like to thank the authors in this volume for the rigor and depth of their hard work on these essays and the intellectual dialogue they have created here and that we hope readers will feel drawn into. We are also grateful to Zahirah Suhaimi for her careful work on the index. We would like to thank each other for being such wonderful coeditor buddies. We thank Ken Wissoker for his editorial oversight and encouragement for this project. Lisa would like to thank her spouse, Graciela, for her support and love. Carlos would similarly like to thank his spouse, Eileen, for her inspiration and companionship.

Carlos Rojas and Lisa Rofel

INTRODUCTION

Contact, Communication,
Imagination, and Strategies
of Worldmaking

Every society exists by instituting the world as its world, or its world as the world, and by instituting itself as part of the world.

— CORNELIUS CASTORIADIS, *Imaginary Institution of Society*

If we proceed on the assumption that communication is the elementary operation whose reproduction constitutes society, world society is clearly implied in *every* communication, regardless of the specific topic and spatial distance between participants. . . . World society is the occurrence of world in communication.

— NIKLAS LUHMANN, *Theory of Society*

In the twenty-first century, China has dramatically expanded its economic and diplomatic engagement with the Global South, including regions in Southeast Asia, Africa, and Latin America. For instance, although China has long maintained extensive contacts with its Southeast Asian neighbors, many of which have large ethnic Chinese populations, its relationship with the region took a significant turn in 2000 when it proposed a free trade region with the ten nations that compose the Association of Southeast Asian Nations (ASEAN). Signed two years later, the resulting agreement was implemented in several stages, ultimately yielding the world's most populous free-trade region. In fact, in the first quarter of 2020, amid the global disruptions caused by the COVID-19 pandemic, ASEAN temporarily overtook the European Union as China's top trading partner. At the same time, robust investment networks have developed between

China and the various ASEAN nations, and by 2018 China was investing USD 150 billion a year in these countries even as the latter were investing USD 60 billion a year in China.

Although China actively cultivated its relationship with many African nations throughout the latter half of the twentieth century, this relationship entered a new phase in 2000 with the creation of the Forum on China-Africa Cooperation, which established a platform for dialogue and cooperation between China and the nations of Africa. One of China's first major Africa-related initiatives following the establishment of the forum was a 2004 low-interest two-billion-dollar loan to Angola, for which Angola was able to use its oil reserves as collateral. The use of commodities or natural resources as collateral for loans came to be known as the Angola model, and China subsequently made similar arrangements with several other African nations. Thanks in part to these investments and the opportunities they created, trade between China and Africa increased substantially. China surpassed the United States as Africa's largest trade partner in 2009, and by 2016 it had established itself as the continent's largest single investor.

President Jiang Zemin's thirteen-day tour of six South American countries in 2000 symbolically marked the beginning of a new stage in China's relationship with Latin America and the Caribbean. China subsequently expanded its socioeconomic and diplomatic ties with many nations in the region, establishing strategic partnerships with Argentina, Brazil, Chile, Costa Rica, Ecuador, Mexico, Peru, Uruguay, and Venezuela. As a result, in 2018 China's Ministry of Commerce announced that China had become Latin America's second-largest trade partner, after the United States, and that Latin America was also the second-largest recipient of Chinese overseas investment, after Asia.

In 2013 these multiregional engagements were aggregated into a top-level policy initiative, with President Xi Jinping's official launch of the One Belt One Road initiative, which was subsequently given a new official translation as the Belt and Road Initiative. The initiative focuses on large-scale loan-based infrastructure investment in nearly seventy countries connected to China via a combination of overland and maritime routes (i.e., the overland Silk Road Economic Belt and the Maritime Silk Road). Given that many of these countries are located in the Global South, the Belt and Road Initiative has therefore become the public face of contemporary China's engagement with the region.

Although China's recent Global South initiatives have received considerable attention around the world, there have nevertheless been sharp disagreements over whether these initiatives are inherently exploitative or benevolent—or, as one commentator pithily put it, over whether China is acting as "monster or messiah" (Sun 2014). The resulting debate, in turn, overlaps with broader discussions of whether the twenty-first century will be viewed as the Chinese century—the same way that the twentieth century is frequently described as the American century and the nineteenth was dubbed the British imperial century—and whether the resulting power shift signals the emergence of a "new world order."

The first prominent usage of a version of the phrase *new world order* was by Woodrow Wilson after World War I, when he predicted the end of large-scale global conflict and a prioritization of collective security within the international community. The phrase was subsequently used to describe the geopolitical realignment that followed World War II, and was also invoked by both Mikhail Gorbachev and George H. W. Bush at the end of the Cold War. In almost every instance, these invocations of a new world order combined an emphasis on reciprocal relationships between sovereign nation-states, on one hand, with an allusion to how this would facilitate the growth of global capitalism, on the other. Many discussions of China's engagement with the Global South engage with different facets of this earlier new world order discourse. For instance, the perception that China is acting benevolently in providing developing nations with much-needed funding (i.e., the "messiah" thesis) views China as following either the liberal new world order model, or its own mid-twentieth-century model centered around cultivating relationships with nations in the Global South in order to promote a network of Non-Aligned third world nations that were nominally outside of the Cold War struggle between capitalist and socialist nations. Alternatively, the perception that China is acting rapaciously in using developing nations to guarantee its own continued access to valuable resources and profitable markets (i.e., the "monster" thesis) may be viewed as a twist on the underlying logic of the earlier new world order discourses, wherein the United States' advocacy of reciprocal relationships between autonomous nation-states was actually intended to maximize its ability to profit from the global economy and wherein America's post–Cold War insistence on neoliberal deregulation of national development projects, thus ending the Bretton Woods agreements, is intended to find new ways to maximize its ability to profit.

Although both the "monster" and the "messiah" theses offer some explanatory value, they are limited by their reliance on a set of dichotomous views of geopolitics based on a twentieth-century Cold War logic and the new world order discourse with which it was inextricably intertwined. Moreover,

3

both of these lines of analysis prioritize economic and diplomatic considerations over other disciplinary methodologies that might offer different perspectives on the transregional phenomena in question, and on the assumptions about the nature of worlds and processes of worldmaking on which they are grounded. Accordingly, rather than focusing on whether China's current engagement with the Global South represents an extension of the nation's midcentury attempts to provide an alternative to the US-led post–World War II new world order or is an embrace of a post–Cold War neoliberal world order, we instead emphasize the processes of worldmaking that this engagement is helping to bring about.

It is important to note that *Global South* does not refer to a fixed geographic configuration, but rather one that is at once contextually situated and collectively imagined. Similar to its predecessor, *the third world*, the label *Global South* highlights the post–Cold War geopolitical and economic relations of globally contested inequalities, along with the historical and cultural processes that shape these inequalities. The terms *Global North* and *Global South* arose out of the Brandt Commission's (named after its first chair, the former German chancellor Willy Brandt) report, *North-South: A Programme for Survival*. Reviewing international development issues in the midst of neoliberal worlding processes, the commission found that developing countries were economically dependent on rich countries, which dominate the international rules of trade and finance, and further, that the former are located largely in the Southern Hemisphere while the latter can be found in the Northern Hemisphere (Bullard 2012).

Each of the regions corresponding to what we now refer to as the Global South has a much longer history, and we are specifically interested in how the emergence of the term coincides roughly with a new set of worlding processes. China, in a modern and contemporary context, has functioned as a crucial fulcrum between the Global South and the Global North. It has long cultivated a set of strategic alliances with nations considered to be in the Global South, even as more recently its own economic heft and approach to international relations has increasingly come to resemble those of some nations typically viewed as part of the Global North. The concept of the Global South, accordingly, underscores the formative transregional relations of domination and resistance, in contradistinction to the nation-state focus of modernization ideologies. As we argue here, many transregional relations of entanglement in the Global South—social, economic, and cultural—occur at a level below that of formal political relations.

The philosopher Cornelius Castoriadis theorizes the central role of the creative imagination in constructing worlds and strengthening their capacity for transformation. Castoriadis's approach developed out of his participation in the French Marxist collective Socialisme ou Barbarie and was informed by his later critique of Marxist thought, on one hand, and by his reevaluation of the human capacity for transformation that he found to be occluded in the Western philosophical tradition, on the other. Castoriadis draws from Marxism a critique of the naturalization of given world orders and an emphasis on historical transformations of them, but he critiques Marxism for its insufficient attention to open-ended and indeterminate creativity—or what he terms self-creation. In his view, the philosophical tradition has had a similar tendency to reduce "being" to "determinacy." He argues that the imaginary element, or self-creation, is the basis of the human condition. For Castoriadis, self-creation emerges in the sociohistorical (what he called nomos) and is manifest in social institutions, culture, and meaning. Castoriadis thus emphasizes both the omnipresence of the creative imagination—its ontology—and the heterogeneity of its modes of enactment. He stressed that the creative imagination emerges ex nihilo, meaning it is not determined by external institutions or powers, be they theological ideas of the divine or the naturalization of social power.

If the social imaginary and hence sociohistorical institutions emerge from self-creation, they also produce an intercultural articulation of the world as a shared horizon. Castoriadis thus imagines the world as both a creative endeavor and as a given context to be encountered. Every society, Castoriadis argues, "develops an image of . . . the universe in which it lives, attempting in every instance to make of it a signifying whole." In this signifying whole, "a place has to be made not only for the natural objects and beings important for the life of the collectivity, but also for the collectivity itself, establishing, finally, a certain 'world-order'" (Castoriadis 1987, 149). Given the creative imagination's ability to produce change, this encounter with a world horizon leads to the possibility of transformed worlds.

The sociologist Niklas Luhmann, meanwhile, similarly emphasizes processes of worldmaking in his description of a transition from a premodern "thing-centered concept of the world," in which communities were relatively autonomous from one another and communication became more difficult as the distance between different communities increased, to a modern world oriented around not things but social relationships, and characterized by a "background indeterminacy ('unmarked space') that allows objects to appear and subjects to act" (Luhmann 2012, 84–85). Luhmann argues that a key factor enabling this transition from a premodern to a modern "world order" was the discovery of the globe "as a closed sphere of meaningful communication" (2012, 85). Just as Benedict Anderson famously contends that the development of print capitalism helped people imagine their position within geographically vast and socially heterogeneous nations (Anderson 2016), Luhmann similarly argues that modern technological developments have effectively linked the globe into a single communicative network, thereby allowing people to imagine their position within a unified "world society." For Luhmann, accordingly, communication is "the elementary operation whose reproduction constitutes society," and by extension "world society is clearly implied in *every* communication, regardless of the specific topic and spatial distance between participants" (Luhmann 2012, 86).

One important implication of Luhmann's emphasis on communication as the grounding of modern world society is that communication generates difference even as it simultaneously provides a shared ground that transcends difference—or, as Luhmann succinctly puts it, "Communication is the difference that makes no difference in the system." This insight applies, in particular, to the various subsystems of which society is composed: "For all subsystems of society, boundaries of communication (as opposed to non-communication) constitute the external boundaries of society. In this, and only in this, do these systems coincide. . . . [Insofar] as they communicate, all subsystems participate in society. Insofar as they communicate in different ways, they differ" (Luhmann 2012, 86). Communication, here, is being used not in the sense of a Habermasian idealized plane of mutual intelligibility (Habermas 1984, 1985), but rather what might be viewed as a more Derridean sense, in which communication is grounded in the necessary possibility of miscommunication (Derrida 1978). At the same time, however, it is precisely the resulting transcommunicative space—which includes not only conventional communication but also the inevitable possibility of miscommunication—that yields a vision of a collective imaginary that is ultimately more consonant with a Habermasian vision of communicative action and collective worldmaking than with a conventional Luhmannian understanding of systems theory.

The worldmaking processes underlying contemporary China's engagement with the Global South may be viewed within the context of three overlapping historical horizons. First, despite the popular perception of premodern China as having been insular and isolated from the rest of the world, the reality is that China has a long tradition of actively engaging with other regions, including regions in what is now called the Global South. This longer history of transregional and transnational contacts, in turn, encouraged the processes of imaginative self-creation that Castoriadis describes. Second, contemporary China's engagement with the Global South may also be viewed within the more specific context of the nation's twentieth-century efforts to cultivate relationships with other developing nations in the name of socialist internationalism. Not only was socialist internationalism a politically novel concept in its own right but it also emerged at a moment when, as Luhmann argues, people's ability to imagine the world itself as a single, unified entity was undergoing a qualitative change. Third, the developments that have unfolded since the beginning of the twenty-first century appear to constitute a new phase in China's engagement with the Global South, which may in turn mark the emergence of a new global configuration, and a corresponding logic of global engagement, that diverges from the twentieth century's Cold War and post–Cold War new world order models.

Even as contemporary China's engagements with the Global South play out against visions of a world society and world order that have their roots in earlier periods, these engagements are simultaneously enabling a myriad of new processes of imaginative worldmaking. These worldmaking processes are inspired by—and intervene with—existing realities, while relying on a variety of ways of understanding and imagining sociocultural relations that underlie and are imbricated in shifting geopolitical orders and the attendant transnational circulations of people, commodities, and cultures. The contemporary engagements between China and the Global South, in other words, reflect a dialectic of unified and heterogeneous visions of the world, insofar as they implicitly rely on a notion of a singular world while enabling a multitude of disparate, and potentially divergent, processes of imaginative worldmaking. In political terms, meanwhile, this dialectic of unified and heterogeneous worlds is reflected in the concept of a new world order, which is explicitly predicated on a vision of a singular world even as the actual processes of worldmaking that unfold in its shadow are similarly multiple and heterogeneous.

Rather than ask whether China's actions are inherently benevolent or exploitative, we instead borrow Laura Doyle's (2014) concept of interimperiality to emphasize the ongoing, multidirectional maneuvers and struggles among competing hegemonic processes. Doyle underscores how people often inhabit spaces where different worlds become mutually entangled, and how people living in these interstices engage and produce the hybridities of interimperial worlds. More generally, we are interested in the processual nature of China's relationship with the Global South, whereby China relies on a wide array of processes to consolidate and extend its influence. As Antonio Gramsci has observed, power needs to be constantly reasserted through hegemonies of rule that pull people into believing what power asserts about itself (Gramsci 1972).

Beyond this emphasis on how communication and imaginative capacities generate a dialectic of commonality and difference, we also attend to how existing processes of worldmaking may foreclose the emergence of alternative worldmaking processes. For instance, Mei Zhan, in her study of the worlding of traditional Chinese medicine (TCM), theorizes the distinction between a process of worlding or worldmaking, with its ruptures and displacements, and of globalism, with its assumption of totality. Zhan illustrates how TCM has been transformed into Western medicine's Other, thereby marginalizing other interpretations of Chinese medicine that avoid such a binary (Zhan 2009). Similarly, we consider how contemporary China's engagement with the Global South not only has the potential to make some novel worlds thinkable but may also simultaneously render other worlding processes nearly impossible to imagine. We place as much emphasis on worldmaking from below as from the state, focusing on what Mary Pratt has called "contact zones"—which is to say, sites of sociocultural transformation where agents negotiate engagements across difference (Pratt 1992).

Worldmaking, in short, is a dynamic process, and the convergence of and ongoing negotiation over various life projects shapes the possible outcomes of worldmaking processes. Our approach does not discount geopolitical considerations, but rather emphasizes the centrality of history, culture, and imaginative processes. Even as powers that expand globally and build new worlds seek wealth and power, these economic and political desires are intricately intertwined with imaginative visions. Expansionist economic and political practices, such as transnational capitalism, are thus contingent—and frequently unstable—assemblages of heterogeneous visions of accumulation, inequality, and personhood that are continually being reformulated (Rofel and Yanagisako 2019).

World Histories

Worldmaking processes in relation to what we now refer to as the Global South long predate the use of the term itself and the geopolitical configurations that it references. Our focus in this volume involves how the emergence of the designation of *Global South* and its lived, imaginative experiences coincide roughly with a new set of transregional political and economic configurations in which China has become an increasingly visible presence. A brief overview of these earlier prehistories will help contextualize the contemporary phenomena we examine here.

The multifarious processes of worldmaking that are enabled by China's contemporary engagement with the Global South build on a long tradition of early processes of worldmaking and corresponding concepts of worlds. In early China, for instance, the closest equivalent to the modern concept of *world* (*shijie* in modern Chinese) was *tianxia*, which literally means "all under heaven." Tianxia foregrounds some of the paradoxes that are embedded within the contemporary concept of the world. Just as the modern concept of world is nominally global in its coverage but in fact is delimited by a narrower set of assumptions that have shaped its development, tianxia is similarly both a paradigmatic figure of universality while at the same time underscoring its own limits. Embedded within a cosmological framework that came to be identified with Confucianism, tianxia theoretically encompassed "*all* under heaven," though in practice it only included those populations who accepted an understanding of the sociopolitical world that was grounded in sociopolitical values associated with China (or, in Chinese, with Zhongguo, which could be translated literally as "Central Kingdom") (Wang, Ban 2017). Unlike the modern system of nation-states, however, this traditional concept of tianxia did not imply a geographically bounded entity. Instead, it was conceived as an outwardly radiating sphere of influence, into which outsiders could become incorporated so long as they embraced Chinese civilizational assumptions and values.

In the late nineteenth and early twentieth centuries, this tianxia paradigm was largely replaced by that of the modern nation-state system, as China's imperial project was overshadowed by Europe's own. While China had long been connected to Europe through trade, in the nineteenth century it was aggressively pulled into a network of Western political ideologies and corresponding political realities, as well as an industrial commodity chain producing mainly textile goods for the European metropoles. European colonialism also resulted in the establishment of foreign communities within China that included British, French, Germans, Americans, Russians, Jews, and non-Chinese Asians. These developments decentered China's own imperial realms and introduced Western-inflected ideas about sovereignty, nationalism, development, progress, and political governance, as well as anti-imperialism, anarchism, and socialism.

Following its mid-twentieth-century socialist revolution, China joined the world of international socialism. In particular, under Mao Zedong China strategically shifted its focus from contacts with what was known as the first world, and instead sought to develop its influence with nations located in the second and third worlds—including not only the Soviet Union and other socialist states, but also an array of developing nations, many of which had until recently been under Western imperial control. Most notably, China played a major role in a landmark 1955 conference held in Bandung, Indonesia, which included representatives from twenty-nine Asian and African countries that collectively accounted for more than half of the world's population. The Bandung Conference played a pivotal role in encouraging alliances between nations in Africa and Asia, just as international socialism sought to transcend national boundaries with a shared political vision.

Mao's death in 1976 marked the official end of the Cultural Revolution (1966–76), and of the Mao era. In 1978 Mao's successor Deng Xiaoping launched the Reform and Opening Up campaign, which sought to stimulate the nation's economic development by transitioning from a socialist planned economy to a hybrid system that was dubbed "socialism with Chinese characteristics." The resulting postsocialist period can be divided into two phases. In the first, beginning in the late 1970s, China focused on attracting foreign direct investment and helped make the nation the proverbial workshop of the world, while during the second phase, beginning in the late 1990s, the nation shifted its attention to securing natural resources necessary for continued economic development. Both phases resulted from China's attempts to reassess its relationship to a socialist project following Mao's death and the subsequent collapse of the Eastern Bloc in 1989 and the dissolution of the Soviet Union in 1991. China's response to these developments was to adopt a hybrid capitalist-socialist economic structure and aggressively pursue economic development, thereby requiring that it enter the global capitalist economy.

Loosely paralleling (but also partially inverting) the Chinese concept of tianxia is the Western concept of empire. In what we might call the era of empires, empires were built on the logic of an expansionist, hierarchical, and incorporative structure that enables a metropole to exercise power over the periphery—a periphery of largely contiguous territories. Empires use presumptions of civilizational superiority to justify their rule, while simultaneously positing unequal distinctions among their imperial subjects to justify differential governing strategies. Empires are established through military conquest, but they are maintained through a broad range of different mechanisms—including economic, bureaucratic, ideological, and socio-cultural processes. Empires tended to share an imagined vision of political rule as a pyramid, with imperial power residing in the apex, radiating down the hierarchy and outward across the territories they worked to incorporate. Imperial borders tended to be indeterminate, such that world "regions" as we have come to know them were not precisely delineated until the last centuries of empire building, when European powers vied for control with one another in an attempt to consolidate disparate geographic regions into a singular world.

Starting roughly in the eighteenth century, colonial strategies of expansion and rule were enhanced by new technologies that enabled domination of more distant lands, located largely in what we now call the Global South, and informed by emerging racial ideologies invoked to manage the production of unequal difference. Racialized distinctions were brought to bear in distinguishing between the metropole and the colonies, as well as to reconfigure local social relations, often hardening differences among peoples living in the same location.

Growing resistance to imperial rule within empires, along with conflict among empires, eventually led to the new political imagination of nationalism. Nationalism is built on the idea of sovereignty and self-rule over a clearly delineated territory. Within each bounded space, nationalism dreams of equality, along with a shared common culture among its population (Anderson 2016). At the same time, nation-states exclude those who are deemed not to fit into their "national culture." Nation-states have incorporated the racialized hierarchies of the previous era, and while there is formal international recognition that all nation-states are equal, earlier colonial powers never ceded their economic dominance over their former colonies. These powers insisted that acceptance of the political sovereignty of these new states be predicated on maintaining their hold on economic power, thus laying the basis for today's transregional inequalities, what now we call neocolonialism or dependency theory and what Ann Stoler calls "imperial debris" (Stoler 2008). At the same time, new imperial powers, especially the United States, grappled with the contradictions of being a sovereign nation-state ruling indirectly over regions of the world that claim political sovereignty of their own.

11

These ongoing transnational relations of inequality informed the world-making processes of the Cold War, in which countries were roughly grouped into first, second, and third worlds. The first world designated the capitalist nations under the orbit of the United States, the second world referred to the Soviet Union and its socialist allies, while the third world encompassed postcolonial nations that were not aligned with either camp. These divisions by no means implied equality within each "world," but rather suggested different imaginations about how worlds should be formed.

A recent point of intersection of these two historical worlding processes (namely, ones grounded on concepts of tianxia and empire, respectively) can be observed in the moment when Xi Jinping—in his first official trip out of Beijing as the newly appointed leader of the Communist Party—visited the southern Chinese city of Shenzhen in December 2012, clearly inviting comparisons with the celebrated Southern Tour (nanxun) that his predecessor Deng Xiaoping had made almost exactly twenty years earlier. In January and February 1992, in the last major act of his own political career, Deng had traveled to the southern Chinese cities of Shanghai, Zhuhai, Shenzhen, and Guangzhou in an attempt to shore up support for the economic reforms he promoted in his Reform and Opening Up campaign. Deng's 1992 Southern Tour, in turn, mirrored yet another trip that Deng himself had undertaken fourteen years earlier, at the very beginning of his term as China's highest leader. At that time, in November 1978, Deng had traveled to Bangkok, Kuala Lumpur, and Singapore to strengthen China's ties with these Southeast Asian cities. A month after returning to Beijing, Deng was anointed China's paramount leader, and proceeded to launch the Reform and Opening Up campaign that would define China's economic and political trajectory in the post-Mao period.

On the surface, Xi Jinping's 2012 and Deng Xiaoping's 1992 trips might appear to be quite different from Deng's 1978 trip. After all, the 1992 and 2012 trips were to southern China, while Deng's was to Southeast Asia. Moreover, the 1992 and 2012 trips were to some of contemporary China's most prosperous and rapidly developing metropolises, while two of the three cities Deng visited in 1978 were located in so-called third world nations. At the same time, however, the symbolic parallels between these three trips (each of which occurred at a pivotal moment in the leader's political career) point to underlying parallels among the southern regions themselves. In particular, the extraordinary wealth and prosperity of the southern Chinese cities in question derive in large part from their ability to capitalize on China's rich network of international contacts—including its contacts with Southeast Asia. Conversely, it is no coincidence that the three nations Deng Xiaoping visited in 1978 all had large ethnically Chinese communities that played an important role in the nations' economies. Collectively, Deng's and Xi's visits to southern China and Southeast Asia reflect the historical significance of economic and cultural contacts between southern China and Southeast Asia, together with the two leaders' expectations that China's future development would be predicated on a continued pattern of international exchange with this broader region.

Since the mid-1980s, China's government has shifted to a socioeconomic structure featuring a market economy, systematic privatization, and the end of social welfare—all of which have contributed to the emergence of a new bourgeois consumer culture and have substantially increased the nation's social inequality. With these initiatives, China has abandoned the objective of world revolution, and instead has begun promoting a stable international environment that would facilitate its own economic development (Z. Chen 2008; Hao, Wei, and Dittmer 2009). China joined the World Trade Organization in December 2001, and by the following year it had surpassed the United States as the most favored destination for foreign direct investment. Hong Kong and Taiwan are currently the nation's largest investors, with Japan and the United States not far behind. China, in turn, has invested heavily in Latin America, Africa, the Middle East, and Asia, while at the same time becoming the largest single holder of US government debt. It has been active in BRICS (a group consisting of the world's five major emerging national economies), has contributed to the development of the Asian Infrastructure Investment Bank (AIIB), and in 2013 it launched the ambitious Belt and Road Initiative to strengthen commercial and economic ties with other Eurasian nations. In the process, China is not only reinventing itself but is also reshaping the world.

These long durée worldmaking histories continue to motivate China's current projects of going out into the world, even as they are revised to distance the nation from previous European, American, and Soviet colonial projects. Historical legacies of civilizational centrality, colonial subordination, nationalist resistance, and socialist internationalism and nonaligned movements continue to shape practices, memories, and narratives. As a result, China and its interlocutors in the Global South continuously invoke, assess, debate, and revise the import of these histories, such that these historical legacies and their revisionist interpretations help shape China's transnational capitalist activities and its ideological portrayal of them.

Contemporary China's engagement with the Global South, accordingly, builds on these earlier traditions of transregional engagement, together with their corresponding concepts of the world and attendant processes of worldmaking. But this raises the question of whether China is displacing the United States as the linchpin of the global economy, or is it simply adapting an existing world order for its own purposes? This question, of course, rehearses the "monster or messiah" debate, which itself is really simply a dispute over whether China is trying to position itself as an exploitative capitalist superpower (on the model of twentieth-century America) or as a benevolent ally of developing, non-allied nations (on the model of mid-twentieth-century China). We suggest that both of these dichotomous visions are overly reductive, and that in order to appreciate the implications of contemporary China's engagement with the Global South, it is not sufficient to ask whether these contemporary engagements are a direct extension of the twentieth-century new world order model (and its discontents) or mark the emergence of a *new* "new world order." Instead, it is important to view these engagements as part of a multiple, heterogeneous, and ongoing process of "new world orderings."

Organization

In the 1980s two influential slogans used to describe contemporary China's attempts to reposition itself on the world stage alluded to the nation's attempts to zouxiang shijie and to yu shijie tonggui. The first phrase means "to enter the world," but could be translated more literally as "to walk or march into the world," while the second means "to match up with the world," but could be translated more literally as "to match the gauge of the world's tracks." While the first slogan offers an inverse version of the paradox inherent in the Chinese concept of tianxia discussed earlier, in that it relies on a concept of shijie that designates both a universal ideal and a delimited sociopolitical space from which China had been structurally excluded, the second instead gestures more specifically to the role of state-driven initiatives in facilitating these same processes of worldbuilding and political realignment.

In particular, the latter reference is to a famous description in Sima Qian's first-century BCE historiographic work *Records of the Historian* (Shiji), of how the First Emperor of the Qin dynasty, after uniting the various Warring States into a single imperial polity in 221 BCE, proceeded to standardize the newly unified empire's units of measurement, its writing system, and even the width of its cart and carriage axles—so that the ruts in the road produced by the cartwheels would be of uniform width (che tonggui). Although

Sima Qian's description of the First Emperor's accomplishments more than a century earlier should be taken with a grain of salt, it is nevertheless worth noting that he suggests the emperor believed such seemingly minor details as carriage axles and wheel ruts could contribute to the consolidation of a new "world" (tianxia).

These concerns with the relationship between broad understandings of the world and the details involved in attendant processes of governance and representation are the focus of Part I of this volume, which examines some of the ways the Chinese state has sought to reconfigure the nation's position in the world in the contemporary period, as well as the narratives and discourses that underlie these geopolitical relations. In the first two chapters, Nicolai Volland and Luciano Bolinaga analyze modern and contemporary China's relationship with Africa and Latin America, with Volland focusing on China's cultural diplomacy with the Africa region during the post-Bandung period, and particularly during the period following the Sino-Soviet split in the late 1950s, and Bolinaga examining the transition, in Latin America, from the so-called Washington Consensus of the 1980s, to the new Beijing Consensus in the twenty-first century. Although both of these chapters focus primarily on state-level diplomatic and economic initiatives, their primary interest is not so much on the strictly political or financial implications of these initiatives, but rather the gaps and disjunctions between the perspectives promoted by these policies, on one hand, and the ways in which these policies actually play out in reality, on the other.

Next, Derek Sheridan argues that the question of whether or not China's actions are imperialistic necessarily relies on a set of state-centric historical analogies, and suggests that we can derive a more nuanced understanding of the implications of contemporary Chinese capital and migration (including but not encompassed by state agendas) if we consider a set of historical precedents that extend beyond European imperialism. Finally, Ng Kim Chew suggests that the literary scholar Pascale Casanova's model of world literature as a "world republic of letters" can be strategically redeployed to help explain the distinctiveness of Southeast Asian Sinophone literature, or what he calls a "World Republic of Southern Letters."

One result of contemporary China's investment in the Global South is a rapidly growing circulation of people and commodities between the regions in question. Many of these individuals are laborers and merchants, and the complex relationships they establish in their adopted communities (either in China or in countries throughout the Global South) constitute an important, and often overlooked, dimension of the larger investment and trade initiatives of which they are a critical component. Part II, accordingly, explores how individuals positioned at different points of contact between the Chinese economy and those of various nations in Africa and Latin America understand their relationship to these local and global economies.

The first two chapters in Part II consider issues relating to communities of West Africans living and working in Guangzhou. First, T. Tu Huynh looks at a community of Africans engaged in small-scale trading in Guangzhou. Arguing that this small-scale trading can be viewed as a form of "globalization from below," Huynh examines the gendered connotations of this practice in Nigeria and other African countries, and how those connotations are transformed in immigrant communities in southern China, where African men are much more highly represented among the small-scale traders. Huynh's primary focus, however, is on the women, and specifically on how they imagine themselves as global entrepreneurs within the context of constantly shifting markets. Next, Nellie Chu turns to a community of West African and South Korean church leaders attempting to establish Christian communities in Guangzhou, focusing on a set of intertwined evangelical and entrepreneurial discourses and activities. In particular, Chu combines ethnographic observation with an analysis of actual sermons to reflect on how these religious figures promote a prosperity gospel that has the effect of helping mask growing socioeconomic uncertainties and inequalities.

The following two chapters focus on China's relationship not with Africa, but rather with Latin America. First, Rachel Cypher and Lisa Rofel examine China's recent investments in Argentina's soybean economy, focusing on the ways in which a set of local narratives about China and the Chinese are generated and circulate. Next, Andrea Bachner considers several literary and cinematic works that address the Chinese presence in Argentina, focusing on how these cultural representations strategically place under erasure the increasingly precarious economic position Argentina and other Latin American nations find themselves in vis-à-vis China.

In his books *Routes* (1997) and *Returns* (2013), the anthropologist James Clifford famously puns on the English terms *routes* and *roots* to reflect on the relationship between migrational trajectories (routes) and the sites of belonging (roots) with which they are intricately intertwined. In particular, Clifford emphasizes the degree to which migration not merely functions as a movement away from a space of the home and homeland but also has the potential to permit migrants to establish new sites of belonging within the very routes they traverse and the foreign regions where they end up. It is precisely this sort of dialectics of displacement and belonging that is the focus of Part III, which examines patterns of migration between China and the Global South, with particular attention to corresponding issues of gender, religion, and culture.

First, Mingwei Huang considers Chinese in Johannesburg, the home of the oldest and largest overseas Chinese community in Africa. To be more precise, Huang examines the relationship between two different Johannesburg Chinatowns—an older one, the history of which is closely tied with the earlier wave of Chinese immigrant labor that helped make Johannesburg's current prosperity possible in the first place, and a much newer one that was established in 2013 in a different part of the city. Huang reflects on how a newer wave of Chinese immigrants to the city actively engage in a process of worldmaking grounded in a set of intertwined beliefs about race and development—a process that Huang also calls globalization from below. In the next chapter Yulin Lee turns from Africa to Southeast Asia, and specifically representations of Chinese migrants in Myanmar in the cinema of the Myanmar-born director Midi Z. Although Midi Z subsequently immigrated to Taiwan and developed a cinematic technique strongly influenced by Taiwan New Cinema, the focus of his films nevertheless is primarily on ethnically Chinese communities from his homeland of Myanmar, many of whom enter into transnational migratory circuits through other regions of Southeast Asia. A theme that runs through Lee's analysis involves a tension, on the part of these displaced migrant laborers, between a desire to return to Myanmar, on one hand, and a nostalgic yearning for a more abstract Chinese homeland, on the other.

The final two chapters examine how literature and literary representations can be used to affirm local identities and to reinforce connections between different communities. First, Carlos Rojas uses a close reading of a short story by the ethnically Malaysian Chinese author and scholar Ng Kim Chew to reflect on a set of intertwined discourses of homeland and diaspora as they pertain to Chinese communities in Southeast Asia while also considering the symbolic and affective significance of the circulation of Chinese-language texts (and of Chinese characters themselves) within a Southeast Asian diasporic space. Finally, Shuang Shen then looks at several case studies from the Cold War period to help illustrate some of the processes that led to the development of Ng's Republic of Southern Chinese Letters. More specifically, Shen considers the writings of Zeng Shengti, who was born in

Guangdong, China, but subsequently immigrated to Singapore in the 1920s, and Wei Beihua, an ethnically Chinese author from Malaya (now Malaysia). Both Zeng and Wei visited Tagore in India, and subsequently wrote extensively about literary, cultural, and political relations between India, China, Singapore, Malaysia, and other regions in Southeast Asia.

In sum, in this volume we attempt to disrupt facile assumptions about China's rising global influence. Instead, our emphasis on multiple histories, cultural representations, and ethnographic narratives of complex negotiations underscores a process by which worlds are continually being made and remade. At the same time, however, we are equally committed to marking the inequalities and disparities that China's engagement with the Global South may produce, and with which peoples throughout the Global South will be forced to engage.

Notes

Epigraphs: Cornelius Castoriadis, *Imaginary Institution of Society*, 186; Niklas Luhmann, *Theory of Society*, 1:86–87.

GEOPOLITICS AND DISCOURSE

Part I

TURNING
THE TABLES ON THE
GLOBAL NORTH

China, Afro-Asia, and Cold War
Cultural Diplomacy

Thousands of ships sail from Shanghai's port,
Across the oceans to every continent.
Standing on the docks we gaze afar,
anti-imperialist flames rage everywhere.
The world people's power is gaining momentum,
Supporting each other, we're mighty and strong.

—On the Docks

After a fierce struggle against American spies and saboteurs, the workers in *Haigang* (On the docks) prevail in their mission: to load a ship with seed grains bound for Africa amid an approaching typhoon. The plot of *On the Docks*, one of the revolutionary model operas (*yangbanxi*) of the Cultural Revolution (1966–76), interweaves three themes: the triumph of man over nature, class struggle, and, most importantly, international solidarity and world revolution. At the opera's critical juncture, the dock workers have to decide between prioritizing either a shipload of glass fiber bound for Northern Europe, or an aid shipment of grain for an unnamed, newly independent nation in Africa. Unsurprisingly, it is South-South solidarity that wins the day.

The approved script of *On the Docks* was published in 1972, at the height of the Cultural Revolution. The year 1972 also marked the climax of public pronouncements celebrating socialist China's solidarity with Africa. The Tanzam railway project, otherwise known as the Great Uhuru (Freedom) Railway, had broken ground in 1970, and by the time of its completion five years later would become the most prestigious Chinese foray into the Afro-Asian world (Monson 2009, 35–70; see also Derek Sheridan, this volume). The ubiquitous propaganda surrounding both *On the Docks* and the railway's groundbreaking ceremonies, however, glossed over mounting troubles. The People's Republic of China (PRC) could ill afford many more capital-intensive offshore investment projects, and the shift in the Cold War to the Southern Hemisphere brought the PRC into direct competition with US and Soviet initiatives in Africa and Asia. As Odd Arne Westad (2005, 4) has argued, the third world turned center stage once the Cold War went global: "The United States and the Soviet Union were driven to intervene in the Third World by the ideologies inherent in their politics." Carrying their conflict to the South, they aimed "to change the world in order to prove the universal applicability of their ideologies." Mao Zedong's China thus faced political and economic challenges as it ventured abroad. The nation's cultural offensive in the postcolonial South had run into trouble as well. Since the late 1950s, the PRC had made extensive cultural overtures to the Afro-Asian world, promoting South-South solidarity with the goal of exporting Mao's brand of world revolution. Cultural diplomacy was a crucial channel to promote the PRC's broader goals in the Afro-Asian world.

The PRC discovered the political potential of the postcolonial South at the Bandung Conference in 1955, but it was not until the Sino-Soviet break of 1960 that China embarked on a full-fledged diplomatic offensive to align itself with the Afro-Asian world, promoting an alternative to the existing Cold War world order. In a doubly insurrectionist move, the PRC thus sought to turn the tables on both the capitalist West and the Moscow-dominated socialist world. The alliance of the revolutionary South was intended to counter what Mao saw as US imperialism and Soviet revisionism (after 1968 labeled "socialist imperialism"), two predatory ideologies deemed structurally analogous that aimed to subdue the peoples of Asia, Africa, and Latin America. Culture was a key means to promote this counterhegemonic agenda. Student exchanges, writers' meetings, and the cross-translation of literary works from the nations of the Afro-Asian world served to build a shared anti-imperialist consciousness that would unite the peoples of the Global South. Against American weapons and Soviet economic aid, the PRC thus proposed culture as a weapon of the weak, to win over the hearts and minds of the peoples of the South, in a global guerilla war of words.

Its intense engagement with the postcolonial world notwithstanding, China has rarely figured in postcolonial studies (Barlow 1993). As Shu-mei

Shih (2001, 30–40) has argued, the fragmented and layered nature of China's encounter with imperialism has resulted in modes of domination that were structurally dissimilar (if no less intense or traumatic) from the experiences in other parts of the South. These challenges have also shaped the discursive landscape, effectively masking vectors of comparison and productive points of contact. Wedged uncomfortably between the capitalist and neo-imperialist North and the recently decolonized South, China posed an obvious challenge to the binary conceptions of global power on which postcolonial theory was built. More recently, the PRC has itself been accused of harboring neo-imperialist motives, and Chinese large-scale investments around the world—and especially in Africa—have further obfuscated the boundaries defining the intellectual topography of postcolonial studies.[1] China's discursive eclipse hence lays bare structural inconsistences and blind spots in the efforts to map the terrain of the postcolonial world. Conversely, it also marks China as an important test case for existing theoretical models. The PRC's self-conscious attempts to define its own position vis-à-vis the South, as well as its position *within* the South *vis-à-vis* the North, provide multiple moments of interpretive intervention.

One such moment of contact and connections between revolutionary China and the Global South occurred in the 1960s when the PRC, driven by geopolitical as much as ideological reasons, intensified its engagement in Asia, Africa, and, to an extent, Latin America. After Bandung, the PRC became, in Shu-mei Shih's (2016, 145) words, "the de facto leader of the Third World," assuming a pivotal position in the "global sixties." China supplied some economic assistance. More importantly, it offered an insurrectionist ideology emphasizing both continuous revolution—a model of politics that, as Fabio Lanza (2017) has shown, appealed equally to postcolonial elites and to leftist Western intellectuals—and solidarity across the South. In this way, it promised a model of transnational ties and collaboration that rejected the developmentalist agenda inherent in discourses of global governance such as that of the United Nations Development Program (Dirlik 2013; see also 2007, 12–15). The PRC recommended the replacement of vertical channels of aid and assistance, which chained the former colonies to the erstwhile metropolitan centers of the Global North, with layered networks of lateral ties running across the South—from Asia to Africa, or from Africa to Latin America, or from Asia to Africa to Latin America. The emergence and proliferation of a discursive idiom foregrounding Ya-Fei (Asia-Africa), or Ya-Fei-La (Asia-Africa-Latin America) as geopolitical as well as ideological entities in the two

23

decades following Bandung, signals a reconceptualization of global power and geopolitics that aimed to challenge Cold War binaries.[2] And it was in the realm of culture, both within Chinese public culture and in the PRC's cultural diplomacy, that South-South or Ya-Fei (Asia-Africa) solidarity found its most elaborate expression.

The PRC, however, quickly discovered the contradictions inherent in its approach to the Global South, and the limits of its cultural diplomacy offensive. Ironically, the PRC had to borrow the means and strategies of its counterhegemonic struggle from its own enemies. The structures of cultural diplomacy and exchange the People's Republic tried to construct were in fact modeled on the network of cultural relations that the Soviet Union had built across the socialist world in the 1950s, and in which the PRC had participated until very recently. Further complicating the Chinese efforts was the aggressive Soviet pivot toward the very same spaces in Africa and Asia, using similar means and arguments. Although ambitious in scope and goals, the PRC's global cultural offensive soon clashed with rival Soviet initiatives, and with US attempts to counter and subvert Chinese propaganda in the Southern Hemisphere. Faced with steep competition and marred by its own ideological inconsistencies, the PRC's global cultural offensive foundered almost as soon as it had begun, and eventually moved from actual engagement to the realm of the imaginary. Set in 1963, *On the Docks* celebrates a brief moment of optimism that had already receded into memory by the time of the play's codification as a model opera. As the PRC turned in on itself at the onset of the Cultural Revolution, the results of Mao's attempts to export revolution remained elusive. The ideal of a new, counterhegemonic world order based on solidarity across the Global South, however, lived on in the cultural imaginary.

This chapter focuses on two dimensions of revolutionary China's forays into the Global South. First, I will outline the institutional infrastructure of the PRC's cultural diplomacy. In the years after Bandung, the PRC systematically expanded its diplomatic corps and put into place an extensive bureaucracy in both the political establishment and its United Front organizations. Bilateral cultural cooperation agreements with an expanding number of nations; cultural exchange work plans; friendship delegations composed of performing ensembles, musicians, and writers as well as student exchanges—they all served to expand the Chinese cultural footprint across the recently decolonized world. At the same time, the PRC moved to increase its role in the Afro-Asian Writers Bureau, a crucial site of transnational cultural politics. Second, I will zoom in on the politics of literary translation. In the late 1950s and early 1960s, leading Chinese literary journals and publishing houses shifted their attention from the Eastern Bloc to the Global South, proposing a radically new cultural geography that consciously redrew the existing literary world map. Tracing the textual construction of the Maoist global literary imaginary, I will document the efforts to import literary works from the Afro-Asian world, following the life cycle of the literary imaginary of Afro-Asia from its inception in the early 1960s to its eventual transposition and afterlife in Cultural Revolutionary works of art. The literary world map, I argue, drew on the institutional infrastructure but gave it a public face by projecting a utopian vision of a new (cultural) world order. The struggle to reconcile these two dimensions of its ventures in the Global South, however, ultimately exposed the inconsistencies inherent in the PRC's approach toward the postcolonial world, and eventually frustrated Maoist China's bold ambitions to reenvision the Cold War world.

Institutions: Chinese Cultural Diplomacy in Afro-Asia

Bandung was a pivotal moment in the evolution of the Cold War world. Yet only in recent years has interest resurged in the ambitious attempts to create a global dialogue outside the East-West monopoly on power and to imagine alternative modes of alliance and cooperation. The Bandung Conference, convened on April 18–24, 1955, aimed to forge what Christopher Lee (2010, 20–27) has called an "imagined *communitas*," a platform to reconceptualize modes of political community beyond and outside the parameters of Cold War confrontation. The summit meeting of high-level delegations from twenty-nine nations and territories offered an opportunity to establish a dialogical mode of cross-cultural interaction, as opposed to the hierarchical or "pedagogical" mode that had dominated the processes of decolonialization (Chakrabarty 2010, 46–47). Bandung created a new language and a new discursive arena to rethink the futures of what would soon be called the third world. The legacies of Bandung, however, have remained ambivalent. Participants were able to put aside, for the duration of the conference, political and ideological differences; yet these disagreements (such as border disputes between the PRC and India) would resurface soon after. More consequential, the dramatic script of the conference proceedings ensured that celebrity political actors such as Nehru, Suharto, and Zhou Enlai occupied center stage; the participating nations' cultural envoys, in contrast, were relegated to the wings. If at all, they were given the task of reenacting the visions outlined by their political leaders in the symbolically coded languages of theater, music, and dance (Wilcox 2017). Bandung, in other words, proposed a new symbolic order but was still driven by ideologies rather than cultural practices. It would take years to actually build the infrastructure for cultural interactions across the Global South.

Chinese political involvement in Asia and Africa began very modestly. In 1950 only four independent nations existed in Africa, and none recognized the PRC. The continent was essentially inaccessible for Chinese diplomats.[3] The regional environment in Asia was not much more hospitable. Although India and Indonesia recognized the PRC in April 1950, the Cold War split the region and complicated Chinese diplomatic efforts; armed conflicts forced the young PRC to take sides (Zheng, Liu, and Szonyi 2010; Hasegawa 2011). At the same time, the PRC was barred from the United Nations, the cockpit of global diplomacy. Bandung, then, turned into a diplomatic coming-out party for socialist China. While the PRC had not been among the meeting's original sponsors, the arrival of Zhou Enlai and his delegation was perhaps the conference's most eye-catching event, at least for the assembled international press corps. Yet Bandung remained a one-off effort and, despite its high profile, failed to put in place permanent structures of cooperation. It was not until the late 1950s and early 1960s that Chinese diplomatic contacts in Asia and Africa strengthened, helped by the confluence of Cold War dynamics, the intensifying Sino-Soviet rivalry, and the quickly growing number of newly independent nations in Africa (Klein 1964; Larkin 1971, 24–37).

The increasing Chinese engagement in postcolonial Africa and Asia can be traced by following the regions' growing institutional footprint within both the governmental and nongovernmental bureaucracies of the PRC. In September 1956, the Ministry of Foreign Affairs (MFA) created a Department of West Asian and African Affairs (Xi-Ya Feizhou si); in late 1964, as the pace of decolonization accelerated and many of the newly independent nations recognized the PRC, the department was further split into a Department of African Affairs (Feizhou si) and a Department of West Asian and North African Affairs (Xi-Ya Bei-Fei si) (Larkin 1971, 26; Zheng and Long 2011). The ministry was assisted in its coordination of cultural diplomacy and exchanges in Africa and Asia by a range of quasi-governmental organizations such as the Committee for External Cultural Relations (Duiwai wenhua lianluo weiyuanhui).[4] The committee and the MFA received support from specialized organizations in charge of expanding the PRC's cultural contacts in Asia and

Africa. These included the China-Africa People's Friendship Association, founded in 1960; the Chinese Committee for Afro-Asian Solidarity, set up in 1965 as the local chapter of the Afro-Asian People's Solidarity Organization; the China Asia-Africa Society, headed by Guo Moruo (1892–1978); and the Chinese Liaison Committee with the Permanent Bureau of the Afro-Asian Writers' Conference, which was founded in early 1959 and located in Cairo.[5]

Ostensibly aimed at the Afro-Asian world and servicing the PRC's solidarity with the Global South, these bureaucracies were in fact intimately tied to China's engagement with the Soviet Union and Eastern Europe. They were either appropriations or expansions of existing bureaucracies built in the early 1950s for liaison with New China's partners in the socialist world, or closely modeled on such bodies.[6] In other words, the bureaucratic infrastructure of the PRC's diplomatic offensive in the Global South was borrowed from the political patterns facilitating the country's Cold War alliances with the Eastern Bloc. The MFA was built from scratch after 1949 and closely followed instructions from its Soviet advisers; until 1956, the bulk of its workload consisted of building relations with the socialist nations of Eastern Europe and the Soviet Union. The new departments, then, were grafted onto existing structures. Likewise, the quasi-governmental organizations closely matched the players involved in the PRC's cultural exchanges with the socialist world. The most important of these was the Committee for External Cultural Relations, which was originally geared toward Eastern Europe, and refocused on the Afro-Asian world only in the early 1960s. The Chinese chapter of the Afro-Asian People's Solidarity Organization seems to have been modeled after its Soviet counterpart, the Soviet Committee for Solidarity with the Countries of Asia and Africa. Chinese outreach to the decolonial states of Asia and Africa thus not only replicated, in structural and functional terms, the organizations in charge of cultural cooperation with the socialist world in the 1950s. Ironically, the Chinese efforts to engage the Global South themselves were patterned on the Soviet model of cultural diplomacy.

The primary vehicle for cultural exchange with the newly independent nations of Africa, Asia, and Latin America were bilateral cultural cooperation agreements. In April 1956, the PRC signed a cultural cooperation agreement with Egypt, the first with a nonsocialist nation. Syria (1956), Iraq (1959), and Guinea (1959) signed similar agreements, followed by more than a dozen agreements with other third world nations after 1960.[7] The agreements themselves were usually brief statements of intent, coded in formulaic diplomatic language. To get actual cultural exchanges going, embassy staff and the foreign ministry annually negotiated work plans that covered, in great detail, all bilateral exchanges under the broadly conceived rubric of culture. The PRC signed a work plan with Egypt in 1955 and with Guinea in 1960; numerous others followed (Zhonghua renmin gongheguo waijiaobu, Duiwai wenhua lianluoju 1993, 1198–1252). Yet both the cultural cooperation agreements and the annual work plans closely followed the routines of cultural exchange within the socialist world. The PRC had signed similar agreements with every single nation of the Eastern Bloc in the years after 1951; and detailed annual implementation plans negotiated through diplomatic channels were the main engine behind the vast amount of cultural traffic between China and the socialist world. The agreements with Syria, Egypt, and others were not only structurally similar but also copied, almost verbatim, the language of the Chinese agreements with its Eastern European partners.[8] Cultural cooperation with the nations of Asia and Africa, then, closely followed precedents and developed along the lines the PRC had established in the 1950s in its interactions within the Soviet sphere of influence.

Intensifying cultural exchanges created multiple opportunities for closer contact between China and the nations of Africa and Asia. The diplomatic forays into the Afro-Asian sphere were spearheaded by Zhou Enlai, the PRC's diplomat in chief. Zhou had led the Chinese delegation to Bandung in 1955. In late 1963 and early 1964, he embarked on an extended tour that led him and his entourage to eight African nations.[9] He returned to Africa three times in 1965 on further diplomatic missions. On Zhou's heels, various Chinese delegations made their way to China's new partners, where they sought to build a network of contacts and initiatives. The China-Africa People's Friendship Association sent a delegation on a four-month tour,[10] and Chinese acrobatics and folk art troupes toured various African nations.[11] Chinese writers responded to the new opportunities opened up by the reorientation of the PRC's external cultural relations. Guo Moruo, in his various roles in "friendship" diplomacy, was a frequent traveler while Yang Shuo (1913–1968), noted for his reportage literature from the Korean War, spent a three-year stint in Cairo as a permanent Chinese representative at the Afro-Asian Writers Conference.[12] Other Chinese writers, such as Mao Dun (1896–1981) and Feng Zhi (1905–1993), also traveled abroad.[13] Meanwhile, writers and artists at home could also become involved with their counterparts from Asia and Africa, as a steady stream of delegations visited Beijing and often other Chinese cities as well.[14] Two particularly high-profile events were the emergency meeting of the Afro-Asian Writers' Bureau in Beijing in July 1966, when Mao Zedong received a group of writers from African and Asian nations,[15] and a June 1967 seminar in Beijing sponsored by the Writers' Bureau to commemorate the twenty-fifth anniversary of Mao's Yan'an talks.[16] All these activities were covered at great length in the Chinese press and celebrated friendship and solidarity across the Global South.

Beyond the level of political and cultural prominence, students played a major role in cultural relations between the PRC and the Afro-Asian world. In the 1950s, tens of thousands of foreign students from all across the Eastern Bloc streamed to Moscow. Their presence contributed to the city's cosmopolitan flair and helped cement the Soviet Union's status as the center of the socialist world. Replicating this Soviet initiative, the PRC tried to admit increasing numbers of students from third world nations to universities in Beijing and Shanghai. Foreign students thus constituted part of the PRC's bid to become the center of the Afro-Asian world. A tabulation from 1962 lists 118 African students in Beijing, the majority coming from Somalia, Cameroon, and Zanzibar (Larkin 1971, 142–43). In China, they joined a much larger contingent of Vietnamese students. Yet, while expanding the intake of foreign students was politically desirable, these efforts clashed with the increasingly radicalized atmosphere on Chinese campuses in the years leading up to the Cultural Revolution. In accounts published in the West, disappointed African students complained of aggressive indoctrination efforts, poor educational standards, and racist attitudes (Hevi 1963; see also Friedman 2011, 78). In the summer of 1966, the Vietnamese government ordered four thousand of their students to leave China, fearing contagion from the Cultural Revolution.[17] Chinese universities suspended instruction shortly thereafter, leaving in limbo the remaining foreign student population. Even at its height, however, the number of students from Afro-Asian countries in the PRC was dwarfed by those studying in the Soviet Union. Trying to beat China's erstwhile partner, the Soviet Union, with its own weapons turned out to be a more complex struggle than the optimistic slogans and public pronouncements of solidarity had suggested.

Texts: Afro-Asia in the Chinese Literary Geography

Arguably the most ambitious of China's ventures into the Global South can be found in the realm of literature. The Sino-Soviet split and the PRC's turn toward the Afro-Asian world fundamentally changed the nation's imagined geography. These shifts necessitated a radical redrawing of the cultural world map. Yet in 1960, when Beijing split with Moscow, the PRC's geocultural imaginary was barely a decade old. In the early 1950s, the PRC had embarked on a bold project to reenvision the geospatial parameters of world literature. If until 1949 Western Europe—primarily Britain, France, and Germany—had occupied the imaginary center of the literary world map, this central position had moved east, to Moscow. Throughout the 1950s, Chinese publishing houses and literary journals supplied Chinese readers with vast amounts of translated Soviet literature, in all genres and from 1917 up to the present day. In addition, readers could find experiences familiar to their own in newly available translations of fiction from across the Eastern Bloc, from countries that hitherto had barely registered in the Chinese literary imagination. The centrality of Soviet literature was justified by the country's being the most "advanced" (*xianjin*) nation of the world, both ideologically and culturally. With the ascent of a globally conceived socialist realism, Western literary experiments such as modernism could be declared aberrant, and their nations of origin, once the main models for Chinese writers, now found themselves relegated to the peripheries of the literary world map (Volland 2017).

The main drawing board of this brave new world map was the journal *Yiwen* (Translations), founded in 1953. It was on the pages of the PRC's most prestigious monthly specializing in translated literature that Chinese readers found fiction, poetry, and essays from nations and territories across the globe, but first and foremost the Soviet Union. Literature from the newly independent nations and colonial territories of Asia, Africa, and Latin America was featured regularly, but in a marginal position compared to that from the Eastern Bloc (Volland 2017, 153–86; also cf. Iovene 2014, 51–79). By the late 1950s, however, this literary world map had become increasingly untenable. The preeminent position of Soviet literature in an essentially hierarchical model of literary prestige and power clashed with the PRC's own ambitions. In an abrupt move, the journal changed its title in January 1959 to *Shijie wenxue* (World literature). If the name *Translations* had indicated a one-way process of literary traffic, the journal's new name suggested a flattened, nonhierarchical vision of literary geography. Notably, the change came on the heels of the October 1958 congress of Afro-Asian writers in Tashkent, capital of the Soviet republic of Uzbekistan. This seminal meeting of authors and literary administrators from more than thirty nations and territories, the first of its kind, aimed to boost cultural diplomacy across the Global South. While not as widely known as the Bandung Conference, the Tashkent meeting was a key event in global literary politics. Among other initiatives, the congress resolved to set up the Permanent Bureau of the Afro-Asian Writers' Conference, which became the Afro-Asian Writers' Association. The PRC sent a high-level delegation composed of twenty-one authors and cultural administrators to Tashkent, led by Mao Dun, Zhou Yang (1909–1989), and Ba Jin (1904–2005) (Yoon 2015, 2018).

The Tashkent meeting, with its focus on Afro-Asian solidarity and lateral vectors of literary contact, came at a crucial moment and helped the PRC to rethink the terrain of world literature. To greet the congress, the journal *Yiwen* published two consecutive special issues featuring translated literary works from across Asia and Africa: poetry from Syria and Mozambique, fiction from South Africa and Thailand, folk stories from Libya and Ethiopia, among many others. These translations—which covered regions hitherto terra incognita on the Chinese literary world map—were accompanied by statements from Mao Dun and other leading writers celebrating cooperation and solidarity among the nations of Asia and Africa (Volland 2017, 180–82). It was to mark this shift toward a truly global vision of literature that the journal adopted its new name, *World Literature*, right after the Tashkent congress. Asian and African literature gained increasing prominence in the journal, and came to dominate its pages by early 1963, emphasizing the PRC's anti-imperialist pivot. Translations from all across Asia and from the newly independent African nations appeared in almost every issue after early 1960, and advertisements on the journal's back cover kept readers informed of new book-length translations from the Afro-Asian world, as well as from Latin America. The journal's new focus was underlined also by thematic issues devoted to literary regions, or to nations that supported the Chinese claim of leadership in the third world. The October 1961 issue, for instance, provided a substantial collection of African literature, followed by a focus on Asia in the following issue. The May 1963 issue was again devoted to leftist literature from all across Asia. A double issue in January–February 1964 brought Chinese readers an unprecedented 160 pages of fiction and poetry from Korea, while the October 1964 issue was designated a special issue on Vietnam. The shift in regional coverage tracked the quickly expanding Chinese diplomatic footprint in the decolonizing world, and gave substance to the anti-imperialist rhetoric. In an afterword to the special issue on Vietnam, the editors explained that the works presented here were selected by the Vietnamese writers' union, which had also supplied the illustrations. The editors further thanked the Vietnamese Embassy, which had helped with editing and proofreading the translations, thereby highlighting newly emerging modes of collaboration.

31

The rise to prominence of the Afro-Asian world on the pages of *World Literature* went hand in hand with the decline and near-disappearance of Soviet literature, and of literature from other Eastern Bloc nations. The South was displacing the Global North, signaling an insurrectionist movement in the realm of world literature. Soviet poetry and fiction still featured prominently in *World Literature* in 1960 and 1961, but Soviet literature had clearly lost the preeminent status it had enjoyed in the early and mid-1950s. As the polemics within the socialist camp heated up, the amount of Soviet literature translated into Chinese dwindled. Soviet critical writings also ceased to function as sources of legitimacy, the arbiters of theoretical trends in the socialist world. Instead, Chinese writers and theorists assumed the task of commenting from a position of authority on the vast array of new literature that reached the journal's readers, thus affirming China's central position on the literary world map. The symbolic victory over the Soviet Union in the cultural sphere, as seen on the pages of *World Literature*, supported the PRC's claim as the new leader of the third world.

Chinese efforts to establish the PRC as the spearhead of Afro-Asian solidarity and the new center of the world Communist movement, however, were fraught with problems. The PRC's prestige in the developing world reached a peak in 1964, but it soon encountered challenges and setbacks (see Larkin 1971; Friedman 2011). Many of China's new foreign partners proved volatile, and the Soviet Union remained a formidable adversary (Friedman 2011; Weinstein 1975). In a sign of troubles on the cultural front, *World Literature* shut down abruptly in December 1964, ostensibly "to undergo improvement work"—at the precise moment when the PRC began to turn inward, frustrated by the less-than-bountiful rewards of its Afro-Asian adventures. Not only did the shrill Chinese anti-imperialist rhetoric alienate many of its more moderate partners abroad, the denunciations of the Global North that dominated *World Literature* during its final years also belied the foundations on which the PRC's Afro-Asian cultural adventures were built. Ironically, much of the coverage of African literature remained dependent on input from the Soviet Union. Most of the translations of African poetry, fiction, and folk stories that appeared in the journal, often in a prominent position, were in fact retranslations from Russian sources. They had first appeared in Soviet books and journals, which remained the most convenient way for Chinese translators to access the Global South. The October 1961 issue of *World Literature*, for instance, featured a thirty-page section on African literature, including poetry and fiction from Mozambique, Nigeria, Congo, Tunisia, and

Algeria, as well as several Swahili folk songs. All but two short Tunisian poems were retranslations from Soviet sources.[18] The struggles of the PRC's premier journal of foreign literature, then, stand symbolically for the problems that plagued the ambitious Chinese effort to assume the leadership in South-South cultural diplomacy. The Chinese attempts to beat the Soviet Union with its own weapons, and in its own game, proved untenable. The PRC's cultural forays into the Afro-Asian world, trying to resurrect structures and models from a bygone era, had lived on borrowed time. Moreover, the utopian aims of the counterhegemonic literary cartography speaking from *World Literature* could no longer mask the incongruencies between the world map and the underlying infrastructure of the PRC's turn to the South. On the eve of the Cultural Revolution, the PRC's projections of cultural power in the Global South hence shifted to the only remaining terrain, the cultural imaginary itself.

"Standing on the docks we gaze afar, / anti-imperialist flames rage everywhere." It was the ideological prerogative of world revolution that had provided the justification, the underlying logic of the PRC's alignment with the Global South. This logic was central to the opera *On the Docks*, as it went through a lengthy process of revisions, from the first version in 1966 to the officially approved script of 1972 and the film version of the same year.[19] *On the Docks* picked up a theme that had been central across cultural forms and media since the early 1960s. The celebration of Afro-Asian solidarity had featured prominently in the initial version of the influential musical extravaganza *Dongfang hong* (The East Is Red, 1964) and its dramatization of the Chinese Revolution, which the "song and dance epic" (yinyue wudao shishi) presented as the mainstream of the world Communist movement (Chen 2016, 153–59). Chinese involvement in the ongoing civil war in the Congo provided the theme for the 1965 spoken drama *War Drums on the Equator* (Chidao zhangu), which was subsequently turned into the musical *The River Congo Is Raging* (Gangguo he zai nuhong) by the *East Is Red* crew (Cook 2019). And friendship with the peoples of Africa and Asia was visualized in propaganda posters and even on postage stamps (see Landsberger and van der Heijden 2009, 118–19, 134, 152, 177). It is in these highly stylized images of solidarity that the Maoist attempt to assume the leadership of the Global South reached its apotheosis, and in which it has entered the collective memory. The iconic images of handshakes and fists pumped in the air are reflections, then, not so much of actual cultural exchanges as of idealized projections, sanitized versions of a decidedly more complex reality. They gloss over the ruptures

33

and refractions under the surface that complicated the ambitious project of South-South solidarity, and that hint at the complexities of the Global South, as a project as much as a paradigm, past and present.

Fifty years after the PRC's first attempt to redefine its position within world politics by way of aligning itself with the "oppressed nations of Asia and Africa," China is once again deeply involved in building contacts across what is now called the Global South. The Belt and Road Initiative, Xi Jinping's signature foreign policy project, has returned the PRC to many of the nations in Asia and Africa that were part of revolutionary China's global outreach in the 1960s and 1970s. Contemporary attitudes toward this earlier initiative, however, remain ambivalent, signaling the highly ambiguous nature of the legacies from the recent past (see the chapters by Luciano Bolinaga and Derek Sheridan in this volume). Rhetorically, the current push for outbound investment gestures much further back into history, invoking the Silk Road as an ancient link between China and Afro-Asia. The theme of South-South cooperation is presented in terms of shared agendas and development goals, rather than class struggle and anti-imperialism, a pivot apparently designed to alleviate fears of the PRC's motives and avoid confrontations on the global political stage. Notably, the language used to celebrate events such as regular China-Africa summit meetings convening in Beijing or the groundbreaking ceremonies for the reconstruction of the Tanzania-Zambia Railway emphasizes the economic rather than the political rationales of cooperation across the South.

The rem(a)inders of the revolutionary PRC's push into the Southern Hemisphere have hence become yet another "red legacy": "ideas, symbols, and sacrifices on the revolutionary path" that have become either "resources or liabilities for Chinese society" (Li 2016, 2). Contemporary proclamations of friendship with the nations of Asia and Africa readily invoke the PRC's long history of engagement with the Global South yet gloss over the historical and ideological conditions of these earlier initiatives. Having turned away from anti-imperialist and anticapitalist agendas in the 1980s, the architects of China's twenty-first-century policies show little interest in conjuring up the ideological specters of the Maoist past. Yet the iconic images of international and interracial proletarian friendship from the visual, dramatic, and fictional representations from the 1960s continue to haunt the protagonists of contemporary China's renewed push into the Global South. Meanwhile, the diplomatic and bureaucratic structures that once conveyed the flows of cultural travelers constitute a form of institutional memory that continues to inform China's twenty-first-century diplomatic outreach.

The biggest irony, however, concerns China's own global status. In the 1960s, the PRC had sided with the nations of the Global South in an explicitly counterhegemonic move, an uprising of the planetary proletariat designed to turn the tables on the Global North. Maoist China called for an overthrow of the existing world order, aiming at both the United States and the Soviet Union, as well as their allies and satellites—a rejection, that is, of the Cold War international system. In the twenty-first century, the PRC once again aims to reshape the structure of global power but with very different means and from a radically different point of departure. Forty years after the onset of the reform period, the PRC in fact identifies more closely with the Global North than ever before—socioeconomically, politically, and ideologically. China's rise to superpower status sits awkwardly with the egalitarian agenda of the past. The legacies from the revolutionary era hence remain ambiguous. They carry the potential to build new bridges and ties, but they also draw unwelcome attention to the PRC's shifting global status. In this sense, then, the legacies of the PRC's efforts to forge Afro-Asian unity in the 1960s and 1970s remain highly symbolic of nothing less than China's always ambiguous status vis-à-vis and within the Global South.

Notes

1 See Luciano Bolinaga's chapter in this volume. For a nuanced study that aims to look beyond the polemics surrounding the PRC's outbound investment spree, see Lee 2018.

2 For an alternative worlding project that aimed to redefine global notions of center and periphery, albeit critical of China, see Ng Kim Chew's contribution to this volume.

3 See Larkin 1971, 15–16. Egypt formally recognized the PRC on May 30, 1956, followed by Morocco on November 1, 1958. By early 1960, the PRC had five partners in Africa; more than a dozen nations followed over the next five years. See also Snow 1994, 289–93.

4 After a 1958 reorganization, the committee had departments in charge of Asian countries, Arab and African countries, and Latin American nations. In 1964 an African department was set up. See Larkin 1971, 217–18; and Su 1993, 449–52, 511–13.

5 For sketches of the above organizations, see Larkin 1971, 219–24; compare also Clews 1964, 143, 156, 163–65. For a detailed account of the Afro-Asian

35

People's Solidarity Organization, see Neuhauser 1968; on the Writers' Conference and its eventual split into pro-Soviet and pro-Chinese camps, see Neuhauser 1968, 36, 43–44, 66–67. A partisan but detailed account of the Writers' Conference can be found in Afro-Asian Writers' Bureau 1968.

6 On Chinese cultural cooperation with the socialist world, see Volland 2008.

7 For details, listed by country, see Zhonghua renmin gongheguo waijiaobu, Duiwai wenhua lianluoju 1993, 76–187.

8 See, for instance, the Sino-Syrian cultural cooperation agreement in Zhonghua renmin gongheguo waijiaobu 1958, 158–59. The texts of agreements with other nations are available in other volumes of the same series.

9 On Zhou's tour, see Adie 1964. Zhou's speeches during this tour, as well as joint communiqués and other documents, are collected in Foreign Languages Press 1964.

10 See Clews 1964, 156. For a tabulation of delegation visits to both Africa and China, see Ogunsangwo 1974, 269–70.

11 Mali, for instance, hosted the Nanjing Acrobatic Ensemble in December 1964 and a folk art group in November 1965; the China Acrobatics Ensemble visited Somalia in February 1966, followed in December 1967 by the East Is Red Song and Dance Ensemble. See Zhonghua renmin gongheguo waijiaobu, Duiwai wenhua lianluoju, 1993, 173–74 and 156–57.

12 Yang Shuo had joined the Chinese volunteer corps during the Korean War as a reporter and had written a book-length account of the war, as well as numerous essays and reportages. In the Writers Union, he had been in charge of foreign affairs and attended the conference of Asian writers in India in 1956 and the 1958 Tashkent congress of Afro-Asian writers. During his tenure in Cairo, he produced a steady stream of essays depicting Afro-Asian solidarity. See Wang Dajun 1979, 2–5.

13 Mao Dun attended the second conference of Afro-Asian writers in Cairo in February 1962. His address to the meeting was published in *Wenyibao* (The literary gazette) 3 (1962): 2–5. Feng Zhi traveled to Cuba in February 1964. See "Wenhua wanglai," *Shijie wenxue* (World literature) 129 (March 1964): 147–48. A travelogue penned by Feng appeared in *Shijie wenxue* 130 (April 1964): 26–30.

14 In May 1963, for instance, writers from Sri Lanka, South Africa, and Indonesia visited the PRC. See "Shijie wenyi dongtai" (World news in literature and art) in *Shijie wenxue* 120 (June 1963): 124. In April 1964, the Algerian writer and philosopher Malek Bennabi (1905–1973), who had authored a book titled *L'Afro-Asiatisme* (1956), led a high-level cultural delegation to China that was received by Mao and Zhou Enlai and visited Beijing, Shanghai, and Guangzhou. See "Wenhua wanglai" (Cultural exchanges), *Shijie wenxue* 133 (July 1964): 148–50.

NICOLAI VOLLAND

15 Only four weeks earlier, a rival meeting had been convened in Moscow that excluded Chinese participants. The two meetings confirmed the split of the Afro-Asian Writers' Bureau. For details, see Afro-Asian Writers' Bureau 1968, 119–20, 125–26; and Ogunsangwo 1974, 230.

16 "Seminar Sponsored by the Afro-Asian Writers' Bureau" 1967, 48–56. For background, see Xiaomei Chen 2002, 151–54.

17 Friedman 2011, 248. At least two thousand of these students had come to the PRC on Chinese government scholarships. See Zhongguo jiaoyu nianjian bianjibu 1984, 666.

18 Similar examples abound. It was somewhat easier to find proficient translators for literature from Asia, yet even in an extensive Asian feature in the journal's next issue, two of the texts, from Turkey and Cambodia, had to be retranslated from Soviet and German translations. Apparently to mask its own embarrassment, later issues of *World Literature* became increasingly vague as to the sources of its translations.

19 See Xiaomei Chen 2002, 146–57. As Chen points out, the third world figured prominently in other plays and operas from the mid-1960s.

FROM THE WASHINGTON CONSENSUS TO THE BEIJING CONSENSUS

Latin America Facing the Rise of China as a Great Power

The peripheral countries of the international system have always—to a greater or lesser extent—been under the influence of the great powers. In the genesis of the interstate matrix, the legal instruments (treaties and agreements) and political instruments (doctrines) had a fundamental value in guaranteeing the interests of the great powers and limiting the political autonomy of peripheral ones. Relevant milestones in this process include the Treaty of Tordesillas in 1494 and the distribution of the New World between Spain and Portugal, the Treaty of Utrecht in 1713, the Final Act of Vienna in 1815, the Monroe Doctrine in 1823, and the Treaty of Nanjing in 1842. However, these instruments did not pursue the construction of a cooperation framework based on the equality of the units of the system, but rather they formed an order based mainly on the interests of the great powers.

With the development of the international system, these instruments started to leave aside the co-optative aspect in favor of more cooperative rhetoric as a consequence of three fundamental factors. The first factor was the institutionalization of multilateral cooperative organizations such as the

Society of Nations (1918) and, later, the United Nations (1945). The second factor was the evolution of the public international law that attenuated the use of strength to two circumstances: for self-defense and under the authorization of the United Nations Security Council. Finally, the third factor was the emergence of a great number of political entities as a consequence of the decolonization process in international politics, which was accelerated during the second half of the twentieth century. The synergy between these three factors limited the co-optative component of the political praxis of the great powers, leading to the genesis of a new set of instruments to exert influence and pressure in the periphery of the system: namely, instruments organized under the concept *consensus*.

The final two decades of the twentieth century witnessed the emergence of the concept of consensus that somehow came to present—at least in appearance—a scheme accepted by all involved parties, and not merely an imposition of the interests of the great powers. Consensus moved away from the traditional legal and political effect that international treaties or agreements had during most of the evolution of the interstate system because it had a greater international acceptance within the new schemes of multilateral cooperation we have been describing and because it was more flexible since it took the form of political "understanding," which can be either tacit or explicit. Consensus is the key to understanding how the capacity to be influenced by the great powers in the periphery of the international system has been reformulated.

The concept of a Washington Consensus was first proposed in an article by John Williamson published in November 1989 by the Institute of International Economy, titled "What Washington Means by Policy Reform." This first consensus consisted of a set of ten economic policies considered by the international financial organizations and economic centers with headquarters in Washington as the best economic program the countries of Latin America and the Caribbean should apply in order to encourage economic growth.[1] The peculiarity of this consensus is that the United States turned principally not to bilateral but rather to multilateral diplomacy. Likewise, it should be pointed out that these economic measures were originally created for the countries of Latin America, but during the nineties they became a more general program for all peripheral economies.

At the time, a direct relation between the international configuration of power and the grounds of the consensus was confirmed. In 1989 the core of international power was clearly in Washington; this suggested the primacy

39

of the United States in the world, and was reaffirmed in 1991 after the collapse of the Soviet Union. The Washington Consensus allowed peripheral countries, and particularly Latin American nations, to internalize the decalogue of commercial and financial policies that allowed them to expand their American influence at the periphery of the system.

Of course, at that point in time, one could think that one was witnessing the formation of a new instrument of the great powers for exerting pressure. The Washington Consensus was not an isolated instrument of foreign policy. While a new configuration of international power was consolidating, the political praxis seems to have been resumed by the emerging power. The reemergence of China as a world power implied an expansion of its area of influence and Beijing incorporated the practice of consensus.

The rise of China reflects its economic expansion and integration into the global economy at the same time that it contributes to a shift in the world economic center from the Atlantic toward the Pacific (Bolinaga 2013). Since 2009 China has been positioned as the world's second-largest economy in gross domestic product (GDP) measured at current prices, but if the GDP is assessed by purchasing power parity (PPP), China actually surpassed the United States in 2017.[2] Due to the rapid growth of its foreign trade, in 2022 China is the largest manufacturer worldwide, which has provided the basis for the idea of China as "the world's factory." Moreover, given its more recent rate of technological innovation, it has similarly begun to be regarded as "the world's laboratory."[3] More than a decade ago, China became the US Treasury's main creditor, and it is currently the world's largest holder of foreign reserves. In addition, since 2010 it has been the world's second-largest recipient of direct foreign investment, and since 2013 it has been the third largest issuer of foreign investment (UNCTAD 2011–14). Inexorably, China is emerging as a leading world power, having left the semiperiphery in order to integrate with a select group of central countries—the oligopoly of great powers (Kissinger 2012, 540; Oviedo 2005, 49–50).

Consequently, due to its new international positioning, China has started to exert more influence over different regions of the periphery. In this way, Latin America and Africa have gained particular importance in China's strategy of "going global" because of the regions' growing reliance on these regions as sources of raw materials. That is to say, over the past decade Beijing has deployed a systematic strategy to guarantee its supply of raw materials and its control over maritime transportation routes, which is the foundation of what is known as the Beijing Consensus. It is precisely for this purpose that China has developed the Belt and Road Initiative.

Beijing did not discontinue the logic of the Washington Consensus, but rather extended it because it saw this logic as an instrument to help guarantee its own interests and help it compete for influence in the periphery of the system with the other great powers. Consequently, the peripheral countries started to internalize other discourses and political practices. Below, we will compare the central postulates of the Washington Consensus and the Beijing Consensus, with the purpose of analyzing the impact in Latin America of the influence that China began to exert, starting in 2004. What implications has the Beijing Consensus had on the trade flows of Latin American countries? What is the role of Chinese investment in regional development? What instruments does China use to impose its interests in negotiations with the region? We hypothesize that China uses the size of its market, its new international positioning as a great power, and its role as issuer of direct foreign investment in order to reformulate its diplomatic and political links with the region. It uses active bilateral diplomacy to secure power asymmetries in its favor while on a discursive level concealing these asymmetries in the name of a putative South-South cooperative relationship that stresses shared profit and symmetrical relations of mutual benefit.

From the Washington Consensus to the Beijing Consensus

The Washington Consensus was established with the objective of finding effective and pragmatic solutions to the crisis of Latin America's external debt, but it also sought to promote an environment with more transparency and macroeconomic stability while furthering the fight against poverty. Its father, John Williamson, recognized that over time the significance of the Washington Consensus had been reformulated: "At least, there are two different meanings. One of them identifies the Washington Consensus with Neoliberalism. . . . The second possible alternative explanation is that the Washington Consensus implies the set of policies that the institutions of that city which advises the developing countries collectively follow: the institutions of Bretton Woods (the International Monetary Fund and the World Bank), the Inter-American Development Bank, the Treasury and maybe even the Federal Reserve of the United States" (Williamson 2003, 11). In practice, however, the application of the Washington Consensus in the Latin

American region has been inseparable from the triumph of the neoliberal system because it came to invert the scenario that the Keynesian proposals had generated.

The Washington Consensus consisted of a set of ten policies:

1 FISCAL DISCIPLINE. A key requirement was to revert the fiscal deficits accumulated by the countries of the region, thereby permitting countries to secure financial aid through programs negotiated with the International Monetary Fund. It was argued that the fiscal deficits generated macroeconomic problems resulting in inflation, imbalance in the balance of payments, and the flight of capital.

2 REORDERING PUBLIC SPENDING PRIORITIES. Washington advocated a reduction in public spending, without an increase in tax revenue. The objective was to divert the unproductive spending of subsidies toward areas such as public health, education, and so forth.

3 TAX REFORM. Washington considered increased revenue as a less effective means of addressing budget deficits than a reduction of public spending.

4 LIBERALIZATION OF INTEREST RATES. The interest rates should follow two fundamental principles: they should be determined by the market, and they should be positive in order to increase savings.

5 A COMPETITIVE EXCHANGE RATE. Exchange rates should be determined by market forces, with the understanding that a competitive exchange rate is the first essential element of an economic policy that is "oriented towards the exterior."

6 LIBERALIZATION OF INTERNATIONAL TRADE. Access to imports of intermediate production factors at competitive prices was considered to be important for the promotion of exports, but the speed at which this was to be accomplished, in order to avoid destroying the national industry, was not specified.

7 LIBERALIZATION OF THE ENTRY OF DIRECT FOREIGN INVESTMENTS. Although this was not a particularly important priority, it was assumed that direct foreign investment could be promoted by means of exchange of Treasury bonds for shares and, in this way, external debt could be reduced. Nevertheless, Williamson did not include the

capital account because he knew that he would not have the support of Washington.

8 PRIVATIZATIONS. Privatizations are able to help reduce the pressure in the government's budget, in both the short term (due to the income from the sales of the company) and the long term (the government already finances the investment). Nevertheless, the potential corruption in the transfer of assets to the local political elite was not foreseen.

9 DEREGULATION. Deregulation was considered as a way to encourage competition in Latin America.

10 PROPERTY RIGHTS. Washington opted to implement some rights that were already firmly established and guaranteed; in the informal sector this was intended to promote the capacity to obtain property rights at an acceptable cost.

The Washington Consensus helped strengthen the neoliberal paradigm and reduce interventionism and the size of the state in the reproduction of capital, although years later Williamson (1999, 2003) refused to recognize it. Privatization was oriented toward eradicating some of the parasitic structures in the search for economic prosperity and accelerated capital accumulation. Nevertheless, strategic sectors for local economic development were lost because, strictly speaking, there was no evaluation. Hence it is often said that the Washington Consensus appeared to recover all those structures that had to be ceded for the establishment of the Keynesian Consensus since the 1930s.

At the beginning of the new millennium, Latin America had more than 450 million inhabitants, but more than a third of the population was still living in poverty, including almost 80 million people enduring extreme poverty. The region's inequality has delayed the reduction of poverty and repeatedly undermines attempts to make progress. Branko Milanovic (2006) mentions that when relating the activities in homes and the traditional indicators of the per capita gross domestic product, it can be concluded that there has been an essential increase of inequity at the international level owing mainly to the economic reforms advocated in the Washington Consensus.

With respect to productive investments and the role of direct foreign investment, Latin America was not favored in the formation of the new economic order. This is in contrast to the case of China and India, which

43

were favored since their states were more present in order to regulate and administrate financial flows and foreign capital. The characteristics of the financing for economic development in the region and the financial opening did not have the expected results. The industrial capacity of the region deteriorated—primarily in Argentina, Brazil, and Mexico, which had more developed industrial capacities. Both Asia and Latin America suffered financial crises in the 1990s, but the developmental policies, reforms, and financial systems of each region were different. While in Asia the financial systems were ultimately strengthened by the crisis, in Latin America the crisis precipitated a denationalization of the financial services sector—leading to drops in income, education, literacy, life expectancy, access to water, health, and nutrition. There has also been a lack of employment opportunities as well as a lack of more equitable expenditure that finances development of the country, not for the service of the external debt or the interest of particular financial markets. The political and economic alignment with the United States, the traditional Western powers, and the main international financial organizations tempted the region as a means of addressing these problems (Svampa and Slipak 2015, 35). With the failure of the Washington Consensus, however, China began to develop as a major power, which encouraged high expectations for an alternative model for local governments, even as a new financial and commercial partnership was being formed. A period of realignment began, in which Washington lost influence in the region and Beijing began to gain influence.

We can divide the relationship between China and Latin America into five distinct stages. The first involves imperial China prior to the establishment of the Republic of China in 1912, during which time there was a significant contrast in the degree of political autonomy. As the young Latin American republics became independent and expanded their capacities, China started to decline in the face of the system of unequal treaties and different antagonisms between Eastern and Western powers. The second stage, from 1912 to 1949, featured not only low levels of commercial exchange but also an asymmetrical power relationship that favored the Latin American nations. The third stage, from 1949 to 1971, was framed by the political standoff between Taipei and Beijing, during which time most Latin American nations maintained diplomatic ties with Taiwan, with the exception of Cuba after the revolution. Some commercial activity between Latin America and China, however, did begin to develop, which encouraged bilateral contacts. The fourth stage, from 1971 to 2004, began with the change of Chinese representation in the United Nations Security Council and the Joint Statement be-tween Mao and Nixon. This geopolitical turn encouraged the normalization of diplomatic relations between Beijing and the countries of Latin America. Bilateral trade and scientific and technical cooperation also increased, result-ing in relationships of relative symmetry. Finally, the fifth stage, from 2004 to the present, is one in which political, diplomatic, commercial, and cultural relations between the two regions have been further strengthened. These bi-lateral ties, however, have developed in conjunction with a set of fundamen-tally asymmetrical power relations, given that the countries of Latin America remain stuck at the periphery or semiperiphery of the world system while China is rapidly emerging as a great power. In this stage, China has become the first, second, or third commercial partner of most of the countries of the region, and one of their main sources of investment and finance. It is in this fifth stage, moreover, that the Beijing Consensus has begun to take shape.

The Beijing Consensus features the following characteristics:

1 ACKNOWLEDGMENT AND ACCEPTANCE OF THE ONE CHINA POLICY. Focused on its tension with the Nationalist government that relocated to Taiwan in 1949, and under the logic that there is only a single Chi-nese state, the People's Republic of China does not acknowledge the existence of two separate Chinese states.[4] The One China policy was established as one of the main pillars of the nation's foreign policy, and Beijing has systematically reduced the international diplomatic acknowledgment of Taipei through its increasing international rele-vance as a power and as a commercial partner. In South America, only Paraguay maintains diplomatic relations with Taiwan and, over the past decade and a half, many of Taiwan's traditional partners in Central America and the Caribbean have normalized diplomatic relations with Beijing, including Costa Rica in 2011, Panama in 2017, and El Salvador in 2018.[5]

2 ACCEPTANCE OF THE PRINCIPLES OF PEACEFUL COEXISTENCE. These principles were sketched out by Zhou Enlai in 1954, and were also part of the central pillars of Chinese foreign policy.[6] In fact, most declara-tions and treaties China signs include some clauses that refer to them as the framework in which the relationships between the signatory parties are developed. This is affirmed not only in all the joint statements be-tween Washington and Beijing (since the days of Nixon to the present)

but also in the vast majority of documents, agreements, and memorandums of understanding that China has signed with the countries of Latin America since the normalization of diplomatic relationships in 1971. Of these five principles, there are two that differ significantly from the Washington Consensus: "no interference in the internal affairs [of other countries]" and "respect for sovereignty and territorial integrity." Williamson himself (1999) recognized the importance of democracy for the institution's stability, such that the implementation of these principles allows China to escape condemnations regarding its political regime, human rights violations, or the Taiwan issue. At the same time, it is also careful not to interfere in the internal affairs of the countries to which it is linked.

3 BILATERALISM OVER MULTILATERALISM. At the moment in which the Free Trade Area of the Americas failed in the Fourth Summit of the Americas, in the city of Mar del Plata (November 2005), China was sitting in the first row observing everything. Beijing understood that multilateral negotiations may reduce power asymmetries, and that the United States was not able to impose its interests. As a consequence, China deepened its strategy under bilateral diplomacy. For the time being, there were no closed agreements with any of the regional blocs. Faithful to the political realist principle of "divide and conquer," China intends to negotiate bilaterally with the countries of the region, delving into power asymmetry in its favor, and in this way guaranteeing the concretion of its interests. One of the clearest examples, which in fact marks the start of a new stage in the link between China and Latin America, is the recognition as a market economy that Beijing obtained bilaterally from local governments (Brazil, Chile, Argentina, etc.). In this way, although at a discursive level Beijing encourages and fosters a multipolar world, at the level of its actions it does the precise opposite, in that it fosters bilateralism in order to reverse a decision of the multilateral World Trade Organization. Other key examples of this tendency are the bilateral negotiation of currency swap with the countries of the region and investment in infrastructure projects.

4 STRATEGIC ASSOCIATIONS OR RELATIONS. The first Latin American country to sign and accept a strategic association with China was Brazil in 1993. Strategic associations or relationships are a key instrument

of Chinese foreign policy, which avoids entering into the sorts of rigid alliances that China maintained with the Soviet Union during Mao's first years in power.[7] Unlike traditional alliances, strategic associations do not operate at the strategic-military level but at the commercial-financial one, and they are not oriented toward generating effects over third parties. Another distinctive feature is that these strategic associations link countries with different political systems and diverse stages of economic development. Generally speaking, they are bilateral agreements, but there are also examples of plurilateralism, such as China's relationship with the Association of Southeast Asia Nations (ASEAN). At the same time, what is striking is the wide range of different types of strategic relations.[8] The conjecture we make is that they are actually signs the Chinese government sends in order to provide guidelines regarding the kinds of businesses or links that local entrepreneurs may carry out with their opposing parties in the country in question. Strategic associations or relationships have become important instruments of Chinese foreign policy, which is oriented to foster a bilateral link.

5 ASYMMETRICAL COMMERCIAL EXCHANGE, FINANCING, AND INVEST-MENTS AND THE "SELL FUTURE" LOGIC. Although within the "peaceful coexistence" principles it is referred to as "mutual benefits," the commercial exchange scheme between China and Latin America is far from that. In effect, it follows the center-periphery logic in which China adopts the position as manufacturer exporter with a high technological content, whereas Latin America embraces the logic of export of primary products and products derived from them. That is to say, the first inequality is established by the impossibility of generating higher added value in exports; there is no exchange of two channels (intraindustrial) and, thus, the industrialization process cannot be boosted in the region. In effect, the trade between China and Latin America tends to be productive primarization in those cases in which there is no certain development of the national industry (Chile, Ecuador, Peru, Venezuela, etc.) and a reprimarization in those in which there are certain developments in the national industry (Brazil, Mexico, and Argentina).[9] The second inequality appears together with commercial imbalances. During the past two decades, the vast majority of the countries in the region have accumulated significant structural commercial deficits. The only

47

exceptions are Brazil and Chile, which not only shows the inequality of the exchange but also the problem of the loss of foreign currency for the countries of the region. A third inequality results from the high concentration of a few products, which are linked to the primary products of Latin American exports to China. Most of the countries concentrate more than 80 percent of their exports in one or two sectors, while Chinese exports to the region are diversified in the manufacturer's sector of low, medium, and high technological content. Finally, a fourth inequality that must be denoted in the commercial area is the importance that China has for the Latin American markets, which is far superior to what the countries of the region represent as commercial partners of the Asian power. This final fact shows how the Chinese market can be used not only to pressure local governments but also to offer an appealing incentive. Regarding financing and investments, the increasing role of China in the region is undeniable.[10] It should come as no surprise that, in both cases, the financial flow is directed mainly to the sector of infrastructure and extractive industries. This is related to the role that natural resources have in the strategy of linking China with the region; it is a key factor in revitalizing and maintaining the process of economic modernization. Related to both the commercial aspect and financing and investment, China deploys its "Sell Future" strategy: it uses the size of its market or its financial capacity to skillfully exchange a political action favorable to its national interest in exchange for a future promise that goes from an increase of exports to the arrival of investments—for example, the recognition as a market economy in exchange for an increase of exports to the Chinese market, as was the case in Argentina in 2004.

If we understand that natural resources are vital for Chinese economic modernization and that the success of the industrialization process provides legitimacy to the Chinese Communist Party—as a conductor of the political process in China since 1949—then the Beijing Consensus can be viewed as one of the most important pillars of China's foreign policy while at the same time contributing to another key pillar: the Peaceful Rise Doctrine.

As a background to this link scheme that China weaves with the region, a course of action was laid out in two key documents. In 2008 Beijing presented a white paper detailing "China's Policy toward Latin America and the Caribbean" (Política de China hacia América Latina y el Caribe).[11] In very idealistic language, it lists key concepts such as "peaceful development and opening strategy based on the reciprocal benefit and the shared profit," "friendship and cooperation with all countries on the basis of the Five Principles of Peaceful Coexistence," "commercial complementarity," and "increase and balance bilateral trade." However, China's political praxis, clearly pragmatic and realistic, stays away from this type of discourse.

That same document makes it clear that the key cooperation areas in commercial matters are agriculture, silviculture, fishery, energy, exploitation of mining resources, and construction of infrastructures. In this way, Latin America is perceived by China as a primary products supplier and, to a lesser extent, as a market for placing its manufactured products (Svampa and Slipak 2015, 44). The result is that Chinese investment and financing for infrastructure in Latin America have been oriented toward fostering the exploitation and extraction of natural resources, always in order to sustain the economic modernization process of China over the years, but collaterally the legitimacy of the Communist Party. We should keep in mind that there exists a synergy between economic development and governance that is expressed in terms of order and progress, and the party is well aware of this. In 2016 Beijing produced a new white paper addressing "China's Policy toward Latin America" (Política de China hacia América Latina), in which the importance of Latin America as a supplier of natural resources was further strengthened.[12] The first part is titled "Latin America and the Caribbean—Wonderful Land" (América Latina y el Caribe—Tierra Maravillosa) and it concludes by presenting a scenario in which the roadmap for cooperation and exchange involves human resources. In this way, the Beijing Consensus appears to substantiate an asymmetrical link scheme, based on the comparative advantage and commercial complementation logic, which implies the large-scale exploitation of natural resources by means of Chinese financial capital.

Maristella Svampa's postulates (2013) suggest that Latin American governments, while immersed in a theoretical discussion regarding the dynamics of accumulation and development models, should take a concrete stand before the rise of China and its growing role in the region. As an opposing party to the Beijing Consensus, the Commodities Consensus began to develop, and while the first emphasizes the new center of world power, the second refers specifically to the practice of the local elites that embraces the economic logic of primarization and reprimarization, under the postulates of an extraordinary profitability (Bolinaga 2018). In sum, the Commodities Consensus and the Beijing Consensus are simply two sides of the same coin.

49

The Impact of the Beijing Consensus in Latin America

If we want to indicate the precise moment when China began to exert considerable influence in Latin America—displacing traditional interlocutors such as European powers and reducing American influence—we would undoubtedly say that it was the year 2004. Since then, Beijing has peacefully but abruptly begun to set foot in Latin America, and especially in South America. Hu Jintao's tour of Brazil, Argentina, and Chile, in November 2004, was essential to understanding the power asymmetry in which China's relations with the whole region would be developed. These three nations recognized China as a "market economy," despite the fact that the World Trade Organization still categorizes it as a "nonmarket economy" (in light of the government's ability to exert control over prices and costs). This was particularly significant in Brazil and Argentina because, as opposed to Chile, their productive structures have some industrial development, which is still primary, but it also shows us how China uses bilateralism to get the most out of power asymmetries and to revert some decisions made in the multilateral field. Also in 2004, for instance, Chinese political forces participated in the United Nations Mission of Peace in Haiti, which maintains diplomatic relations with Taiwan.

China has gradually displaced many Latin American countries' traditional trading partners. Since 2011 Beijing has become the main destination for exports from Chile and Peru as a consequence of the enforcement of various free trade agreements. China is also the main export destination for Brazil, which has long been China's principal trade partner in Latin America and the Caribbean, even though there is no Free Trade Agreement in this case. Meanwhile, Beijing is the second-most important destination for exports from Argentina, Cuba, Uruguay, and Venezuela. Finally, the Chinese market is the third-largest destination for Mexican exports. With respect to imports, the significance of the Chinese partnership for the region is even more pronounced. China is the main supplier for Nicaragua and Panama, the second-largest supplier for Argentina, Brazil, Chile, Colombia, Costa Rica, Cuba, Ecuador, Mexico, Peru, and Venezuela, and the third-largest supplier for Bolivia, Guatemala, and Uruguay. This is important because the commercial dynamics between China and these nations reveal a vertiginous growth of imports over exports, from and to China, which leads us to one of the main problems of the region: commercial deficits with the Asian power.

Only Brazil and Chile have been able to maintain surplus commercial balances, with all other countries running structural deficits, resulting in the loss of foreign currency. That is why China encouraged a currency swap with countries in the region so they could purchase Chinese products with yuan, with no loss of dollars. In practice, however, what actually happened is that countries of the region became tied to China as their supplier of manufactured and industrial materials, further accelerating the growth of imports from China. Therefore, between 2001 and 2010 the commercial link was driven by the high prices of commodities resulting from high Chinese demand, which generated extra income for the countries of the region thanks to several surplus years. Meanwhile, from 2010 to the present, the link has been reformulated in asymmetrical terms due to the fact that not only have exports from the region to China practically stopped but there has also been a decline in international prices. Furthermore, to the detriment of the industrial sector, Beijing has contributed to the breakdown of the intra-industrial structure of the region. The Southern Common Market (Mercado Común del Sur, MERCOSUR) as a case study illustrates how Argentina and Brazil have been displaced as suppliers by their Chinese partner, not only as suppliers to each other but also as suppliers to the Uruguayan market. The most committed sector, and the genesis of the integration process, is the automotive sector. The China factor is reverting and deteriorating the intra-industrial scheme, which had been built during the 1990s and the first five years of the twenty-first century. This is where an inescapable criticism arises, not for the Chinese government, but for the local elites that promote this kind of relationship and do not notice the contradictions in China's rhetoric in what we have characterized as the Beijing Consensus.

This asymmetry ends up being shaped by the high concentration of Latin American exports in a few sectors and, of course, it is about primary products and products derived from them. Between 2001 and 2016, more than 90 percent of Argentine exports to China were concentrated in three major sectors: soybeans, soybean oil, and crude petroleum. Moreover, the sale of soybean oil in that period fell relative to the other two sectors. Brazil concentrated its exports in soybeans, iron, and crude petroleum, with these three sectors making up almost 80 percent of the country's total exports to China in 2016. In that same year, the Chilean export offer to China was even more concentrated in a single product: copper and its derivatives (more than 80 percent). In the latter case, the existence of a Free Trade Agreement (in force since October 2016) did not improve the quality of the exchange, but rather intensified the tendency that was already in progress, associated with a primary-extractive scheme. Venezuela exported crude petroleum and derivatives to

China in such a way that they accounted for more than 96 percent of its total exports in 2016, and 90 percent of Colombia's exports to China were in crude petroleum.

The region as a whole currently faces a challenge of diversifying exports, for which the elite do not seem to have found any solutions—neither by means of bilateral strategies (free trade agreements have proliferated), nor by multilateral strategies (there are no successful commercial negotiations from regional blocs or from other more flexible agreements like the Alliance for the Pacific) (Bolinaga 2018). Meanwhile, in contrast to this homogenization of imports, China's exports to the region are increasingly diversified: the three most important products are cell phone parts and accessories (6 percent), transmitters for televisions and radios (5 percent), and computer parts and accessories (4 percent).

While between 2001 and 2005 the five main exports from Latin America to China represented 50 percent of the region's total exports, in the period from 2011 to 2014 those same products made up 75 percent of the total, indicating that the inability to diversify exports or to improve the quality of the exchange has been decisive.[13] Table 2.1 shows how ingrained China's presence is in the region, and how its presence exceeds the commercial logic, even as it feeds on it. As a common saying puts it: "China set foot in Latin America peacefully but abruptly."

The People's Republic of China currently controls two of the ports of the Panama Canal (San Cristóbal and Balboa), ensuring that it has smooth access to both the Pacific and the Atlantic. Beijing's positioning on the oceans is a key element to the control of maritime flow. Although, as table 2.1 indicates, the construction of a new canal—in Nicaragua—is still in progress, this nevertheless gives us a guide to how the power vacuum left by Washington has begun to be occupied by Beijing. Another project linked to the transportation sector that may have consequences for the region's geopolitics and environment involves the construction of a railroad crossing the Amazon River and connecting ports on the Atlantic and Pacific coasts. It should be noted that China already controls Argentina's Belgrano Cargas railway, which ensures the connection not only for soybeans with the port of Buenos Aires but also for lithium from the northeast and hydrocarbons from Patagonia. Major Chinese oil companies (both state companies and joint ventures) have also landed in the region. For instance, the China National Offshore Oil Corporation (CNOOC) is already operating in Cerro Dragón, where the country's most important hydrocarbon warehouse is located. The China

TABLE 2.1 China increases its presence in Latin America and the Caribbean

AREA	ISSUE	COUNTRY
Sea transportation	Panama Canal: Port of San Cristóbal (Atlantic) and Port Balboa (Pacific)	Panama
Sea transportation	new bioceanic channel project	Nicaragua
Rail transportation	Belgrano Cargas Railway	Argentina
Rail transportation	project to build a bioceanic railway	Brazil Peru
Trade	free trade agreement	Chile
Trade	free trade agreement	Costa Rica
Trade	free trade agreement	Peru
Finance	swap	Argentina Brazil Chile Colombia Peru Uruguay Venezuela
Chinese companies	China Minmetals Corporation	Brazil Chile Ecuador Peru
Chinese companies	China National Cereals, Oils and Foodstuffs Corporation (COFCO) acquired Nidera	Argentina
Chinese companies	China National Chemical Corporation (ChemChina) acquired Syngenta	Argentina
Chinese companies	China National Offshore Oil Corporation (CNOOC)	Argentina
Chinese companies	China National Petroleum Corporation (CNPC)	Brazil Costa Rica Ecuador Peru Venezuela
Chinese bank	Industrial and Commercial Bank of China (ICBC)	Argentina Brazil Mexico Peru
Chinese companies	Sinochem	Colombia Peru
Chinese companies	Sinopec	Argentina Brazil Venezuela

National Petroleum Corporation (CNPC) operates in five countries of the region: Brazil, Costa Rica, Ecuador, Peru, and Venezuela. Sinopec operates not only in Argentina and Brazil but also in Venezuela. Sinochem has positioned itself in Colombia and Peru. China Minmetals Corporation is strongly positioned in Brazil, Chile, Ecuador, and Peru. China National Cereals, Oils and Foodstuffs Corporation (COFCO) bought Nidera and China National Chemical Corporation (ChemChina) bought Syngenta in Argentina, which allows it not only to enter the oligopoly of oilseeds in the region but also to push the price of soy to their own benefit. This process of fusions and acquisitions by Chinese companies reveals that their main strategy is not greenfield but brownfield; there are no significant cases of establishment of new Chinese companies in the region.

China has signed free trade agreements with Chile (2006), Peru (2010), and Costa Rica (2011). With these three countries there has been a noticeable increase in the commercial flow but not in the quality of the exchange itself—which is to say, the interindustrial scheme that severely conditions the generation of greater added value in production has deepened. The cases of Chile and Peru are much more significant in the extractive scheme for copper.

Table 2.1 also brings up the arrival of the Industrial and Commercial Bank of China (ICBC) in the region. It is the largest bank in China and, by market capitalization, in the world. The ICBC has become the revitalizing variable of China's financial flow to the region, whether it adopts the form of investment or financing. Based in Argentina, Brazil, Colombia, Mexico, and Peru, China is consolidating its position in South America; Argentina, Brazil, and Venezuela are the countries destined for 80 percent of China's investment projects in the region.

Conclusion

The progression from the Washington Consensus toward the Beijing Consensus ignites a red light of attention in international relations before what seems to be consolidating itself as a new instrument of the great powers to exert influence in the periphery of the system, under a discursive logic that mitigates the coercive component. Although in both the first and the second consensus there has been verified rhetoric that comes into contradiction with the practices developed by the powers, that is where the coincidences end.

The Washington Consensus favored neither the agricultural sector nor the industrial sector, but rather both were threatened by the increasing liberalization of markets and the expansion of rental-financial activity. Therefore, there was no expansion of the level of employment or a process of economic development that would lead to growth with social inclusion. The real objective of the Washington Consensus was to dismantle the state structure installed in Latin America under the Keynesian State during the post–World War II period.

The Beijing Consensus seeks to guarantee access to essential natural resources to maintain the process of economic modernization in China over a period of time, being vital not only for the stability of the country but for the very legitimacy of the Communist Party as the conductor of the Chinese political process. In this way, a series of discursive and practical instruments that would promote a dynamics of accumulation based on primary-extractive production schemes—which would not allow for the development of significant levels of added value in exports—were developed. Chinese financing and investment were oriented to the primary-extractive sector and to the development of the necessary infrastructure to guarantee its exploitation and connection with the ports. All of this is accompanied by a strong idealistic discourse that combines concepts such as South-South cooperation, reciprocal benefits and shared profit, equality and respect, and increasing and balancing bilateral trade. But the Chinese political praxis verifies that the asymmetric links of power are promoted under the logic of bilateral negotiations, and that the benefits and profits are mainly for China due to the great imbalances—including the concentration of exports in a few sectors, an increase in structural deficits, and a loss of foreign currency—that, far from being corrected, have been exacerbated over time. Finally, the local industry has been weakened by local governments that, to the detriment of the decision made by the World Trade Organization, have recognized China as a market economy, thus losing the possibility of protecting their industries through safeguards and other instruments. The Beijing Consensus, in short, favors this primary-extractive scheme and undermines the intraregional industrial scheme. But it does not question the institutional transparency or the political nature of the regime, which suggests a less interventionist praxis than the American one and also nourishes the support of anti-American sectors that see in the link with China a path toward development and greater autonomy with respect to the great powers. However, they do not seem to understand that the players may change, but the rules of the game will not.

Notes

1 The participants included the World Bank, the International Monetary Fund, the Federal Reserve, some think tanks, and so forth.

2 These measures correspond to the statistics of both the World Bank and the International Monetary Fund.

3 The approval in 2005 of the National Plan of Development of Science and Technology in the Medium and Long Term (2006–20) was the cornerstone of that process. Some of the most significant goals are: (1) to reduce to less than 30 percent the participation of foreign technologies; (2) to strengthen the connection between technological development and economic growth; (3) to form institutions and gather together scientists in research and development of worldwide recognition; etc. (Y. Lu 2010).

4 Unlike the Korean case, where the double acknowledgment is accepted.

5 As of mid-2018, only Belize, Guatemala, Haiti, Honduras, Nicaragua, Paraguay, and the Dominican Republic, Kitts and Nevis, Santa Lucia, Saint Vincent, and the Grenadines still maintain diplomatic relationships with the government of Taipei.

6 These principles include mutual respect for sovereignty and territorial integrity, no mutual aggression, no interference in the internal affairs of other countries, equality and mutual benefits, and pacific coexistence.

7 The disastrous relation with the Soviet Union in the years immediately after Mao's revolution had a tremendous impact on the Chinese worldview regarding strategic alliances.

8 The types of strategic associations include the Friendly Cooperation Association, Strategic Cooperative Association, General Cooperative Association, Strategic Association, Integral Strategic Association, Neighborhood and Mutual Confidence Association, Associative Relation, Associative Relations of Global Liability, and the Constructive Strategy Society. Eduardo Oviedo's article (2006) explains the subject.

9 Regarding the concept *reprimarization*, this chapter takes as a starting point the definition provided by Slipak (2013), which defines the term as a complex process that entails redirecting economic resources toward activities with lower added value, generally primary-extractive activities, as well as the maquila sector. This process restricts the potential of countries in the region to structurally transform their productive matrixes in such a way that would allow them to achieve trade insertion in the international market based on economic activities with major added value (Bolinaga and Slipak 2015).

10 Latin America is positioned as the third most important region for Chinese direct foreign investment, behind Asia and Oceania. The greatest amount of

Chinese investment in Latin America is directed to South America, and the three most important recipients are Venezuela, Brazil, and Argentina.

11 People's Republic of China 2006.

12 People's Republic of China, Consejo de Estado 2016.

13 Those five products were soybeans (20 percent), iron ore (9 percent), copper ore and refined copper (19 percent), crude petroleum (2 percent), and petroleum oil (0.5 percent). During the period between 2011 and 2014, these proportions were soybeans (20 percent), iron ore (20 percent), copper ore and refined copper (21 percent), crude petroleum (12 percent), and petroleum oil (1 percent).

PREHISTORIES OF CHINA-TANZANIA

Intermediaries, Subempires, and the Use and Abuse of Comparison

The China-in-Africa discourse is haunted by the afterlives of European impe-rialism. Discussions about rising Chinese trade, investment, and migration since the turn of the twenty-first century frequently invoke, either directly or indirectly, late nineteenth-century European colonialism. *New York Times* journalist Howard French exemplifies this perspective in his 2014 book de-scribing "how a million (Chinese) migrants are building a new empire in Africa." Focused on the lives of individual Chinese migrant entrepreneurs across the continent, French's concept of empire for the most part reflects a more nuanced understanding of the concept than the casual invocation of co-lonialism found in mainstream media accounts. French appreciates that neo-colonialism does not mean territorial recolonization because "the nature of empire has changed dramatically over time depending on the circumstances" (French 2014, 260). In the end, however, French uses historical analogies to suggest how these processes might turn out. He writes: "What I was wit-nessing in Africa is the higgledy-piggledy cobbling together of a new Chinese realm of interest. Here were the beginnings of a new empire, a haphazard empire perhaps, but an empire nonetheless" (170). While there may be "little hint of a grand or even deliberate scheme [to colonize Africa], . . . in the end, that's not so important. . . . It is outcomes that count" (264). The

Portuguese colonization of Mozambique, he argues, did not begin with the Crown, but with the activities of Portuguese traders. While few may dispute that growing Chinese communities in Africa will lead to greater pressures for Chinese state intervention to protect them (cf. Parello-Plesner and Duchâtel 2015), the suggestion that there is an analogy between the history of European settlers and contemporary migration produces a misleading identity between the situation of postcolonial and precolonial Africa.

Counterarguments that China in Africa *could never be* an emerging empire also rely on problematic historical comparisons. The Chinese foreign minister Wang Yi, for example, has argued that China "absolutely will not take the old path of Western colonists" (Reuters 2015). Like French, Wang implies that the "old path" is even an option in the present world of nation-states. The concept of neocolonialism was invented to describe an array of conditions ranging from dependency on foreign capital to military interventionism, without any implication that countries were being *re*colonized in the traditional fashion (Nkrumah 1965).

Chinese migrants occupy an ambivalent position in this debate in part because Chinese migration precedes the rise of the new China, but also because the economic and political privilege and/or vulnerability of Chinese migrants vis-à-vis others in global hierarchies have long been ambivalent (Nyíri 2005). In this respect, Chinese migrants resemble other Indian Ocean migrants. There is a telling moment in French's book when a representative of a Tanzanian workers' union criticizes the Chinese presence in the language of economic invasion. French asks him how the Chinese presence in the Tanzanian economy is different from the economic strength of Indians, who have a much older history in the country (2014, 212). The man ignores his question but, curiously, French does not address these implications either.

The significance of these omissions is not that a comparison between Chinese migrants and white settlers is unjustified, but that in overlooking the history of non-European migration to Africa, these analogies miss a broader set of relevant comparisons for understanding global inequalities beyond a dichotomy of colonizer and colonized. Asian migrations in the Indian Ocean and Africa not only preceded the rise of European empires, but in many places were more significant to the experience of European colonialism than the migration of white settlers. This is evidenced by the fact that Indian and Chinese communities have *both* been targets of nationalist populism in East Africa and Southeast Asia, respectively, during the postindependence period.

59

The rise of China—like the rise of India—in the Global South cannot be fully understood apart from these histories.

Focusing on the relationship between migrations and state projects, my goal in this chapter is to complicate the dichotomy of colonizer and colonized in China-Africa discourse by calling attention to the shifting and unsettled intelligibility of these categories themselves. In a context where China and Africa have long been interconnected, even if indirectly, through the Indian Ocean trade, I recast the history of these connections as a story of changing modes of global relations. I emphasize *relations* rather than *relationships* to avoid defining Africa and China as discrete a priori cultural/national units with a singular (even if changing) relationship over time. I begin instead with circulations of peoples and goods, their inequalities and mutualities, and changing modes of their governance between the precolonial, colonial, and postcolonial moments. My focus is restricted to the Swahili coast of East Africa, particularly Tanzania, the place where historical narratives have been the most conspicuously mobilized for worlding contemporary China-Africa relations. In particular, these include the fifteenth-century visits of the Ming fleet, and the 1960s–70s construction of the Tanzania-Zambia Railway. Rather than simply casting these moments as signifiers of a Chinese model of power in the present, I instead trace how the meaning of China and the Chinese have shifted in terms of East Africa's own changing relations with the world. I map three "historical horizons" (Rojas and Rofel, this volume) for the contemporary Chinese presence: as Indian Ocean intermediaries, as Asian middlemen in a European colonial world, and as global capital in the postcolonial world. Each of these moments complicates any move to pigeonhole China into a dichotomy of colonizer and colonized but still raises questions about the reproduction of inequality in global relations.

Intermediaries and Subempires

Against the backdrop of East Africa's longue durée, the emergence of China and the Chinese in Tanzania might be situated as the latest chapter in a history of rising and falling trading intermediaries. Before the twentieth century, China and the Swahili coast had long been connected, mostly indirectly, through Indian Ocean trading networks (Kusimba, Zhu, and Kiura 2020). The *Maritime Silk Road* is a recent term invented to describe these networks, and after 2013 the term was adopted by the Chinese state for the Belt and Road Initiative (Kwa 2016). The term evokes the image of a premodern cosmopolitan trading system before European imperialism. China's Belt and Road Initiative has been legitimated by being symbolically linked to a premodern Afro-Eurasian world system characterized to have been a mare liberum over which no single polity, until the Portuguese, was able to—or even sought to—exercise dominion (Sheriff 2010). The fact that the early fifteenth-century Zheng He expeditions did not fundamentally alter the system has supported the narrative of China as what Joseph Needham calls "an empire without imperialism" (Needham 1971, 517–18). But this focus on the state has in turn overshadowed the role of traders and intermediaries. When viewed through the lens of this history, the contemporary presence of China straddles a more complex position vis-à-vis the history of empire.

A desire for globalizations and cosmopolitanisms otherwise haunts some Indian Ocean scholarship as well, which has endeavored to map a world before Vasco de Gama's violent entry into the region. One example is the Zanzibari scholar Abdul Sheriff's Braudelian paean to the dhow cultures of the Indian Ocean (2010). In this maritime economy, trading diasporas, rather than states, were the dominant actors. Sheriff's narrative is nonetheless bookended by a contrast between two new state actors who appeared in the fifteenth century. The first were Admiral Zheng He's expeditions on behalf of the Ming dynasty, the largest state-financed naval operations in human history up to that time, exceeding the subsequent European voyages by several orders of magnitude (296). This alone would have marked them as historically important, but their contemporary significance arguably derives from what the Portuguese did decades later. The Portuguese were "strange new traders who brought their state with them" (E. Ho 2006, xxi), seizing ports and demanding exclusive control over trade. In comparison, the Chinese expeditions became known for what they did not do. The Chinese did not establish a trade monopoly, did not wage religious war by expelling Muslims from their ports, and did not expand the slave trade (Sheriff 2010, 313–14). Finally, court officials in the mid-fifteenth century forced the cancellation of the expeditions, and the destruction of the fleet and its records. Sheriff speculates about what might have happened to the Portuguese had the Chinese remained. In 1521, for example, an ambassador for the Sultan of Melaka, a Ming vassal expelled by the Portuguese a decade earlier, appealed unsuccessfully for aid from China, which "by then had retreated deep into its continental shell" (2010, 313).

The fact that the Ming Dynasty's maritime expeditions of the early fifteenth century did not presage a Chinese overseas empire has facilitated China's

61

exceptional inclusion in the Indian Ocean historical narrative as conspicuously *nonimperialist*. The comparison, however, downplays continuities in imperial practice. One of the goals of the expeditions was to obtain ritual recognition by distant princes and states of the Ming emperor's cosmological centrality (Sheriff 2010, 291). Furthermore, the fleets were armed and sometimes did in fact intervene in multiple local conflicts. The politics were similar to China's imperial interventions on the continent, taken ostensibly at the behest of ritual vassals. However, the further west the fleets went, the less militarized they became, and ultimately they did not fundamentally alter the trade system itself (304, 314).

The expectation that China could have become—or might still become— an empire entails an ideological conceit: namely, if China is retrospectively imagined as having always been a *potential global empire*, it is perceived as being morally superior for having chosen otherwise.[1] This conceit, however, is based on the absence of *maritime* conquest, and therefore is defined in relation to European imperial history. Furthermore, in focusing on state conquest as the measure of empire, the narrative discounts the other ways the Chinese have been participants in the Indian Ocean economy.

The contemporary Belt and Road Initiative—oriented around rail lines, transportation corridors, and ports—is more the heir to European imperial imaginaries of the late nineteenth and early twentieth centuries than to earlier networks of trade and migration (Chin 2013). Nonetheless, the imagery of civilizational concord promoted by the initiative echoes a desire to recover a model of cosmopolitanism and global trade otherwise. The narrative is appealing, but even in the absence of (potential) empires, Indian Ocean connections have also entailed multiple forms of inequality—the most conspicuous for the Swahili coast being the slave trade. Such inequalities complicate the retrospective recovery of the Indian Ocean as an alternative cosmopolitan space, but these complications in turn allow for a more nuanced understanding of power beyond the colonizer/colonized binary.

The role of intermediaries is relevant to this discussion. Intermediaries can be broadly defined to encompass everything from trading diasporas to political formations. Polities emerged along littoral zones like the Swahili coast, capitalizing on the mediation of continental and maritime economies (Sheriff 2010, 5–6). From the perspective of a historical narrative culminating in European imperialism, these political formations—including the Omani sultanate on Zanzibar preceding the German colonization of East Africa—have traditionally appeared in the historiography as *sub*empires:

"satellites" of Western imperialism or "secondary empires" (Iliffe 1979; Curtin 1984). One reason is that the intensification of the slave and ivory trade, and the expansion of the plantation system for cloves and spices in the nineteenth century, were connected to the broader capitalist transformation of the global economy (Sheriff 1987). These involved a range of non-European actors, including Indian merchants invited by the sultan as financiers for armed caravans led by African slaves themselves (Glassman 1995; Burton 2013). During this period, both individual actors and larger political formations could rise or fall within hierarchies of power and prestige based on their control over the out-movement of people and ivory, and the in-movement of foreign commodities, which created chains of patron-clientage reaching from Zanzibar to what is now Congo. Jonathan Glassman writes that "access to credit and foreign markets became the key mechanism by which particularly shrewd and well-placed men acquired wealth to attract large followings of clients and the firearms to protect and empower them" (Glassman 1995, 47). One of these men, the early nineteenth-century Chagga chief Orombo, built a political formation that Sally Falk Moore (1977) equivocates between calling either an African empire or simply an African middleman.

These terminological confusions between the terms *empire* and *middleman* are significant because they highlight the ambiguity, in terms of power and legitimacy, of being an intermediary. Jean-François Bayart and Stephen Ellis have argued that African modes of political-economic action are a "strategy of extraversion" based on the "creation and the capture of a rent generated by dependency and which functions as a historical matrix of inequality, political centralization and social struggle" (2000, 222). These strategies encompassed the colonial encounter and, it is implied, continue with newer external actors. The problem with this framework, however, is the reification of African dependency at the expense of understanding shifting interdependencies between chains of networked actors. There is a long-standing history of cascading trading hierarchies on the Swahili coast—intermediaries replacing or becoming dependent on other intermediaries—which blurs the distinction between concepts of *African* and *Asian*. Nyamwezi traders became porters for the Swahili (Sheriff 1987; Glassman 1995, 58–64), the Swahili became indebted to Arabs from Zanzibar (Glassman 1995, 78), and Arab plantation owners lost land to Indian financiers (Sheriff 1987; Burton 2013). Such patterns have echoed through the colonial and postcolonial periods. For example, although Indian wholesalers dominated in the trade sector during the early period of decolonization, following liberalization in Tanzania they

63

have also faced competition from Chagga traders from the Mt. Kilimanjaro region, and Chagga wholesalers themselves have faced competition from migrant Chinese wholesalers who also face competition from other African traders.

From the perspective of at least this sector, the emergence of a Chinese presence over the past several decades is visualized less by grand state visits and projects than by shifting market geographies and hierarchies within which African actors have played leading roles (Adebayo and Omololu 2018). African traders purchased goods from Europe, the Middle East, and Southeast Asia long before southern China emerged as an industrial center. The inexpensiveness of Chinese commodities, however, has affected local trading hierarchies across Africa, undermining the monopolies of some traders, while opening up opportunities for others. The migration of Chinese traders directly to African markets has only intensified these processes. For example, in Tanzania, traders describe Chinese goods and Chinese traders as having helped African traders enter a market previously dominated by Indian Tanzanians. However, Chinese traders describe their own position in the market as increasingly challenged by Africans, who are themselves migrants from rural areas. While the close relationship between the Tanzanian and Chinese states have played a role in establishing some connections, they do not encompass all the routes through which Chinese manufacturers and trading intermediaries have come together. Many of these routes reflect broader Indian Ocean trading networks that resonate with (without being the same as) longer histories.

Nonetheless, traders have occupied an ambivalent position in mainstream China-Africa narratives, which emphasize states and infrastructure. When contemporary Chinese officials describe the China-Tanzania relationship as long-standing, the privileged actors are Zheng He, Zhou Enlai, and the engineers and workers of the Tanzania-Zambia Railway. In the literature, traders appear with qualifying terms like *low-end globalization* (Mathews 2011). The historian Philip Curtin (1984) concluded his magnum opus on premodern cross-cultural trade with a discussion of the "twilight of the trade diasporas" (230). Dhows, the wooden monsoon sailboats that served as trading vessels for centuries, were replaced, so the story goes, by steamships owned by colonial firms. However, itinerant traders, and even dhows, never completely disappeared from the scene and continue to operate in the margins in the global economy to this day (Mahajan 2019). The (re)discovery of these trading networks by scholars, particularly in the Global South, has spawned terms like *transnational informal economy* (Portes 1997) and, two years before Xi Jinping began talking about them in the language of infrastructure, the *new silk roads* (Yang and Altman 2011).

The compound terminology used to describe these traders illustrates the limitations of teleological histories. Are informal traders to be considered premodern cultural survivals or the paradigmatic subjects of globalization? The answer depends on one's theory of history. From one perspective, they testify to the resilience of horizontal connections outside the West-and-the-rest axis of history. On the other hand, their ideological mobilization as proxies for nonimperial alternatives elides the fundamentally *interimperial* dynamics of their imagining (Doyle 2014): the extent to which contemporary discourses about China in Africa cannot be disentangled from the assumptions and practices of European colonialism, and the interpellation and complicities of Asian middlemen in that history.

Asian Middlemen in a European Africa

The concept of the Maritime Silk Road gestures to a time before European empires, but the recent history of Asian migrations is unthinkable apart from the history of empires. Chinese migration to East Africa was historically negligible compared with their presence in Southeast Asia, but they shared with Indian migrants the fate of being placed between European empires and anticolonial nationalisms (Bonacich 1973). European colonialism in both East Africa and Southeast Asia established a firm dichotomy between the colonizer (white, European) and the colonized (native, African, Malay). The presence of Asian trading diasporas complicated this dichotomy, and the responses they generated uncannily prefigure contemporary responses to the presence of Asian capital in the Global South. The reason for this is not just the enduring hegemony of the West/rest dichotomy in the discourse of South-South relations but also the intimate relationship between trading diasporas and both colonial *and* anticolonial projects.

The earliest story of Chinese settler colonialism in Africa began in the nineteenth century. Francis Galton, the British statistician and eugenicist wrote a letter in 1873 to the *Times* advocating "Africa for the Chinese." Specifically, he proposed "to make the encouragement of the Chinese settlements at one or more suitable places on the East Coast of Africa a part of our national policy, in the belief that the Chinese immigrants would not only maintain their position, but that they would multiply and their descendants

65

supplant the inferior Negro race."[2] The following decade, a similar letter from Sir Harry Johnston appeared in the *Empire Review* advocating making East Africa an "America for the Hindu" (G. Desai 2013, 57). This latter scheme was actually unsuccessfully promoted by some Indian residents of East Africa and sympathetic British officials after German East Africa was transferred to British rule following World War I (Burton 2013, 13–14). The proposals reveal a trope, still present if not explicitly racialized, that Asians, whether Chinese or Indians, are potential "agents of development" (Mohan et al. 2014) whose mere presence as economic actors might be the "catalyst" (Brautigam 2003) to transform Africa. At the time Galton and Johnston wrote, Asians were already being mobilized as a new form of racialized labor for work on plantations and mines from the Caribbean to the South Pacific, and were pitted against the freed African former slaves they were to replace (Lowe 2015). The first large-scale migration from China to Africa would in fact occur during the first decade of the twentieth century when Chinese miners were recruited in the thousands to work in the Transvaal, South Africa.

In European settler colonies, opposition to Asian settlement derived from the same assumption as idiosyncratic subcolonial schemes: Asian economic vitality posing a civilizational threat to white supremacy. In South Africa, as in the United States and Australia, Chinese migrants were restricted from participation in the larger economy (Park 2009). In Africa, opposition to Asian migration was also articulated in terms of the Western protection of indigenous peoples from "Eastern" civilization (G. Desai 2013, 63). For example, German colonial authorities in East Africa justified racial segregation between Indians and Africans in the real estate market on the grounds of protecting Africans from economic exploitation by the Indians (Brennan 2012).

Similar assumptions have continued to inform the grand narratives of China-in-Africa in the postcolonial period, especially as articulated by Western scholars. Early scholarship was framed in terms of China being either a "cure" or "curse" for Africa (Keenan 2009), and only later did attention shift to "reinserting" or "recovering" the agency of Africans in constituting these relationships (Corkin 2013; Mohan and Lampert 2013). The general neglect of African agency—combined with the fact that scholars (particularly non-African scholars) who did attend to African agency conspicuously included the word in their titles—reveals how persisting racial imaginaries shape interpretative frameworks for talking about South-South relations.

The assumption that Asians could be potential modernizers of Africa has also informed Asian anticolonial thought at different points in time. Africa provided a foil for Asian aspirations. Gandhi's anti-Black racism during his mobilization of the Indian diaspora in South Africa is perhaps the most emblematic example, but even in China, the "black race" provided a foil against which the capacity of the "yellow race" to catch up with and challenge the "white race" could be asserted (Dikötter 1992). Anti-Black discourse suffused the writings of prominent late Qing reformers, like Liang Qichao and Kang Youwei, who first embraced the cause of the Boers as anticolonial fighters long before Mao would embrace Black Africans (Karl 2002). When Liang Qichao described the Chinese diaspora in Southeast Asia as colonial, he meant it positively because it indicated the commensurability of Chinese and Western capacities (Perdue 2015, 1010).

The same structural position, however, that afforded the discursive complicity of anticolonial nationalism with racial theories and subcolonial fantasies, also afforded the imagining of more inclusive anticolonial aspirations. Besides the contributions of Indian and Chinese communities to popular anticolonial nationalist movements in both East Africa and Southeast Asia, some historians have argued more controversially for their distinct *economic contribution*. For example, Robert Gregory (1993) sets up a contrast between the Indian pursuit of free economic exchange with East Africans, and the paternalistic "socialism" of the British. The idea that market exchange was more egalitarian than colonialism is reflected in the words of the early twentieth-century Indian Ugandan capitalist Nanji Mehta, who wrote that "the Indian merchants have never dreamt of establishing their power anywhere; they rather chose to mix freely with the sons of the soil, sat and talked with them on the same carpet, carried on their trade and remained for years to earn their livelihood" (Desai 2013, 129). Gaurav Desai characterizes such statements to be "non-conquest narratives" (127). In Mary Louise Pratt's (1992) original definition, nonconquest narratives are found when "expansionist commercial aspirations idealize themselves into a drama of reciprocity" (Desai 2013, 127). Indian settlers never established a political regime, a colonial state, and therefore the economic relationships they established with Africans were premised on the equality and reciprocity of trade (notwithstanding the tensions of economic relationships themselves).

Nonconquest narratives have reemerged as a prominent discourse of South-South cooperation, although this is now articulated by state elites. The discourse of South-South cooperation and "win-win" development replicates the *drama of reciprocity*, asserting equality, fairness, and free exchange between non-European partners against the paternalist attitudes and policies (conditionality) of the West (Mawdsley 2012). In some respects, this drama of reciprocity differs less from "the West" than is commonly assumed. As Sankar Muthu (2003) has demonstrated, a current of eighteenth-century European enlightenment thought idealized market exchange as anti-imperial, based on reciprocity rather than conquest. Does not the ideology of neoliberalism itself depend on the romance of equal rational economic actors freely engaging in exchange without any aspirations to political power or rent seeking?

The discourse of South-South cooperation is a legacy of mid-twentieth-century third world solidarity. This legacy can be at odds with the earlier legacy of Indian Ocean mobilities. Indeed, decolonization involved both China and India distancing themselves from their diasporas. In the case of India and its East African diaspora, there was, as Gerard McCann explains, a "broad transition from those transnational linkages within the 'diasporic nationalist milieu,' which had impacted early African political protest, to more avowedly internationalist foundations as Nehruvian visions of Afro-Asian order soared onto the global stage" (2013, 279). India's first prime minister, Jawaharlal Nehru, urged Indians in Africa, traditional supporters of Indian nationalism, to align themselves with African nationalism, and not seek any special privileges sanctioned by India (McCann 2013). During the Bandung Conference of 1955, the Chinese premier Zhou Enlai followed a similar path by publicly renouncing claims on the overseas Chinese in Southeast Asia. What China and India shared in the age of decolonization and the normalization of the nation-state system was the pursuit of *internationalism* rather than *transnationalism*. Global connections meant the society of sovereign governments rather than the diasporic linkages that had characterized earlier periods and had only now become *trans*national.

Indian "Bloodsuckers" and Chinese "Friends": Two Meanings of Asian in Postcolonial Tanzania

The creation of diplomatic networks between legally equal postcolonial states required the disavowal of the expectations of extraterritorial privilege that characterized relationships within colonial empires. Hierarchies, inequalities, and exploitation had long infused these networks, but under the sign of nationalism they became questions of who was to be included and who was to be excluded from the emergent national communities. This situation posed dilemmas for diasporic populations throughout the Indian

Ocean. As Anne Bang (quoted in Burton 2013, 20) writes, "Contrary to the Empire . . . the nation state demand[s] full identification." This situation entailed far more than national identification alone, as it also exposed racialized economic inequalities to political scrutiny. In 1965, four years after Tanzania's independence, 77 percent of bank assets were held by Great Britain, 40 percent of industry was owned by foreign capital, and 32 percent of industry was held by Asians, meaning Indians (Aminzade 2013a, 37). The place foreign capital would have in national development posed a dilemma for a state promising substantive change from colonialism, and this in turn problematized the position of Indian capitalists who held African citizenship.

In what would become Tanzania, anticolonial nationalism among Africans was directed toward the Indian community as much as, or even more than, the Europeans (Brennan 2012). One reason was that Africans interacted with Indians more than Europeans. Indians were shopkeepers, creditors, and employers, and it was through the everyday politics of these interactions that the dislocations and economic inequalities of colonialism were felt. The official nonracialism of the Tanganyika African National Union (TANU) included Indians as members of the new national community, but this conflicted with its goal of addressing the economic inequalities and trading hierarchies that had survived the ascendance of an African political class (Aminzade 2013a, 104–34). Despite the founding president Julius Nyerere's frequent denunciations of anti-Asian populism, his promotion of socialism after the 1967 Arusha Declaration, particularly the nationalization of real estate, was popularly understood in racialized terms as removing the dominance of Asian "bloodsuckers" (Aminzade 2013b; Burton 2013). Forty thousand Indians would leave Tanzania voluntarily, only half the number that left Uganda following Idi Amin's active attempt to expel them.

As Indians were leaving, however, Tanzania was officially welcoming up to thirty thousand Chinese engineers and workers as "friends" assisting in the construction of the Tanzania-Zambia Railway (Monson 2009). This was at the same time that diasporic Chinese communities themselves were facing populism in Southeast Asia. The contrast in attitudes is instructive for understanding the paradoxes of national independence and international interdependencies. The railway, intended to bypass routes through the white settler colonies of southern Africa, had been rejected by the World Bank for funding because it was considered to be a political decision (2009, 15–16). Tanzania and Zambia, as frontline states for liberation movements, had hoped to increase their geopolitical autonomy. They solicited offers not just from China, but from other countries too, but in the end, China supported the construction of the railways with both financial and technical assistance. The engineers and others who worked alongside Tanzanians and Zambians between 1970 and 1975 were not diasporic migrants in the sense I have been describing, but their mobilization was functionally equivalent to earlier colonial schemes for using Chinese or Indian labor in the construction of African infrastructures. Transnational labor migration was now being mobilized for nation-state building rather than colonial-state building.

President Nyerere considered nation building to depend on the application of hard work. Thus, in his exhortations to Tanzanians about self-discipline and labor, longer-standing colonial tropes about the challenge of recruiting the African peasantry for wage labor were repurposed as the summoning of a new postcolonial socialist subjectivity (Monson 2008). China and the Chinese were upheld by Nyerere as models for Tanzanian subjectivity. The Chinese, according to Nyerere, worked hard because they accepted that they were poor, while Tanzanians did not recognize their poverty (Lal 2014, 103). The idealization of China stemmed in part from its geopolitical stature. Nyerere argued that China was the only "developing country" that could "challenge imperialism on equal terms" (2014, 102). Besides the early success of the Chinese revolution as a model for subsequent liberation struggles, the testing of the first Chinese nuclear bomb in 1964 had had an effect among anticolonial movements globally, similar to that of the Japanese victory over Russia in 1904 (Kelley and Esch 1999). China's status as an anti-empire in the Global South, in other words, was as much a product of non-Chinese anticolonial aspirations and imaginaries as any product of Chinese diplomacy.

Nonetheless, despite the welcoming of China as a nonempire, imperial specters accompanied China even at that early date, and in both Kenya and Tanzania, scattered discontent about Chinese influence appeared (Lal 2014, 112). Chinese development projects in Tanzania and elsewhere in the Global South were governed by regulations designed explicitly to efface imperial potentialities. Chinese experts and engineers were required to live in conditions equal to those of local experts and engineers. In China's 1964 white paper "Eight Principles for Economic Aid and Technical Assistance to Other Countries," it is written that "in providing aid to other countries, the Chinese Government strictly respects the sovereignty of the recipient countries, and never asks for any privileges or attaches any conditions."[3]

In his speeches and writing, Nyerere frequently warned that foreign states, particularly Western powers, would never willingly provide aid or technological transfers that would help poor states to develop, and that if they did, such aid would place these states into continued dependence (Nyerere 2011). Nonetheless, even at the height of *Ujamaa*, Tanzania's socialist project, in the mid-1970s, Tanzania was highly dependent on foreign aid from a wide range of global actors, which included, but far exceeded, China. Self-reliance was itself a product of dependent connections with actors outside of Tanzania. Nyerere recognized this, but he sought to preempt its capacity for reinforcing North-South inequalities by diverting interdependence to South-South cooperation. Nyerere promoted international cooperation among the poor states themselves as means of mutually reinforcing autonomy through the matching of complementarities. For example, in a speech delivered in 1970, he argued that if Tanzania needed industrial goods, it should first look for other developing states producing those goods before procuring them from the West. Complementary sourcing would embrace comparative advantage, but within a proscribed global sphere. As an example, Nyerere pointed to China as a potential supplier of industrial goods and asked, "Do we know what she produced?" (2011, 8). The imported goods might be more expensive or of lower quality, he added, but that was a short-term sacrifice in exchange for mutually supported long-term economic growth. These principles were in fact applied to the funding for the railway. In order to finance the salaries of Chinese rail workers, and to provide the Chinese with the funds necessary for the procurement of local supplies, an arrangement was reached where Chinese commodities, including bicycles, would be sold in Tanzania, and the revenue would be used for paying day-to-day costs (Monson 2009, 30). In the end, however, these economic interdependencies proved to be limited to the completion of the project itself (Yu 1975, 70). China's importance as a supplier would decrease in the following decade and it would ultimately be Tanzania's and China's liberalizations under the pressure of ascendant neoliberal norms and institutions that would end up bringing together the complementarity of Chinese manufacturers and Tanzanian consumers.

China in Tanzania: Another "Face" of Liberalization

The discourse of the New Maritime Silk Road portrays the Chinese presence in East Africa as the resumption of premodern connections, but it is also in many ways a single component of a much broader process of new forms of global capital entering the region. Since the liberalization of the Tanzanian economy starting in the 1980s, Canadians, British, Norwegians, and Australians have been joined by Gulf Arabs, South Africans, Indians, and finally, the Chinese, as foreign investors (Aminzade 2013a, 276–319). The China-in-Africa narrative focuses on China at the expense of this larger context. Nonetheless, what China means in Tanzania is shaped by this context.

The early phase of neoliberalism in Tanzania replicated familiar forms of racial capitalism. The success of Indian capitalists prompted a revival of anti-Asian populism in national politics (Aminzade 2013a, 320–55). The arrival of South African capital following the end of apartheid in 1994 was also controversial. Having served as a frontline state throughout the anti-apartheid struggle, it was not without a popular sense of irony that Tanzania welcomed white South Africans as new investors, bringing along the same attitudes and labor practices associated with apartheid, and creating new islands of expatriate privilege within Dar es Salaam (Schroeder 2012). Neoliberalism in Tanzania, as Richard Schroeder argues, was racialized. Capital had a "face."

Chinese migrants and investors are—to borrow Emmanuel Akyeampong and Liang Xu's terms—only the latest phase/face of China in Africa (2015), but perhaps the most consequential. Nonetheless, to understand how they fit into the story, one must know whom they are being compared to, and the medium of comparison. For example, the Chinese presence in Tanzania is most visible in commodities such as shoes, clothing, plastic goods, kitchenware, cell phones, and electronics. As Huruma Sigalla (2014, 73) observes, "When you ask an ordinary Tanzanian about China, you most likely get an answer that is related to Chinese products," a phenomenon found globally (see Bachner, this volume). In Tanzania, commodities are more widespread than Chinese traders themselves, who mostly stay in the wholesale sector, in contrast to other countries where retail "China shops" or groceries are more familiar parts of the neighborhood (see Cypher and Rofel, this volume). As elsewhere in the continent (cf. Fioratta 2019), Chinese commodities have engendered ambivalent reactions. For some, they have opened both consumer mobilities and economic mobilities for traders who deal in them. At the same time, the specter of "fake" and "cheap" continues to surround these products; although "fake" often refers primarily to point of origin. German and American goods, for many Tanzanians, are by definition not "fake." Chinese commodities of high quality are sometimes not even recognized as "Chinese." There are long-standing patterns to be found here too. During the nineteenth century, for example, East African consumers valued Merikani cloth produced in Salem, Massachusetts, over textiles produced by

British manufactures, some of whom began to counterfeit American designs (Prestholdt 2008, 77).

If one is talking about labor practices and economic opportunities, however, the axis of comparison might switch from East-West to South-South. For example, among African wholesalers who have faced competition from Chinese wholesalers, the Indians cease to be outsiders. During a conversation between a Chinese and a Tanzanian interlocutor of mine that turned into a debate about whether Chinese wholesalers should operate shops in Dar es Salaam, my Chinese interlocutor, himself a wholesaler, echoing Howard French's interview, asked his Tanzanian counterpart, "What about the Indians?" "They are a part of us," his friend responded. On the other hand, a Tanzanian manager working for a Chinese factory praised his bosses for training people like himself, unlike his former Indian bosses, who kept "secrets" and only gave management positions to their family. But if one is asking about marriage and intimacy, some Tanzanian men will say the Chinese are "just like the Indians," refusing the possibility of marriage or intimacy because of racial prejudice.

The Chinese presence in Tanzania, if properly contextualized within a long and ongoing history of successive (and coexisting) forms and degrees of foreign presence and business, appears not to be a new imperial formation analogous only to European colonialism, but rather an assemblage of processes and practices that are analogous to many things, running the gamut from middlemen trade (like the Indians) to natural resource extraction (like the Canadians).

Conclusion

Rather than starting with China and Africa as discrete entities to be defined (such as colonizer and colonized), it is more productive to begin with specific connections and relationships, how these connections and relationships are understood by different actors, and how these understandings lend themselves to myriad worlding projects (Rojas and Rofel, this volume). The regions we now call Africa and China have been connected for centuries, although the directness, scale, and mode of relations have varied over the centuries. Among the varied analogies used to describe contemporary China-Africa relations, an Indian Ocean–centered portrait of shifting hierarchies of trade and prestige has at least the advantage of decentering state actors and highlighting how both contemporary Tanzanians and Chinese contend

73

to find profitable niches in a globalized Afro-Asian trade. At the same time, the cosmopolitan drama of reciprocity invoked by the Indian Ocean also overlooks the histories of inequality and hierarchy in these relationships. While discourses about empire and nonempire in turn reduce the complexity and nuance of these connections, close attention must nonetheless be paid to the critical function of these discourses. When Tanzanian traders talk about a "Chinese invasion," for example, they are talking about market hierarchies and spaces for local economic mobility, and they hold their own government responsible above any plans by China. Also, despite recent efforts to rethink "dependency" and "distribution" as African contributions to political economic thought (Bayart and Ellis 2000; Ferguson 2015), industrial futures—or what Achille Mbembe calls "the challenge of productivity" (2001, 57)—continue, rightly or wrongly, to inspire ordinary understandings of African development. When anxieties are expressed about China, these anxieties are often less about China itself than about the state's ability to successfully negotiate with foreign capital. Understanding these contexts may require decentering China as the focus of global China. The paradigm of China-in-(insert location) merely globalizes a Sinocentric framework. A view from Africa, but also not Africa alone, is necessary to keep these questions decentered and truly global.

Notes

1. An example of this argument in the China-Africa literature is the use of the story of Zhuge Liang and Meng Huo in the *Romance of the Three Kingdoms*. According to the legend, Zhuge Liang obtained Meng Huo's submission to Han rule voluntarily by releasing him after each capture (S. Chan 2013, 70–76).
2. Francis Galton, "Africa for the Chinese," *Times*, June 5, 1873.
3. The irony of these principles was that at the time the average Chinese worker, if measured in per capita GDP terms, was far poorer than the average urban Tanzanian resident. For many Chinese workers, accordingly, coming to Dar es Salaam meant an opportunity to purchase goods that were inaccessible in China itself (Jin 2008; Monson 2009).

A WORLD
REPUBLIC OF
SOUTHERN
LETTERS

In *The World Republic of Letters*, Pascale Casanova borrows Pierre Bour-
dieu's model of cultural production and extends it from a focus on individual
nations to a broader approach covering all of Europe, and even Asia (Casanova 2007). Casanova's goal is to describe the Eurocentric field of "world literature" that emerged in the nineteenth century, for which she convincingly
outlines the conditions for recognition, the different linguistic and narrative
strategies, and the translators who made it possible for a wide array of authors to be introduced into the field of world literature—including figures
such as Kafka and Faulkner; "Irish miracle" authors such as Yeats, Joyce,
and Beckett; Latin American Boom authors such as Asturias, Paz, Borges,
and García Marquez; Anglophone South Asian authors such as Naipaul and
Rushdie; as well as diasporic authors such as Nabokov.

    In this field of world literature—the center of which was originally
Paris, but which was extended to include London and New York—Chinese-
language literature does not receive even as much attention as Vietnamese or Korean literature. One of the key reasons why the literary center has
accepted works by some authors from peripheral nations is because they
all wrote in major European languages such as French, English, German,
Spanish, and Portuguese. This is true even of authors from Africa and Latin

America, and those who are fluent in multiple languages are better able to manage the quality of their translations. The former imperial powers are the birthplace not only of these so-called major languages but also of modern literature and civilization. They are the birthplace of modernity, and where capitalism first emerged.

The literary geography described by Casanova has a corresponding political and economic background, and it is this background that constitutes the system's primary power. Just as third world nations' literary modernity is always belated (and even if the nations already have their own literary traditions, those traditions are viewed as merely classical or premodern), those previously colonized nations were forced to measure their culture against a Western standard. They were required to industrialize and accommodate national reconstruction projects driven by the operation of capital (so as not to "fall behind" or be consumed by stronger nations). The literary organization of these third world countries, accordingly, adopted an array of modern Western literary institutional structures. These institutional structures include taxonomies and their valuations, publication systems, media networks, critical practices, university structures and curricula, and so forth. In reality, there are only two paths that third world literatures can take if they wish to be recognized by the West. First, these authors can rely on "successful" translation, as many Japanese authors do. Second, these authors can write in a major European language, as English-language figures such as V. S. Naipaul, Salman Rushdie, Kazuo Ishiguro, and Ha Jin.

Here, it is not difficult to discern the influence of Immanuel Wallerstein's world systems theory. Adapting capitalism's division of labor, Wallerstein divides nations or territories into a system of center, periphery, and semiperiphery. From the beginning of the modern period, Europe has always been positioned at the center, while third world nations, even if they previously enjoyed an imperial status, have been relegated to the periphery—at least until they are fortunate enough to be promoted to the semiperiphery. However, this theory also suggests that any region can also have its own center—though even these regional centers continue to occupy a semiperipheral position. In early modern Asia, the role of the regional center was played by Japan—which ultimately succeeded in leaving Asia and joining Europe. In literary terms, this process of figuratively leaving Asia began with Yasunari Kawabata and Kenzaburo Oe, and recently Haruki Murakami has received even greater global recognition. Prominent modern Chinese authors like Lu Xun, Yu Dafu, and Guo Moruo were nourished by modern Japanese literature, and early modern Chinese scholarship was also deeply influenced by Japanese translation.

Literature's Galápagos Archipelago

Although the world has inexorably been absorbed by global capitalism's system of profit and loss for more than a century, literature and culture are partial exceptions to this process. For instance, modern literature written in Chinese remains outside of the world republic of letters that is currently centered around Euro-American languages. In fact, Chinese occupies an even more marginal status in this regard than other East Asian languages—to the point that one could almost say that Chinese-language literature is world literature's Galápagos archipelago. At the same time, it could also be said that Chinese literature shares the fate of other literatures written in minor languages such as Indonesian, Malay, and Thai. The rapid pace of globalization has contributed to the extinction of many of the world's weaker languages, and even if a language happens to have its own writing system, it may be difficult for its spoken version to survive. Moreover, even if a language does survive, it would need to be established as the national language of a new nation—but if the nation hopes to survive, it must always compromise with English.

Even today, nearly a century after the birth of modern Chinese literature, the Eurocentric world republic of letters continues to view Chinese novels as merely second-rate. For instance, the US-based Chinese author Ha Jin recently remarked:

> Our classic novels are completely different from Western ones—as different as apples and oranges. Our modern and contemporary novels are imported products . . . and therefore it appears that the English-language world looks down upon our novels. If you plan to edit a global collection of short stories in the English-language world, you will naturally include many European and American authors. . . . However, it is not uncommon for such a volume to not include a single Chinese-language author, and in fact those authors wouldn't even be missed. We find a similar problem when it comes to novels. I've been living in the United States for thirty-one years, and when I interact with Western authors I can see that they truly look down on modern Chinese-language novels. Every time a Chinese author wins an international literary award, some of the Western writers I know will inevitably ask me what is good about the work

in question. The implication is that after they read the work, they feel unconvinced by it. Of course they are biased—but to be perfectly honest, it is true that modern and contemporary Chinese literature hasn't yet produced a work that the world would recognize as truly great. (Ha Jin 2016, 34)

Needless to say, to claim that a work is recognized by the world "as truly great" necessarily means that it accords with Western standards. In fact, it is almost as though such a work enters the world through a process of mimicry, not as an original creation.

Similarly, Howard Goldblatt, the most important English-language translator of modern Chinese literature, states:

Like Korean novels, Chinese novels have not been very well received in the West, or at least in the United States, though Japanese, Indian, and even Vietnamese works fare somewhat better. This is perhaps due to the perception that the characters in Chinese novels lack depth. . . . Modern Chinese authors' "obsession with China" has made it such that they have been unable to establish connections between the circumstances in their own nation and those of people outside of China. . . . Contemporary authors have a similar problem, in that they remain excessively focused on things relating to China, and consequently they overlook an important aspect of literary creation—namely, that literature has to read well, and only then will people buy it! . . . There is, of course, nothing wrong with focusing on China's social situation, but if one therefore overlooks the universality that a literary work should have, there may well be unfortunate consequences. (Goldblatt 2014)

"If it is good, people will buy it!" This is global capitalism's law of the commodity. Fredric Jameson took a version of Goldblatt's charge and developed it in his discussion of third world literature as national allegory—using it to critique the phenomenon whereby first world readers inevitably view third world literature with a sense of déjà vu (Jameson 1986).

It should be noted, however, that Jameson advocates a process of historical contextualization, whereby first world readers must approach third world texts through a process of sincere (and *complete*) historicization in order to appreciate the works' underlying *allegorical resonance*. For consumers who simply treat the novel as leisure reading, this is probably unrealistic. Goldblatt even suggests that this limitation may be the fault of traditional

NG KIM CHEW

Chinese novels—meaning that this critique is directed toward China's entire narrative tradition. He asks:

> Why is it necessary to add so many descriptions and details, to the point that a novel becomes a veritable literary encyclopedia? Is it really helpful to the narrative to describe every single character, major or minor, in exhaustive detail? Is it really necessary to keep breaking up the main plot and adding additional unrelated subplots? Is this really helpful to the reader? I think that this tendency is perhaps related to the underlying influence of the traditional Chinese linked-chapter novel. Virtually all of the contemporary Chinese authors I know would read these linked-chapter novels as they were growing up, and their underlying influence cannot be ignored.
>
> If a classic Chinese novel like *Dream of the Red Chamber*, also known as *Story of the Stone*, were to be judged by the standards of contemporary Western fictional criticism, it would certainly be seen as an entertaining read but would not necessarily be considered a great novel. This is because it contains too many unrelated and unimportant details, and consequently the reading experience is not very fluid. *Dream of the Red Chamber* could perhaps be viewed as a documentary of an aristocratic lifestyle during the Qing dynasty, but can it really be considered a well-structured novel? It has a lot of what it doesn't need, but doesn't necessarily have what it does need. (Goldblatt 2014)

Given the size and breadth of Goldblatt's contributions to the translation of Chinese literature, together with his professional identity and the evident sincerity of his reading practice, his opinion may be considered fairly representative of contemporary Western attitudes toward Chinese literature. His discussion here of Chinese literature's distinctiveness is one that only a minority of Sinologists would find interesting, or would even understand—but it nevertheless has its own internal consistency corresponding to a different form of narration, and is the product of different standards.

From these commentaries, we can observe world literature's aesthetic politics. Who has the authority to determine which elements should be present in a literary work? And does not the phrase "does not accord with the standards of great Western literature" imply that within the Eurocentric world republic of letters there is some sort of international law that applies to literature? By extension, if China were to be accepted into this group, it would be merely as a representative of a part of the world that Western imperialist powers have already carved up like a melon (Wang Hui 2004, 695–706; Lin Xuezhong 2009). The claim that China lacks a "well-structured novel" is no different from the assertion that China has no philosophy (which, in turn, led generations of Chinese philosophers to imitate Western idealist philosophy), and is based on reliance on a single Eurocentric standard.

Chinese was once a powerful language in East Asia, and in the Tang and Song dynasties classical Chinese began to be used as the written lingua franca in what are now Japan, Korea, and Vietnam. During the imperial era, Chinese literature became part of the tributary system, and came to function as its own world system—with China, of course, positioned at the center. After the fall of the Ming, these hierarchies were inverted, with Japan and Korea briefly usurping the current Han civilizational orthodoxy, though this inversion did not last long.

Korea and Vietnam were repeatedly colonized throughout the early modern and modern periods. As a result these regions, which had previously been part of the Chinese Empire, were effectively "de-sinified." Moreover, although Japan succeeded in becoming a Europeanized, modern empire, Korea and Vietnam initially remained colonial territories. In the process of becoming modern nation-states, Korea and Vietnam both established their own national languages and rejected their former reliance on the Chinese language and writing system. In cultural terms, they removed themselves from the regional systems to which had they previously belonged, and instead began imitating European nations in their pursuit of modernity.

The category of *Huawen* (or "Chinese-language") literature is actually a modern creation. Like the term *Huaren* ("ethnic Chinese"), Huawen is a product of historical sedimentation. Following the early twentieth-century language reform movement, literacy in China improved and Chinese became easier to write. As a result, the barrier to entry into the literary field was lowered since it became possible to write without needing to have a deep training in the Chinese classics. During the Republican Era, the modernization of the national education system and the diversification of the newspaper supplements and literary journals also helped disseminate these modern writings more widely. Beyond China's borders this kind of system of literary production was not difficult to replicate, and within a few generations of migration the resulting body of overseas literature began to develop its own history. After China's Reform and Opening Up movement in the 1980s, Huawen literature was reestablished as an academic discipline, and consequently Chinese-language literature from outside of China came to be viewed as a unified field known alternatively as world Huawen literature, overseas Huawen literature, or "Taiwan, Hong Kong, and overseas Chinese literature." Its status, however, is not so much academic as political, as it takes its inspiration from the nationalism of "cultural China." Literature from mainland China is typically not included in this category of *Huawen* literature, although it is obviously positioned at the center of the "Chinese-language world system" (Ng 1996).

US-based academics have recently begun using the term *Sinophone* to refer to what in Chinese I am calling Huawen literature. I am not opposed to this translation, and am grateful to professors David Der-wei Wang and Shu-mei Shih for helping promote the concept and encouraging a group of younger American scholars to conduct further research in this area. However, I do not particularly like the popular reverse translation of *Sinophone* back into Chinese as *Huayu yuxi* (literally, "Sinitic-language language system"); instead, I prefer the older term *Huawen literature*. The term *Huawen* dates back to the Republican Era and refers to literature originating from outside of China, including Taiwan, Hong Kong, Singapore, and Malaysia. This literature was influenced by the popularization of writing in the vernacular, the system of modern literature, and immigration following the founding of Republican China. Because China was the birthplace of new vernacular literature, the earliest instances of modern Chinese-language literature all came from May Fourth generation writers (most of whom had studied abroad). Similarly, the earliest modern literary genres, literary techniques, and systems of literary valuation all came from China. Even the first anthology of modern Chinese literature, *Collection of Chinese New Literature* (Zhongguo xinwenxue daxi), which was published in 1936 at the encouragement of Zhao Jiabi, provided a model of a large-scale collection system that could be used by Sinophone literature from other regions.

China had long been the undisputed center of modern Chinese-language literature. After 1950 Taiwan continued to regard itself as China (calling itself "Free China"), but Taiwan's rural literature debate in the 1970s was followed by the rise of a nativist consciousness, which came to describe itself as Taiwan literature. Meanwhile, Sinophone literature from Hong Kong, Singapore, and Malaya was defined by its geographic origin, all of which became part of the Chinese-language literature's Galápagos archipelago. This constitutes what I call Huawen literature, which has typically been viewed as a local phenomenon approached in the context of these respective regions and has rarely been integrated into a single field of study. In particular, Sinophone

81

literature from Singapore and Malaysia has been positioned at the periphery of the periphery, in that for a long time it was strongly influenced by Hong Kong and Taiwan literature. Meanwhile, Hong Kong, and particularly the Republican of Taiwan, have consistently occupied a semiperipheral position in relationship to the center as represented by mainland China.

The "Mute" South: Singaporean Chinese

Taiwan, Hong Kong, and Singapore/Malaysia all have a historical context that is distinct from that of mainland China.[1] This is particularly true with respect to their experience of having been long-term colonies—as a result of which they were each deeply influenced by a colonial culture, and were also exposed to modernity before mainland China. Even if individuals in regions to the south of China and elsewhere—including colonial territories—received modern Huawen education (an imitation of Republican China's nationalist education), their use of both standard written Chinese (Huawen) and oral Chinese (Huayu) was still influenced by the daily use of colonial languages, Minnan and Cantonese dialects, and other local dialects. As a result, literary development in these regions ended up being quite different from that within mainland China.

The explosion of Huawen literature in the wake of the new wave of Chinese emigration in the 1980s includes works by Chinese immigrants to the United States, Canada, and Australia, as well as some second-generation authors—many of whom continued to maintain close connections with mainland China, to the point that their literary works could even be seen as a kind of "overseas edition of Chinese literature." Meanwhile, Southeast Asian countries like Indonesia, Thailand, and the Philippines—each of which had a long history of Chinese immigration—all developed a Huawen literature in the 1930s that was made possible by their respective Chinese-language newspapers, journals, and education systems. However, the nationalist policies of forcible assimilation that emerged in each of these regions in the 1950s virtually eliminated the regions' corresponding Chinese literary traditions.

In this respect Singapore was an exception, in that in the 1970s Lee Kuan Yew's government succeeded in abolishing the island's left-leaning Chinese educational system, and then implemented a program encouraging the nation's Chinese majority to speak Huayu while prohibiting them from using local dialects. In order to join the world and to meet the requirements of the international market, Singapore removed Huawen from its educational

NG KIM CHEW

system (including primary schools, middle schools, and universities) while promoting "standard spoken Chinese" and trying to eliminate local dialects. In 1978 the government began promoting the "speak Chinese" movement, while prohibiting the use of local dialects in all radio and television broadcasts. In the Straits Settlements, which had always had a large concentration of Chinese residents, not only did the Chinese-language movement succeed in suppressing dialect-based provincial guilds, multidialect temples, local opera troupes that performed in dialect as well as the ordinary language used in the market but it also undercut the ability of local dialects to be passed down from one generation to the next.

With respect to his promotion of the use of Huayu in Singapore, Lee Kuan Yew explained:

> I definitely don't want to follow the lead of countries like Mauritius or Luxembourg, and let a coarse Hokkien dialect become the lingua franca of Singapore's Chinese population. Nor do I want to let the dialect interfere with our promotion of bilingual education, or fracture Singapore's Chinese society. I understand that if Singapore were to permit Hokkien, Teochew, Hakka, Hainanese, Shanghainese, and other dialects to persist, it would become very difficult for students to simultaneously learn Huayu—because for them, these would be two completely foreign languages. People tell me that many Singaporeans even view English as a foreign language, and that Hokkien is their daily language, and they ask why I don't simply make Hokkien Singapore's common language, the same way that Cantonese is Hong Kong's common language? Actually, during the post-War period Hokkien had already become Singapore's de facto common language—but unlike Hong Kong, where nearly everyone speaks the same high-level version of Cantonese, in Singapore people instead speak a version of Hokkien that is actually twelve different subdialects rolled into one. In Hong Kong, schoolchildren use Cantonese to read, write, play, debate, and hold meetings, and if our Hokkien were of the same high level as Hong Kong's Cantonese, then it might be an option for us to keep it. However, Singapore's Hokkien is very rudimentary, and doesn't even have a writing system. (Lee 2015, 188–89)

Lee believed that it was necessary to choose between local dialects and standard Huayu, though this belief had no real academic basis. Even if children spoke a dialect at home (as was common), they could nevertheless quickly learn Huayu in preschool or primary school. The situation Lee had in mind, however, is one in which the educational system does not use Huayu at all, and instead offers instruction entirely in English—which is basically the "language relief" system he set up for Singapore's ethnic Chinese. When Lee speaks of "fracturing Singapore's Chinese communities," "a language that is entirely foreign to them," and so forth, he is using political slogans that reflect the linguistic positionality of a local Chinese like Lee himself, for whom both Huayu and Hokkien were effectively foreign languages (Lee was ethnically Hakka and did not learn Huayu and Hokkien until later in life).

In advancing this argument, Lee Kuan Yew noted that Huayu had entered into wide usage in mainland China and Taiwan (Qiu 2012). In reality, however, the standard languages in mainland China and Taiwan are known as *Putunghua* (literally, "common language") and *Guoyu* (literally, "national language"), respectively, neither of which is exactly the same as Huayu. Before Singapore and Malaysia were founded, these two regions inherited a version of Huayu from the reform movement and the Xinhai Revolution, which subsequently spread into the South Seas region. Actually, this was the national language of the Republic of China in exile and therefore it carried strong emotional resonances, even as the Greater Malaysia Chinese educational movement inherited the same tragic sensibility. Lee Kuan Yew probably did not realize that the Huayu used in Singapore after the nation was founded was actually a different kind of invention, but was nevertheless one of the most important driving forces. Because Lee probably did not understand Taiwan's "Free China" period, he did not mention the situation of Taiwan's Hokkien, which is quite similar to that of Cantonese in Hong Kong. At the same time, Singapore's Huayu movement also had a deep and long-lasting impact on Greater Malaysia's ethnically Chinese residents, particularly the residents of Southern Malaysia who had access to Singapore's radio and television broadcasts.[2]

In a 1991 article titled "A Drifting Language" (Piaobo de yuyan), the mainland Chinese author Wang Anyi—whose father was an ethnically Chinese Singaporean who had returned to China—described her recent visit to Singapore as follows:

> I notice that [local Singaporeans'] Chinese vocabulary is limited and their syntax is constrained. They are all quite estranged from the Chinese language, though they remain deeply curious about it. Similarly, the current generation of children are mostly educated in English and cannot speak Chinese, though their parents can often speak Cantonese or Minnan dialect, and with difficulty may be able to speak a bit of Putonghua

and English. Members of their grandparents' generation, meanwhile, can usually only speak Cantonese or Minnan dialect. This is the background of Singapore's literary scene. (Wang Anyi 1996, 216)

Wang Anyi focuses here on the first generation of ethnic Chinese born in Singapore following the founding of the nation in 1965—which is to say, members of my own generation. For anyone who aspires to adopt a standardized writing system, it is a tragedy for someone to say that their "vocabulary is limited, and their syntax is constrained."

When Wang Anyi mentions "their parents" in this passage, she is referring to individuals born around World War II—including the first generation of native-born ethnically Chinese Singaporean and Malaysian authors, many of whom have some proficiency in different Chinese dialects, as well as Malay and English. Their reading ability in classical Chinese was often quite good, which helped make their vocabulary much richer than that of the "standardized generation." Wang Anyi's essay outlines how the various political systems in these regions have contributed to a markedly different Chinese language environment, although, in her account, Malaysian Chinese authors' ethnic culture appears to be in danger of perishing.

In Singapore, the languages officials promote as "standard English" (which is to say, London-accented English) and "standard Chinese" (which is neither Beijing-accented Mandarin nor the Chinese spoken in Taiwan), respectively, are both relatively dry, almost like a foreign language. The languages people actually use in their day-to-day interactions, meanwhile, are actually creoles, of which "Singlish" (Singapore-style English) is the most representative example (Goh and Woo 2009). Singlish is a transethnic hybrid language that takes English as its base and incorporates elements from other languages and dialects, including Hokkien, Malay, and Tamil. The result is similar to the "bazaar Malay" (Pasar Melayu) that formed in the Straits Settlements a century ago—which took Malay as its base and also absorbed a large amount of Minnan vocabulary. The ethnic-Chinese population of Singapore at the time consisted primarily of Fujianese immigrants who, as a result of the Qing dynasty's antimaritime policy, ended up marrying local women and then developed a new creole. When Lee Kuan Yew critiqued Singapore's Hokkien dialect as being "very rudimentary, and even lacking a writing system," and claimed that it "consisted of twelve different subdialects mixed together," what he was describing was an "ethnic Chinese Singaporean lingua franca" that could also be called a "bazaar Hokkien"—

85

which he felt needed to be destroyed precisely on account of its richness and diversity. However, Lee's critique did not prevent this dialect from becoming even more standardized as people began to use it in more formal settings—the same way that Hong Kong also has a kind of "bazaar Cantonese." Similarly, the Huayu that people speak on a daily basis is a kind of creole consisting of a mixture of different dialects and local languages—or we could perhaps call it a "bazaar Huayu." Southern Chinese literature is grounded precisely in this sort of discursive movement operating below the level of a "standard" language.

Huawen: Local and Foreign Accents

Ha Jin—who has been living in the United States for over thirty years and who writes primarily in English, even as he continues to struggle with standard American English—notes in his "In Defense of Foreignness" that "in Conrad's fiction, we can sense a linguistic boundary demarcated by the English dictionary—he would not invent words and expressions that might sound alien to the English ear" (Ha Jin 2010, 463). Then Ha Jin notes that immigrant authors like himself "do not work within the boundary of dictionaries. We work in the border areas of English, in the space between languages, and therefore our ability and accomplishments cannot be measured only by the mastery of Standard English" (2010, 467).

After Malaya achieved independence from the British in 1957, local authors writing in Huawen generally abstained from using local dialect. This was particularly true after the 1970s, when they began to display a preference for a smooth Chinese influenced by Taiwan's literary circles (and also perhaps by Singapore's Huayu movement). After the 1990s, this phenomenon was compounded by the impact of contemporary mainland Chinese literature, which resulted in an even stronger preference for a so-called standard Chinese that seemed to predetermine the linguistic preferences of readers in other Chinese cultural regions.

During the first two decades following the founding of the nation of Malaysia—apart from the literary language acquired from 1940s China via literati who relocated to the south and tended to have good literary training, such Fang Tian and Bai Yao—literature tended to be lyrically expressive, though occasionally it could be excessively aesthetic (as with Wang Ge). In the hands of some locally born authors, who were not interested in the operations of language itself, this gradually came to constitute a kind of local dialect (such as Yuchuan)—a kind of fractured Chinese that used many clichés, set phrases, and redundant sentences. This literary form lacked distinctiveness.

At the same time, there were also some authors who, after having endured hardship, developed a distinctive linguistic sensibility—a kind of "Malaysian-born Huawen." Occasionally, there emerges a kind of out-of-place aesthetic sensibility—this is a Malaysian peninsular tropical character, and it could be said that a Huawen variant has evolved naturally under the influence of local dialects and colonial heritage. For Chinese and Taiwanese jurors for major literary awards, this kind of Huawen carried an uncomfortable, foreign tone. For instance, the two finalists for Malaysia's 2015 Huazong literary award were Wen Xiangying and Li Zishu; needless to say, the latter ended up winning the top prize. It seems as though things have always been this way—with fluent Chinese invariably winning out over broken Huawen. From the perspective of the center, the former is perceived as more familiar, more domesticated, and safer. However, if one only follows this path, one is unlikely to create a true distinctiveness that would generate a meaningful difference with respect to the presumptive center. Below, I will examine several related issues by considering examples from Taiwan and Hong Kong—two islands that make up what I call Huawen literature's Galápagos archipelago.

Hong Kong and Taiwan did not suppress Huayu to the same degree as Singapore and Malaysia. In Hong Kong, Cantonese enjoyed a natural development that influenced the tone of Hong Kong's written Chinese. In Wong Bik-Wan's novel *Portraits of Martyred Women* (*Lienü zhuan*), for instance, we find a good example of the complex negotiation between standard Chinese and Cantonese:

> When your grandmother first arrived in Hong Kong, the areas that are now Shanghai Street, Guangdong Street, and New Landfill Street were all ocean. At that time, there was only Temple Street. Similarly, what is now Nathan Street was just mountain. At that time, you couldn't sleep in the afternoon, because the foreign devils might come to inspect your house, and if they saw you sleeping, they'd assume you were dead, so they'd drag you away and either give you a deadly shot, or hospitalize you to death. When cleaning out the mortuary, people would be afraid that they'd get sick, so everyone would take their mattress and disinfect it. They'd go in with a large metal pail and a wooden bed board, and soak it. When the foreign devils arrived, they would take a sniff—and if there wasn't any

87

foul water, they'd take the bed board and go wash it. Your grandmother Song Xiang would soak her bed board in foul water, so that she wouldn't have to wash it. (Wong 1999, 56)

This is a Cantonese that is soaked in sewage water and full of foreign devil idioms and truncated sentences. Ordinarily, however, in works written in the Cantonese script, the word 是 ("is") would be rendered as 係, the word 不用 ("no need") would be rendered as 唔使, the word 睡覺 ("to sleep") would be rendered as 瞓覺, and the word 拿 ("to take") would be rendered as 攞. The kind of compromise that we find in Wong Bik-Wan's passage is also very common, as it preserves a Cantonese tone while including many lexical items from standard Chinese. Accordingly, readers who do not know Cantonese are still able to understand this sort of passage, while those who do know Cantonese will be able to discern additional layers of meaning.

During Taiwan's period of Japanese occupation, Minnan was used as a distinctive "Taiwan vernacular" by writers such as Lai He and Yang Shouyu, and although the dialect subsequently endured a long period of suppression by a dominant "national language" (during the period of Japanese colonialism, this "national language" was Japanese, and during the subsequent Republican Era, it was Huayu), there remained a few writers who were willing to experiment with it. After 1949 a representative precursor who devoted himself to the carnivalesque was Wang Chen-ho. In his novella "An Oxcart for Dowry," a rural character remarks: "This is a stinky ear! Don't be afraid of him. If he could hear, we probably wouldn't have had this kind of incident!" (Wang Chen-ho 1996, 73). Here, the phrase "stinky ear" is Minnan dialect and means "deaf," but the remainder of the remark—"Don't be afraid of him. If he could hear, then this sort of thing probably wouldn't have occurred"—is standard Huayu. If the passage had been written entirely in Minnan dialect, then the expression 不怕 ("don't be afraid") would have been rendered as 唔驚, the expression 不會 ("wouldn't have had") would have be rendered as 袂 (膾), and the expression 這種事 ("this sort of thing") would have been rendered as 這款代誌. For readers who do not know Minnan, however, these alternate renderings would have been extremely difficult to understand.

After continuing to evolve for several more generations, this sort of local language came to assume a nearly untranslatable form, as in the line "咸菜脯一樣的臉望了一會爛瓜一樣的天" in Wu He's novel *The Bone Collector* (*Shi gu*) (Wu 1995, 100), or the line "我悚矣!欲去倒一下，各人毋通膾記敆你个書搬轉去" in Huang Handi's novel *Renzhi* (Huang 2015, 80). Even readers who are very proficient in standard Chinese will find it extremely difficult to make out the meaning of this sort of passage if they do not have a background in southern dialects.

As discussed earlier, the shared exteriority of Taiwan, Hong Kong, and Mahua literature; their southern conditions, southern dialect, and experience of colonization; the excitement and anxiety of entering each of their respective histories and searching for the position of their respective literatures—all of these factors invite us to view these regions as a "Southern Chinese Republic of Letters," a never-never land within Chinese literary history.

Whereas Casanova focuses on how authors from the periphery attempt to be accepted and recognized by the center, I am primarily interested not in narrative strategies of "entering the center," but rather in strategies of "being outside," even though this is not necessarily a question of "removing the center." Relevant writing strategies do not attempt to follow the center in establishing literary standards, nor are they constrained by the limits imposed by Communist ideology or bound by its prohibitions. Accordingly, my phrase *Southern Chinese Republic of Letters* tropes ironically on Casanova's *World Republic of Letters* because what I am describing is actually a republic without a center and without borders.

Our Galápagos Archipelago

My own exploration of these issues began with my essay "Sinophone/Chinese: The South Where Language Is Lost and Reinvented," originally published in 1995, which took as its starting point Wang Anyi's reflections on how the literary language used by authors on either side of the Taiwan Strait after 1949 evolved in two different directions (Ng 1998; English translation available in Ng 2013b). In this way, I sought to problematize the concept of the South, and to conceptualize the notion of the Sinophone. In another essay, for instance, I considered how Malaysian middle schools currently teach courses in Guowen or Huawen, which may be viewed as a local and denationalized version of Taiwan's courses in "national language" (Ng 2015a). I attempted to distinguish between two different linguistic strategies employed by overseas Chinese authors. On one hand, there are authors who use an elegant and fluid Chinese, which in the 1970s was promoted in Taiwan as a form of "pure Chinese"; on the other hand, there are authors writing in Huawen who use translation, local dialect, and so forth to undermine the language's fluidity.

89

Casanova's *World Republic of Letters* describes how authors positioned in peripheral regions can be divided into the categories of those who use local languages and those who use the language of the former colonial powers. If authors in the first category desire to enter the center, they need to have their works translated into major European languages. As for the authors belonging to the second category, they can be further divided into two subcategories: those who use a beautiful and fluent form of the imperial language and those who use dialect to explode that standardized imperial language. Accordingly, in my article "Chinese Modernism" (Ng 2001), I considered the possibility of creating a field of Chinese world literature in contradistinction to the West's world republic of letters—arguing that the latter would be positioned at a distance from the West's center so that it could create its own modernism.

Support for this notion of a republic of southern Chinese letters can be found in the fact that there remain many historical and geographic links between the literary traditions of Taiwan, Hong Kong, Malaysia, and Singapore. During the colonial period, for instance, Huawen literature in the Malayan peninsula originated via "Southern literati" who came from China via Hong Kong, including figures like Fang Xiu, Fang Beifang, and Wei Yun. Similarly, expatriate Chinese authors like Li Kuang, Ma Boliang, Yang Jiguang, and Huang Ya were viewed as "Hong Kong authors." The leading modernist Bai Yao came to Malaya from China, after passing through Hong Kong and studying abroad in Taiwan. From the 1950s to the 1970s, the literary fields of Taiwan and Hong Kong were intimately connected with one another. In this way, Taiwan established itself as a center of Chinese literature. Meanwhile, from the 1950s onward, British Malaya—and later the nation of Malaysia—continued to rely on Hong Kong and Taiwan literature for its literary nutrients.

After the 1960s, overseas Chinese students who went to study in Taiwan were able to enter Taiwan's literary scene through actual participation. To a limited degree, this repeated the path of what Casanova describes as "seeking recognition." However, since the turn of the millennium many young Malaysian Chinese authors, having been recognized by Taiwan's major literary awards, have used the publication of their works in Taiwan as their first step toward literary recognition. In addition, during the first three or four decades after 1960, Taiwan literature served as an important model for these young Mahua authors, and literary criticism in these two regions directly influenced Singaporean and Malaysian authors' literary imagination and literary judgment, resulting in a kind of internal intimacy, and even interdependence. Comparatively speaking, the literary traditions of these regions were not severed as a result of political interference, but rather continued to evolve at their own pace. This resulted in the production of some works that could not possibly have appeared in mainland China—including the multifaceted works by Xi Xi and Leung Ping-kwan in Hong Kong; modernist works by poets like Ya Hsien, Yang Mu, and Hsia Yu in Taiwan; and the nearly untranslatable writings by Wang Wen-hsin and Wu He. However, a text's putative untranslatability should have been an important objective to begin with because therein lies the abstruseness and profundity of literature's Galápagos archipelago. Of course, Taiwan's literary writers should not just pay attention to their own literary production and to a world literature that is perceived as being positioned above theirs while in the process ignoring their own minor literary fields and the contiguous cases of Huawen literary fields.

Of course, our Galápagos archipelago is the product of a set of historical contingencies, including the collapse of the Chinese empire, the sealing off of the People's Republic, Hong Kong's colonization, the establishment of Taiwan's republic and the attendant suppression of nativist elements, and the status of Huayu within the Malayan emergency. It is within this set of unique historical circumstances that our Galápagos archipelago has evolved, but eventually the day may come when these contingencies will disappear and these differences will fade away.

Notes

This is an abbreviated translation of a revised version of the keynote address that Ng Kim Chew delivered at a conference, "Sinophone Studies: New Directions," held at Harvard University on October 14–15, 2016. The chapter was translated by Carlos Rojas.

1 For strategic purposes, Singapore and Malaysia could be viewed as a single entity. See Ng 2016c.

2 This did not just affect southern Malaysia, but further research needs to be done to determine exactly how far this influence spread.

LABOR AND EXCHANGE

Part II

NEW LIVELIHOOD STRATEGIES AND WAYS OF BEING FOR AFRICAN WOMEN AND MEN IN CHINA'S WORKSHOP OF THE WORLD

The increased presence of investment, manufactured products, and people from China in nearly every African country today has drawn international attention to developing China-Africa relations in the twenty-first century. At the same time, the number of African people in China has not gone unnoticed. Small-scale traders seemingly constitute the majority of the Africans in China. The attention paid to them over Africans of other professions can be attributed to several factors, one being the rising trade volume between China and African countries. While China's imports of natural resources occupy a significant role in the exponential rise in trade, exports from China to Africa are equally important in augmenting circulation of affordable manufactured goods, strengthening connections between China and African countries, and accelerating the rate of capital circulation in both directions (Haugen 2018). Studies focused on African traders in China as well as Chinese traders in Africa agree that clothes, textiles, and footwear as well as other everyday products constitute the bulk of their intercontinental trade. Just as importantly, they suggest that these small traders have a role in contributing to China's trade relations with Africa (e.g., Yang Yang 2011; Haugen 2011, 2018; Mathews 2015, 2017; Bodomo, Che, and Dong 2020).

This chapter offers a close ethnographic analysis of the African traders in Guangzhou. It expands on the available literature that either explicitly focuses on Nigerian men in trading roles or implicitly assumes that the African traders are predominantly men. By drawing attention to African women's trading activities through the stories they share, this chapter explores why and how gender roles and relations appear in a particular setting of low-end globalization or globalization from below. Globalization from below, according to Arjun Appadurai (2000), involves grassroots institutions mobilizing to redress sociopolitical inequities generated by the continual extension of capital. Considering its grassroots nature, others describe globalization from below as the nonhegemonic part of economic globalization (Mathews, Ribeiro, and Alba Vega 2012, 1). Suitcase tourists-cum-traders, prevalent in regional cross-border trade, are also part of this process. The risks, market uncertainties, small profit margins, and aspirations that are endemic to low-end globalization seemingly reinforce a neoliberal ideology that thrives on market freedom and competition, and which exalts the figure of homo economicus, or what Shoshana Pollack and Amy Rossiter call an "individualized entrepreneurial subject" (2010, 156). Having become a source of cheap and low-quality goods that the developing world can afford to consume and a city where the rule of law has been relatively flexible up until recent years, Guangzhou, with its extensive export-oriented production and wholesale trade centers, qualifies as a node of globalization from below—even facilitating it.

Small-scale trading as a means of surviving the continual extension of capital at the grassroots of globalization is filled with contradictions and contingencies. It appears to be anticapitalist, for the people involved are those who are or have become economically marginal in their societies as neoliberalism weakens their countries' economic autonomy. Their strategy to survive with little state support is trading at the grassroots of the global market regardless of their level of experience. Yet their aspirations for upward economic mobility—becoming rich, as Nellie Chu's chapter in this volume reveals—present a paradox. The competition, self-interest, risk-taking, and investments in status-endowing titles that underpin the desired ends are compatible with neoliberalism. The neoliberal mindset that permeates small-scale trading and is rampant in the Chinese market contributes to furthering not only the extension of what Pollack and Rossiter describe as an "economic calculation into traditionally non-economic arenas" (Pollack and Rossiter 2010, 156) but also the alteration of long-standing social relationships and social roles or ways of being, or as Jason Read puts it, "from 'homo economicus' as an exchanging creature to a competitive creature" (Read 2009, 28). Globalization from below is therefore not opposed to capitalism, but assists it by enabling and fostering a new subjectivity among the marginalized who, as entrepreneurs, are now locked in competition with one another.

Focusing on how African women and men struggle in the cracks of the global market while redefining their gender roles, this chapter puts African women's trading activities in Guangzhou into the picture of globalization from below. In doing so, it aims to modify how one analyzes changing gendered labor among African women and men and to show how both women and men operating as homo economicus simultaneously contribute to the production of new gender inequality in a particular setting of globalization from below, rather than equality as Appadurai envisions. Whereas in the past African women did not have to assert their right to engage in small-scale trading activities, now they do. This is all the more the case when the neoliberal shift enables women to deal in high-value, profitable goods and use professional titles to assert their equality with men. By contrast, in the past African men did not engage in nonessential economic activities that included small-scale trading of everyday goods, as it was subsumed under reproductive labor. But now, with structural adjustment (and continuous liberalization), men have been pushed to enter this realm. These changes have produced struggles as well as paradoxical gender assertions from both women and men. Guangzhou illustrates the contingent nature of gendered labor, how globalization from below is constitutive of and enables uneven development.

To understand the findings from my fieldwork conducted in Guangzhou (2013–14 and intermittently in subsequent years) and their connections to the effects of neoliberalism, some background to African women's prominence in labor processes, especially in small-scale trading, and the policy of structural adjustment in African countries is necessary. The next section reveals how the co-option and appropriation of small-scale trading extend free-market rationalities into postcolonial African societies. This transformation redefines gendered labor and relations among small traders. This can be seen as well in Guangzhou, which contributes to the transformation in African social relations from abroad. Additionally, an analysis of a hypermasculine discourse emergent in Guangzhou sheds light on a rising consciousness based on professional titles and, moreover, the neoliberal notion of homo economicus. This chapter concludes with the view that, despite significant changes in gender relations, the ideology of homo economicus is making the male-dominated representation more rigid and stronger in the Chinese market and in China-Africa relations more generally. This suggests that new world orderings, despite new possibilities, can either reproduce existing social inequalities or generate new ones among already economically marginal groups of people.

African Marketplaces: Old and New Livelihood Strategies

The social organization and types of economic activity that women and men undertake in certain societies are inseparable from the market systems that are particular to their societies. In an internal market system dependent on agricultural production, Sidney Mintz (1971) points out that women take up the distributive activity (also referred to as petty commerce or trade) independent of their husbands' economic activities. Gendered labor, he explains, follows family relations and culturally prescribed sex roles (247). Studies focusing on African entrepreneurial women substantiate this point. The literature reveals a long history of women's labor as intermediaries, distributing agricultural produce, selling foodstuffs, and marketing household goods (e.g., Afonja 1981; Robertson 1984; Pietila 2007). Small-scale trading entails conveying, packaging, and processing products, not to mention being a source of credit for customers (Mintz 1971, 248). For market women, these activities were subsumed under household reproductive labor that included work on family farms owned by men. Grier (1992), discussing the Akan women in southern Ghana, notes that their high value as farm laborers made them ideal for male relatives to pawn off for money to purchase land for cocoa production. Trading activities extended throughout the colonial period for women with business acumen and accumulated knowledge (passed down or acquired from informal information exchange), enabling them to become successful intermediaries for the European trading firms that threatened African men's dominance of international markets and lucrative commodities (Robertson 1974; Chuku 1999; Clark 2010).[1] That African market women have had hundreds of years to acquire experience and refine their business techniques can be seen in the Nana Benz of Togo's wax-print fabric trade (Sylvanus 2016). These successful traders have historical ties to influential precolonial trading clans and had credit relationships with major European textile companies in the colonial era until their displacement by

Les Nanettes. By contrast, Les Nanettes—lower-class women who consti-tute a new generation of Togolese women traders with no historical ties to the wax-print textile trade—represent the unraveling of the nexus between small-scale trade and kinship on one hand, and the continual expansion of capitalist relations to small-scale trade on the other.

Women's distributive activity creates essential connections between the local producers, trading firms, and consumers; the subsistence sector and commercial economy; and supply and demand. Women also supply other "incidental services" through their intermediation, such as augmenting transportation and communication facilities, substituting their own labor for capital, providing market intelligence, and offering training for younger entrepreneurial women (Mintz 1971, 249). However, as part of reproductive labor, trading was regarded as a secondary or nonessential activity under-taken by wives and children (Bauer 1963, 11). While the trading activities of women are important to the development of especially underdeveloped economies, Mintz (1971, 250) points out a prevalent view that "facilitat-ing the operation of such economies is not the same as making them grow." This view implies that women do not accumulate capital sufficient for other investments, thus hindering full capitalist development. The policy of struc-tural adjustment—enforced in the developing countries that had accepted loans from the International Monetary Fund and the World Bank—would give new importance to small-scale trading in postcolonial African societies.

Neoliberal economic reforms would transform what had previously been viewed as part of everyday existence into a distinct occupation. Rather than improving African societies and economies, such reforms have contributed to a rising trend in unemployment, poverty, and inequity. Women noticeably took on more reproductive responsibilities as men's economic capacity diminished in the midst of massive layoffs brought about by government measures to re-duce budget deficits, especially by reducing public expenditure. Saskia Sassen's (2003, 55) concept of "feminization of survival" encapsulates the data showing that family livelihoods, capitalist profits, and debt servicing of governments have been realized on the backs of women whose numbers in alternative global labor circuits (e.g., domestics, nurses, sex workers, etc.) have increased. In African contexts, structural adjustment programs have presented multiple moments of change/crisis and adaptation/negotiation in women's and men's roles that have ramifications for maintaining as well as reimagining gender relations. For example, while some women who had historically dominated trading of particular products were able to use their accumulated knowledge of the market to minimize new risks (Chalfin 2000), the Nana Benz were not as fortunate; by the 1990s, these successful textile traders had lost their socio-economic position in Togo to Les Nanettes (Sylvanus 2016).

In other African contexts, changes in gendered labor occurred through careful negotiation, as observed in interactions between Wolof men, who were farmers in rural Senegal, and their wives (Perry 2005). While men lost their ability to procure inputs essential to cultivating cash crops after the elimination of state programs (e.g., import substitution), Wolof women were able to access microloans, allowing them to take up distributive activity full time. As the men were catapulted into a crisis of masculinity, a moral discourse emerged that implicated market women in a growing tide of social decay, including prostitution. Nonetheless, the women emphasized the importance of the conjugal contract to maintain a facade of patriarchy, so that they could continue trading.

In other countries, such as Ghana and Tanzania, some men identified opportunities for profiting from the food and secondhand clothing trade in the streets and local markets, traditionally women's domain (Overå 2007; Pietila 2007). Their entry into these activities situated the men in direct competition with women. The process of transforming these previously conceived nonessential activities to new male niches has been achieved by asserting pressure aimed at usurping women's position in local markets, such as men sexually harassing women or using conspicuous and aggressive market strategies that include donning women's wear (e.g., bras) to mock them (Pietila 2007, 37). Another strategy is to emigrate, allowing African men to undertake small-scale distributive activity without feeling restricted by local gender norms (Overå 2007, 559).[2] Europe and North America were important destinations before rising entry barriers directed migration toward more accessible countries, such as China, within the developing world (Lehmann and Leonard 2018). Not only would large numbers of African men arrive in Guangzhou but the Chinese market would also increase the capacity of women to deal as equals with men.

The Guangzhou Market:
New Livelihood Strategies of African Women

When China initiated open market reforms in the late 1970s, the special economic zones in Guangdong Province (that Guangzhou is part of) played a critical role in the country's transformation. By the late twentieth and early twenty-first centuries, Guangzhou's neoliberal transformation—supported by export-oriented production and a vast assemblage of wholesale trade centers—was crucial for the current formation of African trading communities in the city (Haugen 2012). According to Brigette Bertoncello and Sylvie Bredeloup (2007), the early African traders were those studying in China. The 1997 financial crisis in Southeast Asia also forced the African textile and apparel traders who were doing business in the region to seek new markets, including Hong Kong and, soon after, Guangzhou (Le Bail 2009). "Chocolate City" and "Little Africa" (Li, Lyons, and Brown 2012), the neighborhoods where the African traders live and transact with Chinese entrepreneurs in Sanyuanli (in Baiyun District) and Xiaobei (in Yuexiu District), augmented Guangzhou's reputation as an international trading hub. The number of Africans who have temporary residence in this city is estimated to be between fifteen and twenty thousand (Bodomo 2010, 689; Li, Ma, and Xue 2013, 709; Qiu and Feng 2014).

Within this population, Adams Bodomo's (2010, 699) survey indicates that 87 percent of the Africans regard their occupation as businessmen and 9 percent see themselves as traders, while the remaining 4 percent include "artists," "education service officers," "housewives," and "lecturers." While the survey does not further reveal the gender of each occupation, the category of housewives exposes the implicit masculine assumption of the other occupational categories. The survey does not further reflect on why and how the category of traders—and, possibly, businessmen—has been evolving. Though one could see African women with children around Xiaobei who fit the description of housewives, one woman I interviewed, when asked about the activities of Africans in Guangzhou, replied simply that "we're all trading."

A closer look at women's trading activities in Guangzhou presents an idea of how gendered labor is undergoing changes. While conducting fieldwork in Guangzhou from 2013 to 2014, I spoke to a number African traders, both women and men, and I will draw on their accounts of their experiences here and for the remainder of this chapter. For instance, Tammy's first trip to Guangzhou was initiated by her husband after a bad investment.[3] When her husband first traveled to China in 2007, he unknowingly returned with copied spare car parts that could not be sold in Ghana. A month later, he asked Tammy to travel with him to China. The reason she gave for this was that he recognized her ability to learn languages quickly and to communicate with the Holy Spirit that would enable her to guide him toward success. Her business acumen was clear even if unacknowledged. Soon after their arrival, she

New Livelihood Strategies

made contacts with Chinese businesses and identified two provinces to source reliable car parts. After the birth of their first child, the couple decided that Tammy would remain in Guangzhou while her husband returned to Ghana. She was responsible for caring for their child and continuing to source spare car parts for her husband to sell at home. Additionally, she learned about the wholesale centers and opened a shop selling women's apparel in Xiaobei.

In 2013 African women and men could still be seen selling goods out of shops in wholesale centers located in Xioabei and Sanyuanli. Viv's experience demonstrated the challenges of being one of these shop owners. Before coming to Guangzhou, Viv had a shop in Uganda and traded in Dubai, Ethiopia, and Thailand. In Guangzhou, she had a shop as well. However, in our second meeting, she talked about having to leave the shop due to rising rent and the fact that she had no one to share the cost with. Even after she received financial assistance from a sister in Uganda, who gave her money to rent a new shop, Viv still had to wait to find someone with a Chinese identification card to help her sign the lease. Viv was not alone in needing to rely on local Chinese business partners to lease a shop. Given the difficulty of registering businesses locally, this strategy allowed her and others to bypass local regulations.

In her new shop in a wholesale center in Sanyuanli, Viv sold jeans to African customers. From regular visits to her shop, I soon realized that she also provided other services, such as taking purchase orders over mobile phones and shipping consumer goods to her family in Uganda as well as to African customers in other parts of Africa, Europe, and the United States. To complete these orders, she made trips to other shops and wholesale centers. This particular service is part of the intermediary work she undertook after closing her shop in late 2013 due to stricter enforcement of Chinese work requirements. In Guangzhou, intermediaries are brokers or middlemen for the traders who buy commodities for African markets. They are also called "agents," and the most visible African agents in Guangzhou are men. However, as Viv and other women I interviewed revealed, women also brokered for traders from their home countries.

Faiza and, to an extent, Yafiah were examples of such intermediaries. As Fazia explained, these women assisted "clients" with "completing supply chains." Agents provide services such as doing market research prior to the clients' arrival, accompanying clients to meet Chinese suppliers or manufacturers, and inspecting products before they are loaded into containers. This final step is crucial in a setting where African traders have reported being cheated by Chinese manufacturers who sent poor quality products or the wrong items. When I met her, Faiza had already been in Guangzhou for nearly seven years but still could not speak Chinese, which is a requirement for agents. Her disinterest in learning the language was linked to the fact that she was only willing to stay in China temporarily for the economic opportunities and stability it offered.

During my visit with her in Kenya, Faiza described her neighborhood as a "slum," where different business ventures her family had pursued yielded little profit. To help her family, she moved to Nairobi for work after finishing high school. She soon started to buy handbags from downtown to resell at her workplace. Once she had some savings, Faiza began crossing the border to Uganda to buy women's undergarments to sell. A friend's invitation to work as an English teacher brought Faiza to Guangzhou in 2006, but when she arrived she discovered that the position was no longer available. Rather than return home, she accepted a Kenyan man's offer to teach her about the Chinese market. The number of agents increased after she started this line of work, and she felt that the younger Kenyan men, who competed with her, were the most aggressive. In addition to these competitors, shipping and logistics companies had also moved from Dubai or Hong Kong to Guangzhou and started to offer brokering services. These are mostly dominated by African men with more socioeconomic resources. In such a competitive environment, Faiza began to focus more on church activities, eventually leaving Guangzhou in 2016 when the opportunity to do missionary work in the United States arose.

Meanwhile, Yafiah, although she was also an agent, expressed her disdain for the types of goods Faiza dealt in. The small profit earned from textiles, apparel, and small household goods presented little motivation for Yafiah to accompany traders all over Guangzhou and neighboring cities to find cheap suppliers. As she put it, she preferred to deal in "the big things." Yafiah had left Sierra Leone for Nanjing in 1996 to learn Mandarin before enrolling at a university in Shanghai. After studying and working as an English teacher in Shanghai for fourteen years, she wanted a change of environment and moved to Guangzhou. A shortage of capital delayed her dream of starting a shipping and logistics company. Instead, with her knowledge of Chinese, she partnered with a small local Chinese shipping business. Yafiah supported this business by accompanying customers from her home country who traveled to Guangzhou to purchase construction and building materials. Such commodities are the "big things" that require more capital and earn higher profits. They can easily fill a cargo container, thereby lowering the cost of shipping and eliminating the waiting period that African traders with less bulky goods

103

have to endure while sharing containers. When business was profitable, Yafiah was a shipping agent, but when business declined, as it did when travel was hindered during the Ebola outbreak in West Africa, she became "just a shopping agent for African countries" because she could not choose to turn down the "small things." By the end of 2017, Yafiah announced that she had achieved her dream of having her own shipping company, even though it put her in debt and she was nearly cheated by her previous Chinese partner.

Among the African women in Guangzhou, there are also itinerant traders who stay there for a few months at a time on short-term visas. For instance, Atoofah described herself as a trader when I met her in 2013. She already had over fifteen years of experience as an itinerant trader, beginning in Karachi and Dubai while she was still living in Somalia. She subsequently resettled in Kenya, and had traveled to Turkey, Indonesia, India, Hong Kong, and Bangkok to purchase women's apparel to sell in Nairobi. Atoofah explained that with one business card for a hotel and another for a supplier, she headed to Guangzhou for the first time in 2007, and returned regularly in the years that followed. Her husband managed the shop and her sister cared for her children in Nairobi while she made the thirty-hour round-trip flight to Guangzhou three to five times a year. Her stays there ranged from two weeks to a month or longer, depending on her visa, and when asked why she is the one who travels, she explained that she has the eye for identifying good clothes "for ladies— big ladies, small ladies."

Another trader in a similar position was Mama G from Nigeria, who started traveling to China in 2005. She brought samples to Guangzhou to have them made under her brand name that she then sold at a market in Abuja. Mama G explained that frequent travel allowed her to change fashion quickly and stay ahead of customers' rapidly shifting demands, especially since her brand was expensive by local standards. Having time and money to travel as well as accumulated knowledge, traders such as Mama G and Atoofah could mitigate the risks associated with market uncertainties.

Some women with fewer resources or who have full-time jobs also work as part-time traders. Small-scale trading supplements their income. For instance, Aaida is a Nigerian holding an Irish passport who works as an assisted-living nurse in Ireland. As a mother of two school-age children, she required childcare whenever she traveled to Guangzhou to purchase children's apparel to sell to parents from her children's school. Reflecting the moderate quantity of goods that part-time traders like Aaida purchase, they are also referred to as suitcase traders.

A closer look at African women's trading activities in Guangzhou reveals other distinctions. Not all of them identify as traders. For instance, Mariam, a Comorian, prefers the title of businesswoman. This preference seems to be connected with the fact that she works full time load-shedding aircrafts at the airport in Comoros, and sources building materials and home furniture for her shop during her vacation time.[4] She purchased these materials in Dubai beginning in 1993 before turning to Guangzhou in 2010. Similarly, Ms. C views her businesses in Zambia and Ms. M's, whom she occasionally travels with for trade, as belonging in the high-medium scale, making them "businesswomen." By this she means that both have several businesses in Lusaka, including restaurants and shops that sell specific types of products. They also source commodities globally, traveling to countries such as Japan, the United States, Hong Kong, Dubai, and China. Ms. M, whom I spent the most time with, left a career in journalism in 1992 and took up regional cross-border trade because she had just become a mother and "wanted the luxuries in life." When she started going to Johannesburg in 1995, three-quarters of the passengers on the bus were women traders. Her account of traveling and carrying goods back to Zambia on a bus and sharing accommodations with other women resonates with Manisha Desai's (2009, 380) observation that such cross-border trade is "regional, hard, arduous, and open to many risks and harassments," requiring the women involved to create personal networks to help facilitate their movement of consumer goods.

Ms. M and Ms. C were indeed part of a network of women who provided support to one another, especially when buying "big things" such as second-hand cars from Japan. As I learned from a visit with Ms. M in Zambia in 2014, this type of network facilitates information exchange and is jealously guarded to control gossip and rumors. Gossip is often intertwined with accusations of witchcraft or commentaries on wealth accumulation that could be used for political ends or to ruin reputations (Pietila 2007, 90). Ms. M's reputation as a global and successful businesswoman has attracted unscrupulous business proposals that put her reputation at risk. She shared that, prior to my visit, a Zambian man had wanted to know if she would collaborate with him in what was basically trafficking of children, which she quickly declined to prevent rumors from spreading. Ms. M's concern about her reputation suggested that to be a businesswoman is also to hold a certain position in the community; it is a status-endowing title that is built over time and guarded.

Clearly, some African women have decades of experience and accumulated knowledge while others are new traders who draw on the precedents of others.[5] Aaida's mother was a trader in Nigeria and Faiza's was a nurse who engaged in Kenya-Uganda cross-border trade. Atoofah seemed to have been an apprentice to her mother, who traded in Somalia before resettling in the United States. Their mothers were models and readily offered advice. Ms. M had aunts who traded regionally and offered guidance. Regardless of the length of time these women had been trading, they came to Guangzhou with experience from other settings of low-end globalization. Their presence in China suggests that their trade circuits have continued to expand with shifts in the global market and with their ability to accumulate capital in the cracks of the global market. They have been able to adapt to the neoliberal landscape. The women who are full-time traders and are dealing in construction/building material as well as shipping in the Chinese market further reveal that some African women traders/businesswomen have amassed enough capital to be economically independent. This gives them the capacity to compete as equals with African men, who have had access to land, which gave them the resources to monopolize trading in high-value commodities. When women go into the "big things" and use professional titles, they are asserting that equality.

However, women are not alone in blurring gender roles in trading as they acquire more freedom and capital to deal in high-value commodities and become full-time traders in low-end globalization. While the Chinese market is increasing some African women's ability to assert their equality with men, it is also presenting new opportunities for African men who either have no prior trading experience or have previously held professional jobs. The next section examines how these men assert their entrepreneurial role in trading activities by reinterpreting them. Paradoxically, while gender roles are being blurred and redefined as these men are pushed to enter this realm, once regarded as nonessential, gender discrimination has actually intensified.

Reimagining "Women's Work" and Masculinity

African women in Guangzhou often have to respond to moral discourses that negatively represent them, and their myriad ways of coping reflect tensions among women of various nationalities or ethnicities, who have different ideas about gender relations. For example, one Cameroonian woman initiated a fight with a Nigerian man at his shop for disrespecting her by delaying payment for the goods he had received from her. When she recounted this fight at Viv's shop, Viv responded that the woman should not have acted like a man, and instead should have spoken nicely to the man so that he would bring her the money. This is how women should conduct business, Viv maintained. This view resonates with the Senegalese women traders in Donna Perry's (2005) study, who tried to demonstrate a commitment to upholding the conjugal contract, precisely in order to continue working as full-time traders.

In another example, Atoofah stated that relations with African men in small-scale trade could be symbiotic, but only if the men did not also buy and sell women's apparel. When the men crossed that line, which a few did by copying her designs, Atoofah had to stay ahead of the competition. One strategy involved traveling frequently to Guangzhou and Bangkok to search for new designs, and she also constantly changed her "shipping name/mark" to prevent her competitors from imitating her designs. The increased competition from African men in the Chinese market, with its low prices, different scales of production, and flexible copyright, requires Atoofah to use her accumulated knowledge to keep prices low and offer quality goods while still earning a small profit.

Details about the relation between women and men traders can also be gleaned from the discourses concerning African women that circulate in Guangzhou. A Somali man's conversation with a woman trader offers one example. The man viewed the "ghetto-like" behavior of boys in a Nairobi community as being the result of irresponsible mothers traveling for trade. The woman, defending herself, insisted that the social environment influenced the children's behavior, thereby justifying her family's decision to live in a suburb where there are better schools. The implication was that this living arrangement, made possible by her earnings from trading activities, made her a good mother.

Paralleling this gendered dichotomy is another dichotomy between "bad girl" and "respectable woman," alluding to women's sexual freedom and individualism (Pietila 2007, 87). The "bad girl" imagery circulated in Guangzhou through claims that the majority of African women were prostitutes. When asked for an estimate of the percentage of African women in Guangzhou who worked in the sex trade, one African man answered 20–40 percent, or even as high as 80 percent. Such a view implicitly asserts control over women by making them responsible for their own reputations. This was evident in Yafiah's comment that she avoids walking alone at night in the streets of Xiaobei. This sort of association between female African traders and prostitution is not uncommon in African contexts, especially in places where men's socioeconomic status and sense of masculinity are already in crisis. Stigmas associated with being rape victims, HIV carriers, or "witches" who use magic to accumulate wealth and gain success, portray women as destructive, manipulative, and individualistic (Desai 2009, 383; Pietila 2007, 109).

These stigmas also undermined African women's value as economic actors. Even when African men attempted to acknowledge women's economic agency, they implicitly portrayed them as inexperienced. A self-identified Ghanaian procurement manager shared that the female customers he worked with had plenty of money, but unlike the African men, the women usually did not know what they wanted when they arrived in Guangzhou. He elaborated that, except for one South African woman who sourced car parts—which put her in the same realm as the men who purchased high-value machinery beneficial to economic development—the female customers mostly purchased apparel or washing powder, tissue paper, and other household goods to sell in local African markets. Though his intention was not to disparage these women, he nevertheless reinforced the perception that small-scale trading of everyday products is a nonessential activity.

Ironically, this manager did not recognize how his own role straddled traditional gendered divisions of labor in trading. That female traders had been intermediaries in the past, connecting peoples and everyday products, eluded him. He was one of the group of men I encountered in Guangzhou who used professional titles such as agent, broker, CEO, designer, or businessman to distinguish themselves from itinerant traders. The agent or broker is the intermediary who connects two markets. A CEO is a partner in a foreign-owned shipping and logistics company in Guangzhou that facilitates the flow of consumer goods, information, and capital. The designer is fundamentally an apparel trader, while the businessman cannot be bothered with such low-value commodities. On one hand, these professional titles reveal how the services of small traders have been dissected, commoditized, and modernized under neoliberalism. Even the processing of goods is done by Chinese export-manufacturers. On the other hand, such titles create an image of legitimacy (belonging), respectability (value), and rationality (systematism). These men have become entrepreneurial subjects whose rational and efficient conduct enables them to maximize their interests (Pollack and Rossiter 2010, 159). Accordingly, through status-endowing titles, these African men also blur gender roles in relation to trading, reinterpreting and normalizing a seemingly nonessential activity as always-already a male niche (Overå 2007, 558).[6]

T. TU HUYNH

These men enter this realm of activity and, along with it, develop a form of hypermasculinity. One particular song, "Ife Neme Na China" (Things that happen in China), highlighted in Heidi Haugen's (2012) study about Nigerian men's "second state of immobility," captures the elements that inform a hypermasculine imagining of place and identity. This song forms part of a general trend of Africans self-publishing music in hopes of breaking into the industry via China (Carli-Jones and Lefkowitz 2015; Castillo 2015). Haugen notes how this song contains descriptions of "police harassment, imprisonment, forced repatriation, casual sexual relations with Chinese girls, economic difficulties and betrayal by family in Nigeria" (Haugen 2012, 8). Dibaocha, a Nigerian Igbo R&B singer who is important in the African music scene in Guangzhou, also elucidates African men's experiences in his lyrics, but in more romantic ways. For example, his song "I Feel Good" includes a Chinese singer who expresses her love and unconditional commitment to the African singer in the song (i.e., Dibaocha). And "Asia Money" affirms that "if you get the money, you are somebody."[7] Nonetheless, further reading of "Ife Neme Na China" indicates that the described threats are not just experienced, but are also utilized to mobilize a new masculinity in, as one lyric puts it, "China [that] is very difficult/China [that] is very hard."[8] The song addresses Nigerian men as "brother," warning them to "be alert" and "know how to retreat from fuck-up," and also expresses camaraderie by noting that "what we are doing in this China is not easy." The song's conclusion celebrates a muscular masculinity among these men because "only hard people will stay here," and then declares: "And if it is too hard for you/*zou ba* [Chinese: 'go!'] to the country you came from!"

This gesture of claiming entitlement by telling others to leave resonates with Loren Landau and Iriann Haupt's (2007, 9) observation of African migrants' experience with exclusion in South Africa. For the African men in Guangzhou, their stay in China is presented as a challenge that they alone can shoulder. There is a sense of triumph in the discourse of hardship in Guangzhou. Stories about Chinese people who cheat, the challenges of renewing visas, and encounters with racism contribute to the unique responsibility for African men to persevere. Other risks—involving the fickle nature of market trends, currency exchanges, and customs officials—exacerbate the already difficult situation that is favorable for imagining masculinity (Mathews and Yang 2012).

All of these examples speak to the hardship of low-end globalization. To borrow Gordon Mathews and Yang Yang's phrase (2012, 110), these African men imagine themselves confronting "the 'wild west' of contemporary capitalism." They are not alone in their description. The South African founder of an international advisory and procurement firm in Beijing also refers to the China he first encountered as "the wild west."[9] This concept draws on ideas of conquest, expansion, persistence, and survival by "real men" in the process of settling the American frontier. The "many things happening in China," including promiscuity, as the song illuminates, enable African men to rework their masculinity in a poststructural adjustment period of diminished economic opportunities and status.

Whether there are multiple masculinities alongside a hegemonic one, as Robert Morrel (1998) reminds us, the real and imagined world of hardship, risk, and casual sex in Guangzhou excludes "not-real men" as well as women and defines how putative "real men" should behave. "I am a man" is what a Sierra Leonean man repeated several times during our conversation. For him, it meant being able to survive on purchase orders and shipments of consumer goods to African customers elsewhere, along with occasional basketball contracts. Moreover, it meant having the ability to budget money and withstand numerous challenges. His explanation excluded the possibility for African women to survive in Guangzhou. From this standpoint, the Chinese market contributes to the intensification of gender discrimination, keeping gender inequality intact.

Conclusion

This chapter contributes to understandings of the transnational economy from below or low-end globalization by focusing on how African women and men struggle in the cracks of the global market while redefining their gender roles in relation to trading in Guangzhou. I have identified two paradoxes linked with both processes: (1) the competition, self-interest, risk-taking, and investments in professional titles observed among the African women and men struggling at the grassroots of globalization are compatible with neoliberalism, which subsumed traditionally noneconomic arenas under capitalism; and (2) operating as homo economicus, both African women and men trading in the Chinese market contribute to the (re)production of gender discrimination and inequality.

By focusing on African women, the chapter contributes to our understanding of ongoing transformations of gendered labor among Africans in China. Many scholars have written about how neoliberal economic changes have forced African women into the global labor market or have driven them to seek alternative types of work, as men's role as breadwinners diminishes. But low-end globalization centered on small-scale trading also offers other possibilities for both women and men. On one hand, the African women who have accumulated capital to go into the "big things" are blurring gender roles because high-value commodities are typically not part of the distributive activity that women have undertaken in the past. On the other hand, African men who have been pushed to enter the realm of small-scale trading in the aftermath of structural adjustment are also redefining gendered labor in ways that put women traders on the defensive. Through moral discourses, reinterpretation of services integral to small-scale trading with the use of professional titles, and articulation of a hypermasculinity in Guangzhou, African men's encroachment on distributive activity that was subsumed under reproductive labor has been normalized, and trading that was viewed as a nonessential activity has become essential work. It is important to delineate these processes of gendered transformation, as they allow for a deeper understanding of how gender ideology continues to shape spaces, scales, and subjects in specific contexts. What we observe in Guangzhou illustrates the contingent nature of gendered labor, how globalization from below is constitutive of and enables uneven development in ways that reinforce gender discrimination.

Notes

An earlier version of this chapter appeared as "A 'Wild West' of Trade? African Women and Men and the Gendering of Globalisation from Below in Guangzhou," in *Identities* 23, no. 5 (2016): 501–18.

1 The predominance of men in international markets and lucrative commodities reflected their privileged access to capital, land, labor, and time (M. Desai 2009, 379; Overå 2007, 544; Perry 2005, 211). But when the European trading firms took over these markets, the African men who had rights to lineage land shifted toward large-scale agricultural production. Furthermore, since men were also privileged in receiving formal education, most were equipped with the skills to assume professional occupations (Robertson 1984, 643).

2 Though not avoiding gender norms, Somali men, for example, affected by diminished public sector employment opportunities, see immigration and small-scale trading as opportunities to augment their socioeconomic status, according to the CEO of a shipping and logistics company.

3 All names are pseudonyms.

4   The consumer goods she purchased complicate the notion of suitcase tourist/ trader.

5   Sylvanus's 2016 study focusing on cloth traders in Togo sheds light on the tension between the two groups.

6   This process finds parallels in other fields, as Monica Green's (2008) documentation of the masculinization of women's medicine, namely gynecology, in the sixteenth century shows. According to Green, the development of a learned masculine culture, combined with change in what constituted authoritative knowledge, allowed men to assert authority over women's medicine.

7   As of 2020, some of Dibaocha's songs have been made available on YouTube.

8   Haugen shared with me the rest of the lyrics of this song and the translation, which are not included in her article.

9   Unlike the African men mentioned in this chapter, this was the only white South African interviewed. The chapter does not examine the racial differences among Africans.

PROPHETIC BECOMING

The Prosperity Doctrine in Guangzhou, China

In the heart of Guangzhou's Xiaobei district in southern China, migrants from different regions across West Africa, including the Ivory Coast, Liberia, Nigeria, Guinea, and Gambia, assembled in a compact office room on the 31st floor of a semidilapidated building, where services for the Global Pentecostal Living Faith Fellowship (GPLFF) took place. From 2011 to 2014, the GPLFF was an underground church in Guangzhou. This fellowship constituted one of numerous licensed and unlicensed Christian churches that served the transnational and multilingual diasporic communities. Dressed in their Sunday finest, congregants gathered regularly to sing songs, recite prayers, and reflect on sermons led by Pastor Thomas, a charismatic leader from the Congo, and by Pastor Johnson, a preacher-in-training from Liberia. Like Pastor Thomas and Pastor Johnson, many congregants in this underground fellowship were itinerant traders who exported commodities in relatively small volumes to retailers and wholesalers in all regions of Africa. Here, the faith-based and profit-driven endeavors of the pastors and their congregants served as key nodes through which transnational Christian and business networks articulated with practices of capitalist accumulation and religious conversion in southern China.

One Sunday, Pastor Thomas approached the podium to give the day's sermon. As he delivered his sermon in French, his wife, Christina, stood next to him, translating his lecture word-for-word into English. With their heads bowed and their eyes firmly closed, parents, children, and young couples in the audience listened intently to his words, occasionally breaking their silence by reciting songs of praise in French and in English. Pastor Thomas began his homily by narrating his recent travels to Dubai, where he frequently visited so as to conduct his export business. There, he encountered a fellow male trader of the Muslim faith. During the course of their conversation, the two men built an unusual rapport, and the trader convinced Pastor Thomas to lend him an undisclosed amount of money as a loan to cover a long-standing debt. The acquaintance promised to repay him in three weeks. They decided to meet at a specific time and place, where the man would repay the pastor. When the day came, the man failed to show up, leaving Pastor Thomas feeling misled and betrayed. A portion of this sum was reserved for a business transaction that he had planned during his stay in Dubai. Without the money, Pastor Thomas could not proceed with his business plan. In his anguish, Pastor Thomas prayed, asking God for spiritual guidance and comfort. Nearly a week later, to the pastor's surprise, the Muslim trader found Pastor Thomas as he entered the hotel lobby to return a portion of the money that was owed to him. The man apologized profusely, explaining that one of his family members had suddenly fallen ill, but he somehow managed to collect half of the money in time (albeit a week late). The pastor thanked him for his consideration, forgave the remainder of his debt, and took his act as a sign of the man's renewed faith in God.

The central message Pastor Thomas sought to convey through his story was that an important aspect of one's faith in God was to spread his love by expanding his kingdom. On a large screen directly behind him, he projected a slide that displayed these words written in bold letters: "Let FEAR, LOVE, and COMPASSION motivate you to expand the Kingdom!" Underneath, he listed the following bullet points: Personal Quality and Quantity, Church Quality and Quantity, and Territory. Pastor Thomas then proceeded to emphasize that in a kingdom, a king, namely God, rules over his territory. As believers, love compels us to expand God's territory. However, as Pastor Thomas elucidated, before we are able to fulfill this mission, we must first ask for God's help. We must first ask and receive God's grace before we share our love for him with others. Pastor Thomas concluded his sermon by reminding us of how he demonstrated his obedience to God by asking for help during his time of financial need in Dubai.

In *The Protestant Ethic and the Spirit of Capitalism*, Max Weber (2002) theorizes how certain ethical values and dispositions exemplified by followers of Protestantism—such as asceticism, hard work, and modesty—predispose Protestants to achieve entrepreneurial success in modern capitalist activities. His seminal essay on the "spirit" of capitalism challenges Karl Marx's critique of political economy, which is based on theories of historical materialism, by focusing on the psychology and moral economy of a people. Weber's study of the Protestant ethic shows how emphasis on one's rational engagement with the economic world is intricately linked with the fulfillment of one's spiritual destiny (without necessarily the mediation of the church). This link, in turn, has paved the way for the emergence of modern capitalism.

In the contemporary period of globalization and transnational migration, Weber's notion of the "spirit" of capitalism is exemplified by what observers and believers like Pastor Thomas describe as the prosperity doctrine, otherwise known as the prosperity gospel, which preaches that faith in and devotion to God ensure health and prosperity in the bodily world. According to the prosperity gospel, modest monetary contributions from followers are given as "seed offerings" to God in exchange for bountiful health and wealth (Haynes 2013).

Based on the ethnographic research that I conducted among West African migrant entrepreneurs in Guangzhou's GPLFF from 2012 to 2014, this chapter analyzes the sermons and testimonials through which migrant "pastor-entrepreneurs," such as Pastor Thomas and Pastor Johnson, preached the prosperity doctrine. It shows how these pastors interpreted the prosperity doctrine while they created for themselves a particular "worlding" project in which their Christian beliefs intimately intersected with their transnational business activities.

My research was part of a larger project that compared South Korean and West African pastor-entrepreneurs who engaged in the fast fashion commodity chains in Guangzhou. Throughout this period, attendance at GPLFF's Sunday services peaked and the congregation's outreach activities thrived. During my attendance at the church, I participated in regular weekly services, as well as postservice dinners and activities organized by young members of the congregation. More importantly, I developed friendship bonds with the pastors and with their congregants, enabling me to formulate a

115

deeper, more nuanced understanding of their worldviews based on their life histories and personal stories.

Prophetic Becoming

Living along the margins of mainstream society in China, this underground congregation viewed its activities as a hub of globalized Pentecostal faith in which West African migrants in China discursively linked their interpretation of the prosperity doctrine to what Weber described as a spiritual "calling" (Beruf) through their personal experiences of transcontinental migration and worldly travel to China (2002, 28). As Pastor Thomas's sermon revealed, his belief in God and in the prosperity doctrine were frequently tested and reinforced through his business transactions and personal encounters with local partners and clients.

Through their personal experiences of racism, debt, and displacement, I argue, believers of the prosperity doctrine cultivated a sense of entrepreneurial personhood. This was achieved through the actualization of their personal desires while accumulating God's graces in order to attain eternal salvation. The processual construction of believers' entrepreneurial desire and subjecthood constituted what I call "prophetic becoming," by which I mean discursive constructions of entrepreneurial desire that are intimately shaped by individuals' experiences of crossing transnational and oceanic boundaries in order to escape wars, disease, and sociopolitical crises in their native places in West Africa.

Prophetic becoming entails the ongoing transactional exchange—often characterized by faith, dependency, and uncertainty—between a believer and God. West African pastors and congregants express their faith through the discursive constructions of desire and freedom, while they negotiate their encounters with racial discrimination, policing, debt, and theft in China. Such journeys and faith-based conversions are driven and accompanied by a personal sense of self-transformation and devotional renewal upon their arrival in China, where their ambitions for material wealth and eternal salvation are activated and deepened. Much like the heterogeneous processes of "imaginative worldmaking," as described by Carlos Rojas and Lisa Rofel in the introduction to this volume, African migrants' journeys of self-discovery as followers of the Christian faith are characterized by disruptions and displacements. In this exchange, the believer must demonstrate her devotion to God by performing particular actions and possessing certain qualities in this world, such as hard work and asceticism, even though the majority of believers will not be saved.

While Weber insightfully highlights the faith-based dimensions of capitalist motivation, particularly key aspects of profit-driven action that challenge conventional ideas around rationality and calculation, West African migrants' journeys of prophetic becoming deepen Weber's analysis of the Protestant "spirit" of capitalism by casting faith not simply as a given totality that the congregants may or may not possess based on their calling or *Beruf* (2002, 28). Rather, the West African pastors describe their relationship to God as an uneven, dialectical transformation of the self; their journeys to otherworldly salvation involve ongoing uncertainty, divergence, and reaffirmation. As Pheng Cheah (2008) argues, a worlding practice is found in "intervals, mediations, passages, and crossings." West African migrants move not only between national borders but also between the boundaries of the spiritual and the secular. Their experiences of displacement, debt, and discrimination in China and in the material world sometimes cause them to question their faith in God. This is particularly true when their beliefs are mired in disappointment, doubt, and uncertainty.

Because Protestants believe that their faith is continually being tested, many believers are compelled to demonstrate their faith through actions carried out in this world. Through these actions, a believer accumulates God's grace in the face of ongoing uncertainty about whether she is actually one of God's chosen people. Such actions thus involve the dialectical processes of uncertainty, action, and devotional renewal frequently epitomized by the maxim, "God helps those who help themselves." For Pastor Thomas in particular, accumulation of God's grace through action in the material world is not enough to become a true believer. Rather, prophetic becoming entails a transactional exchange in which faith-based action must necessarily accompany a personal desire for wealth and other forms of prosperity in order to receive God's grace in this world and the afterworld. In other words, pastors of GPLFF seek to cultivate entrepreneurial subjects through the language of desire so that congregants may meaningfully witness and receive prosperity, thus deepening their devotion to God.

Pastors' experiences of transnational migration lead them to interpret and to preach the prosperity doctrine in specific ways. Though their project of "worlding" remains along the margins of Chinese society, West African migrants imagine themselves at the center of these faith-based transcontinental crossings and otherworldly conversions. Their boundary-crossing journeys and transformations, however contingent, unstable, and risky they may be, entail three aspects of their faith-based conversion and self-renewal.

First, their stories of personal risk and unpredictable moments of fortune and wealth enable these transnational migrant entrepreneurs to redefine themselves as respectable members of the transnational Christian faith community as well as the global capitalist economy, both of which exceed the spatial-political confines of the nation-states from which they began their transcontinental journeys. Second, their unpredictable and uneven experiences of crossing spiritual and material worlds are punctuated by times of wealth and fortune, as well as bankruptcy and failure. Based on these events, the pastors convey lessons of becoming proper entrepreneurs through business and risk management in order to evidence their faith. The prosperity doctrine's language of desire is thus closely linked to the experiences and discourses related to economic risk and loss. Third, the uncertain and precarious conditions upon their arrival in China lead the migrants to feel vulnerable and displaced, leaving their Christian faith as a primary source of their continual transformation and renewal in the face of ongoing instability, poverty, state-led oppression, and communal violence. These experiences heighten migrants' faith though their renewed devotion is not necessarily a result of them. Moreover, their uncertain future increasingly compels these itinerant traders to view China as a temporary site of economic accumulation and religious conversion before they must seek opportunities elsewhere. The relative fluidity through which these transnational migrants move across regions in the Global South thus challenges the assumption that their understandings of entrepreneurial personhood remain certain and stable.

As a case in point, this particular congregation—like many unlicensed churches in this transnational migrant community—remained vulnerable to the racial profiling, heavy policing, and various rent-seeking activities that regularly plagued the migrant district of Xiaobei. As T. Tu Hyunh explains in this volume, coping with precarity has been a reality for many of Guangzhou's African migrants since China's laws controlling their movements in private and public spaces have often been vague and discriminatory. In fact, congregants would find themselves sitting through the service in the dark whenever landlords decided to cut off their electricity because of late rent or unpaid bills. In addition, African migrants were often intercepted by police officers who frequently demanded inspection of their IDs, residential permits, and business licenses. Those who failed to show valid paperwork were thrown in jail and heavily fined, leaving many migrant traders stuck in China without money or familial support. For many African traders, their experiences of racial profiling and other forms of discrimination brewed a sense of distrust toward Chinese residents, particularly those who were nonreligious and had not shown active support in their faith-based community. Such distrust left some African groups isolated from Chinese communities in Xiaobei. In fact, Pastor Johnson once shared with me his preference for cooperating with Korean business partners over his Chinese counterparts in Guangzhou, primarily because of their shared devotion to Christianity.

Racial tensions that often characterized this neighborhood thus colored migrants' experiences of religious and entrepreneurial life in Guangzhou. In some instances, police officers would even close an entire wholesale market where African traders frequently shopped for garments, household goods, novelties, and other accessories for an entire day, thus interrupting the business and personal activities of shopkeepers and visitors. During this time, officers would inspect business licenses of African shopkeepers as they searched for counterfeit goods. In other instances, officers shut down unlicensed churches and other religious activities.

The pressures of surveillance and harassment ultimately forced Pastor Thomas to close the doors of the GPLFF in 2014, during a time when African communities in Xiaobei faced even tighter restrictions by the police and other law enforcement officials in Guangzhou. In recent years, intensified crackdowns on undocumented African migrants, through heavy policing and racial profiling, have led many traders to close their businesses and leave Guangzhou in favor of more religiously tolerant and business-friendly cities such as Yiwu in Zhejiang Province. Unyielding surveillance and aggressive restrictions on mobility by the city police forced African church leaders and their congregants to go further underground, moving their sites of worship and limiting communication with those outside of their congregation. The uncertain conditions of their religious and work lives demonstrate the enormous personal and economic risks that African traders take in order to establish their practices of profit-making and worship.

The Prosperity Doctrine and the Making of Entrepreneurial Subjects

In recent years, social scientists have examined the ways in which pastors and other religious leaders have called on and mobilized entrepreneurial subjects through the spread of the prosperity doctrine in Pentecostal churches across

Africa and other regions in the Global South. These scholars have cogently observed that the emergence and subsequent popularity of the prosperity doctrine within Pentecostal congregations in Africa during the 1980s have occurred in conjunction with the privatization and restructuring of state-sponsored welfare programs through large-scale loans and other debt schemes introduced by the World Bank and the International Monetary Fund among developing economies. This socioeconomic development, commonly described as the global emergence of neoliberalism, has led anthropologists, sociologists, and human geographers to interpret and critique the prosperity doctrine in the Global South through several distinctive analytical frameworks.

Some scholars, such as Jean Comaroff and John Comaroff (2000), have argued that the prosperity doctrine emerged at a historical juncture when post-Fordism became the dominant mode of labor and production within the global economy. In this mode, production and productive labor no longer serve as the fundamental sources of personhood, family, and moral order; at the same time, the sovereignty of nation-states and public institutions has gradually eroded. The Comaroffs call this development a "neo-Protestant manifestation," based on a future-oriented, transactional form of devotion that "fuses the messianic spirit with the speculative force of financial capital" (2000, 77). For the Comaroffs, the practice of separating out the immediate accumulation of wealth and other material desires in this world from the speculative promise of eternal salvation by God in the spiritual world distinguishes contemporary forms of neo-Protestantism from the "old" Protestant ethic as described by Max Weber (2002) in *The Protestant Ethic and the Spirit of Capitalism*.

The Protestant Ethic and the Spirit of Capitalism

For other scholars, the historical convergence of neoliberalism and the prosperity doctrine has masked the deleterious effects of post-Fordist production and finance capitalism. Ebenezer Obadare (2016) has argued that the principle of self-actualization through entrepreneurship and the accumulation of capital, which underlies the prosperity doctrine, encumbers progress toward more egalitarian forms of economic development while exacerbating poverty and social inequality. Moreover, as other scholars have argued, the prosperity doctrine depoliticizes religious movements through its emphasis on individual wealth as symbolic of one's relationship with God.

In this sense, the prosperity doctrine obscures the dynamics of power and inequality in the accumulation of capital. In her study of a Nigerian Pentecostal congregation in southern China, for instance, Heidi Haugen (2013) argues that the prosperity doctrine accentuates the congregants' sense of ethnic isolation, which is reinforced by the racial and religious discrimination held by the many Chinese people African migrants have encountered. Since Africans in China believe that they are chosen to spread God's message, Haugen has found that the prosperity gospel exacerbates interethnic tensions in China. In this Nigerian congregation, Chinese-run churches, particularly state churches, are frequently dismissed as lacking in authentic faith and are thus deemed meaningless (2013, 98).

Meanwhile, a growing body of anthropological scholarship has challenged the argument that the prosperity doctrine leads only to apolitical and asocial effects by elucidating the sociopolitical worlds through which the gospel has been created. As some scholars have observed, the prosperity doctrine has facilitated the deepening of hierarchical relationships and social obligations that congregants have with one another based on their unequal material possessions. In his examination of migrant women's Bible study groups in a Pentecostal congregation in Botswana, for example, Rijk van Dijk (2009) demonstrates how the prosperity doctrine offers female entrepreneurs ways to minimize economic uncertainties and to control unpredictable market dynamics by promoting a business-administrative outlook. Van Dijk thus challenges the Comaroffs' view that the prosperity doctrine merely offers congregants various mechanisms of passively coping with economic precariousness and market uncertainties.

In a similar vein, Simon Coleman (2015) challenges the assumption that the prosperity doctrine promotes a singular notion of the atomized individual, rooted in the Protestant (namely Lutheran, as Weber observes) emphasis on private devotion and interiority. Through his study of a Protestant congregation that drew its supporters from the Pentecostalism movement in Sweden during the 1980s, Coleman describes the multiple and competing forms of personhood promoted by the prosperity doctrine through what he calls the gospel's transactional character (295). He argues that this particular sect of Protestantism promotes engagement with the carnal world, in which "interactions with others may involve mediations of the self with anonymous others," through transactions and other forms of mutual constructions (301). Such transactions include acts of giving to others through charity and other forms of aid in order to open oneself up to receive abundance and prosperity from God.

Likewise, in her study of Pentecostalism in the Zambian Copperbelt, Naomi Haynes (2012, 2013) emphasizes the notion that the prosperity doctrine generates its own diverse forms of sociality, based on spiritual hierarchy as well as economic inequality. The health and wealth gospel attempts to resolve the tensions and contradictions believers face when the promise of prosperity and wealth fails, and when the principle of entrepreneurial freedom intersects with the values of charity and social obligation.

Drawing from the works of Haynes and Coleman, who emphasize the tensions and contradictions that underlie the prosperity doctrine, I elaborate on the notion of prophetic becoming, in which followers cross oceans and national boundaries in order to become transnational entrepreneurs and to spread God's Word. Their experiences of becoming entrepreneurs entail transnational and otherworldly journeys that fuel their personal ambitions for wealth while encountering socioeconomic risks along the way. As Haynes and Coleman have shown, the particular forms of personhood and sociality that are determined by the prosperity doctrine materialize in parts, or gradients, in the processes of emerging entrepreneurial agency and spiritual becoming, which are anchored in their precarious livelihoods and cross-cultural exchanges in China. Their sense of entrepreneurial agency and potentiality becomes incrementally actualized through their transactions and cross-cultural engagements with the material and non-Christian world.

The process of becoming an entrepreneur unfolds and materializes through a personal journey and life experiences that entail transactional risks, losses, and failures. This view, then, justifies why and how some migrant entrepreneurs are spiritually and materially more successful than others, while it perpetuates the promise of prosperity without necessarily delivering on that promise. Moreover, pastors do not view economic risks and uncertainty as a personal calculus of opportunity costs or economic losses. Rather, they view misfortune and risk as transactional, as an exchange for a deeper devotion to God along an otherworldly trajectory that articulates with the material world of unequal possession and hierarchies of spiritual ambition. Their transcontinental journeys help migrants to realize their respective faith-based potential in accumulating wealth, while their ability in becoming successful entrepreneurs is the ultimate testament of their devotion to God.

Narratives of Entrepreneurial Transformation

For the West African pastors in Guangzhou, their journeys of prophetic becoming started with the initial realization of their otherworldly potential. This process involved their transformation into desiring, entrepreneurial subjects upon their arrival in China. A central theme that Pastor Thomas and Pastor Johnson often highlighted in their sermons on the prosperity doctrine was the role of self-transformation in fulfilling one's prophetic destiny as directed by God. According to the pastors' worldview, the pathway to self-liberation entailed the re-creation of one's self as a worldly entrepreneurial subject, one that is mobile and endowed with money. In other words, wealth and prosperity were closely enjoined with devotion and religious conversion. Their sermons not only conveyed messages of spiritual empowerment and uplift but they also demonstrated how congregants—the majority of whom were small-scale itinerant traders—could learn to become proper entrepreneurial subjects through a business management outlook in order to serve as personal manifestations of God's Word.

As Pastor Thomas once declared in a sermon on the ways in which congregants could serve God's will through entrepreneurship, "A man must have a vision, a higher goal. Dreams and aspirations are what separate human beings from animals. Lofty visions unite us as moneyed traders and self-made entrepreneurs who are predestined by God to carry out His message." He thus reminded his congregants that money alone could not yield a deeper sense of meaning in life, yet the spreading of God's message would not be possible without financial success. Money, in and of itself, held no intrinsic value if one did not have faith in God. Without money, however, worldly projects of faith-based conversion would not be possible.

As a case in point, Pastor Thomas and Pastor Johnson frequently explained to their congregants that money served as a necessary bridge linking their past lives in Africa with their entrepreneurial lives in China. In their search for material wealth and divine redemption, these religious figures saw themselves as leaders, chosen by God, who crossed expansive oceans and transcended worldly temptations, such as greed and egoism, in order to follow their prophetic destinies in China and beyond. To illustrate this message, the pastors shared their personal stories of transcontinental experiences of mobility and profit.

Pastor Thomas recalled his first journey to China when, as a youth, he traveled by boat, passing through Ivory Coast to Sierra Leone. At that time, a long-standing civil war was ravaging the country, leaving thousands of people dead and millions displaced. Thomas's boat suddenly came to a halt when it encountered several military vessels that were blocking the mouth of the river. Armed soldiers unexpectedly approached Thomas's boat. Pointing their rifles directly at him, they demanded a toll fee. Moments later, gunshots ripped through the sky, leaving Thomas stricken with fear. He ducked down and thought for a second that he was dead. When he finally found the courage to open his eyes, he realized that the soldiers were merely demanding a small payment and had no intention of killing him. After the young Thomas paid the fee, he proceeded on his journey. In that instant, as Pastor Thomas recalled, he realized that the tokens of his prosperity, including his youth, health, and survival, had been given to him by God in order to fulfill his personal mission of creating a Christian fellowship in China.

Pastor Johnson experienced his childhood during the late 1980s and early 1990s in the war-torn country of Liberia. As a son of a relatively well-off businessman, he managed to avoid the spaces of heavy conflict incited by two civil wars by retreating from the city of Monrovia and escaping into the countryside, which he referred to as "the bush." Johnson was raised by his paternal grandmother—who was one of four wives—and grew up surrounded by his forty cousins. His father ran his business from home, so Johnson lived mostly in the countryside until his teenage years. Since, for the most part, schools were closed during the two long-standing conflicts, Johnson was home-schooled, learning to read and write by reciting passages from the Bible with his grandmother. He also picked up his business acumen from his father. Influenced by his family's faith in Christianity, the teenage Johnson decided to visit China in his search for economic and religious opportunity. With a modest amount of capital saved by his relatives at home, Johnson left Liberia through informal smuggling networks by way of Sierra Leone. He worked for a friend of his father in Dubai for a few years in order to amass some personal savings, before arriving in China on a one-month tourist visa in 2009. He eventually enrolled as a university student in a business college in Guangzhou in order to maintain his resident visa in China. Meanwhile, he taught English part time to Chinese youths while struggling to grow his export business. When he met Pastor Thomas through a business exchange that year, Johnson was overwhelmed by the pastor's devotion to God and decided to train as a preacher under his guidance.

When Pastor Johnson described the early years of GPLFF's establishment, he reiterated the centrality of China's rise to the world stage. The pastors saw themselves as religious and entrepreneurial intermediaries who brokered between God and the Chinese people in negotiating financial deals while spreading God's word. In fact, the discourse of territorialization often echoed the religious leaders' motivations to accumulate wealth and to extend the geographic boundaries of global Christianity. For example, one of the fly-ers advertising their Sunday services displayed the thematic message, "Ex-pand God's Territory." In the pastors' view, China's expansive land, its dense atheist population, and its emergence on the global platform facilitated the pastors' shared visions of evangelical conversion as well as economic accu-mulation. As Pastor Johnson once explained to me, "China is for business. China is the world."

Their determination in establishing a fellowship in Guangzhou, however, entailed a number of challenges. When Johnson and Thomas arrived in Guangzhou, they started conducting services in their apartments in Xiaobei while slowly collecting donations from their community members. Several months later, they rented office space in a neighborhood high-rise to hold the growing number of congregants who attended their services. The rent was 6,000 RMB a month, a sum that vastly exceeded their budget.

The pastors also found themselves frequently being called on for financial assistance when many of their community members were arrested and jailed for overstaying in China on expired visas. Over time, the pastors learned that economic survival in China required more than merely paying the bills and renewing their visas. It also required building close relationships with Chi-nese people based on trust and reputation, a challenge the pastors and their congregants continually struggled with in their everyday, cross-cultural interactions. Eventually, they managed to build friendships with Chinese pastors from various regions in China as well as with local friends who helped them resolve various bureaucratic matters, including illegally switching on the electricity when they could not afford to pay the utility bills.

Despite these challenges, however, the pastors and their congregants emphasized the significance of China in facilitating the fulfillment of their religious and economic endeavors. They articulated this point through the discourse of entrepreneurial freedom. For instance, Pastor Thomas once ex-plained to me, "Anyone can be a boss in China. Most of the world's commodi-ties are sourced here, and the quality of goods are low enough that almost anyone can buy and own branded goods. In Africa, consumers want brand names for the 'look.' They want to look like celebrities for a cheap price." He then extended his role as an entrepreneurial broker into his religious life. "In China, you can fulfill your holy destiny determined by God. But God is our boss, our provider. He comes before business. No business is possible without God. If money grows on trees, then God nurtures those trees."

Actualization of Entrepreneurial Desire
through Transaction and Exchange

Another critical aspect of their self-transformation into entrepreneurial subjects, as Pastor Thomas and Pastor Johnson emphasized, was the cultivation of their worldly and material desires. In a sermon that followed his entrepreneurial encounters in Dubai, Pastor Thomas underscored the importance of the principle, "Seek and you shall find." Here, he highlighted the significance of material desire, which he conveyed in a single slide that displayed the following question written in bright yellow letters, "What do you want?" In his view, desire served as an implicit driver in expanding God's kingdom in his name, one that was cultivated through transactional exchanges with God and was measured through material possessions.

During his sermon, Pastor Thomas asked the congregation to close their eyes. He asked who among the congregation was in need of money (no one seemed to have raised their hand). He then asked who needed a job (about five people raised their hands). Lastly, he asked who needed personal guidance or knew someone who strayed beyond the path of goodness and needed faith (one person raised her hand). Pastor Thomas then emphasized that, as believers, they should inform the sick (that is, the nonbelievers in China and beyond) that they needed to be open and welcome faith in God. He ended with a final message: A.S.K. Him (ask, seek, and knock)—"God wants to give us good things." Thus, the language of personal want and need (in conjunction with asking for and seeking help) served as a central theme in his message that day. He then said, "Prayer is not just about asking for yourself! It is about asking so we can give to others, and so we can receive time, energy, and resources to "EXPAND THE KINGDOM. WHAT DO YOU WANT TO ASK FOR?" Pastor Thomas gave this answer: "Expand the kingdom and join the family." At the end, he asked his congregation to think about ways in which they had encountered nonbelievers (the "sick") and how they could spread God's word.

In short, the language of evangelism resonated quite strongly with the language of entrepreneurship and enterprise, particularly the message about expanding God's territory. It called for reflecting on the desires of believers and thinking about the ways in which they aligned with the mission of expanding God's territory (through acts of conversion). In this example, the prosperity doctrine's transactional character was demonstrated through the language of desire since desire fueled religious and economic ambition. It foregrounded the believers' relationship with God and their evangelical mission on earth. As Coleman's (2015) study showed, a believer's agency was realized and "carried forth through the circulation of money and of (Biblical) words," thereby revealing the transactional character of person-formation inherent within the preaching of the prosperity doctrine (310). The personal cultivation of worldly desire thus served as a stepping-stone to becoming a faith-based entrepreneurial subject. In other words, the making of the entrepreneurial subject began with the construction of a desiring subject.

Discourse of Risks and Desires

While Pastor Thomas and Pastor Johnson saw dreams and desires as sources of self-empowerment that enabled Christian followers to realize their entrepreneurial potential, they recognized that the project of transformation into faith-based entrepreneurial subjects involved unforeseen economic loss and spiritual risks. Key to this personal transformation was learning and adopting the mindset and skills from the business and management worlds in order to learn how to hedge spiritual and economic risks. Pastors often drew analogies of business risk, loss, and debt to describe their relationships with God and with their evangelical missions in China. Just as African traders in China often encountered debt, bankruptcy, and imprisonment, believers' personal relationships with God must involve trust and, ultimately, a leap of faith.

For this reason, the pastors frequently echoed the message "Take a risk with God" in their sermons and in the congregants' testimonials. In this congregation, risk meant the linking of economic and spiritual loss, since one's engagements with market exchanges in the material world mirrored and reinforced the follower's transactional obligations with God in the spiritual realm. This dynamic underscored what Haynes (2012, 2013) identified as the tension between personal ambition and social obligation inherent in the prosperity doctrine. On one hand, a believer's entrepreneurial agency was gradually realized through worldly transactions and encounters; the adherent's confrontation with business risk, on the other hand, reinforced the notion that God was the ultimate authority who decided how that transaction, including its associated risks, unfolded.

This belief became apparent during the service one day when Pastor Johnson asked Mary, a forty-something-year-old woman from Angola, to stand up and introduce herself to the congregation. With her hands neatly folded, Mary explained that she had recently arrived in Guangzhou after a treacherous journey. Prior to her arrival in China, a neighbor had placed a curse on her family members through what she believed was witchcraft. Her mother became extremely ill, requiring over 50,000 RMB for surgery and medication. In desperation, Mary had prayed continuously for seven days, and turned to a Christian pastor in Angola for help. The pastor advised Mary that in order to cure her mother, she needed to marry a Christian man who lived in China. As the pastor explained, Mary's marriage to this devout Christian was the key to her spiritual freedom.

Fearing the risk of losing her mother, Mary followed the pastor's guidance and quickly prepared for her trip to China. Then she met a stranger. Within a few days, she married the man and converted to Christianity. Days after her marriage, as the pastor accurately predicted, her mother miraculously recovered. Mary took the unexpected reversal of her mother's health as a sign that Christianity—namely, her belief in God—had cleansed the curse that had been put on her family back home. Mary's journey and arrival in China, though filled with uncertainty and risk, strengthened her belief in God vis-à-vis the operation of witchcraft as well as the regulatory dangers of the Chinese state. Mary viewed her marriage to the man as symbolic of her new bond with the Christian faith.

China as a Territory of Capital and Religious Accumulation

While Pastor Thomas and Pastor Johnson emphasized the significance of business, management, and interpersonal skills in attaining health and prosperity, China served as a testing ground for their faith as well as their entrepreneurial destiny. Congregants frequently drew comparisons between China and the rest of the world, emphasizing the number of unique business opportunities they found there, which would not be possible anywhere else.

The emphasis on China as a place of economic possibility was affirmed to many other African migrants in 2014, when news of Ebola-related sickness and deaths among friends and loved ones spread throughout the African communities in Xiaobei. Curfews, quarantines, and closing of borders to people, money, and goods across West Africa disrupted many congregants' businesses in China to the extent that they had to temporarily suspend their businesses. For example, Pastor Johnson relied on his part-time work as an English teacher as an alternative source of income, while congregants turned to alternative trading connections in countries across North America, the Middle East, and Southeast Asia. Though such anxieties and disruptions would seem to challenge the delivery of health and wealth as promised by the prosperity doctrine, the global health crisis paradoxically renewed the pastors' and congregants' faith in the gospel.

In my private conversations with Pastor Johnson, he frequently emphasized China's role in donating money and research efforts to the crisis. In fact, congregants often stressed to me that China and Africa relations were rising in political and economic importance on the world stage. The recent Ebola crisis had confirmed their beliefs. Though Pastor Thomas and Pastor Johnson subscribed to a future-oriented view of economic progress and eternal salvation in their financial and spiritual trajectories, their notion of development was not tied merely to the unpredictable actions of the state or the uncertainties of the market. Rather, their financial and faith-based futures were tied to their capitalist and evangelical actions in China as stepping-stones to the global platform and to the afterlife. For them, China served as a growing church, and the body of that church symbolized the body of Christ. In expanding their evangelical and capitalist pursuits in China, pastors and congregants followed the principle of manifest destiny, where they could become "kings" of their land and of their destinies. Following this belief, the pastors often echoed the following catchphrases to their congregants, "China is the Kingdom, and You are the Kingship. Expand Your Territory!"

Moreover, the possibilities promised to the congregants by the prosperity doctrine provided them with a language through which they negotiated the sense of alienation and displacement they experienced as migrants during their stays in China. Faced with structural poverty in their home countries, as well as structural violence and racism in China, their presence in China in light of the socioeconomic crises unfolding in West Africa led to a certain sense of being in the world, one that was tied to a particular cosmopolitan identity as well as a universalistic belief in expanding the territories of God. For example, in one instance, Pastor Thomas told a story about a salamander climbing up a tree to demonstrate self-empowerment in light of widespread debt, poverty, and disease. In drawing this metaphor, the pastor related the congregants' roles in China as God's chosen people in helping spread the gospel. While China was described as their kingdom in the spiritual sense, their transformation as entrepreneurial and faith-driven subjects always developed in relation to God. Though they were financially poor and politically powerless, believers saw themselves as chosen by God in fulfilling their evangelical destinies.

Within this logic, some African migrants viewed their experiences of racism and structural violence in Guangzhou as obstacles in adapting to the business world in China and on the global stage. As African migrants who protested against the Guangzhou police following the death of a Nigerian man in 2012 had shown, many felt anger, disappointment, and frustration with the institutional challenges they faced. For those who had already experienced financial debt and bankruptcy, the policing and racial discrimination they encountered in Guangzhou became part and parcel of the enormous risks involved in attaining the health and wealth that were promised to them by the prosperity doctrine. In 2015, for example, a group of young men from Gambia found themselves destitute and nearly homeless in Xiaobei after a group of snakeheads had lured them to China and robbed them of their money and passports (Carling and Haugen 2020). With generous contributions from various community members, the young men were able to travel to Thailand and other parts of Southeast Asia to try to achieve their entrepreneurial destinies.

Conclusion

As of 2018, the GPLFF had been driven underground to the extent that services were no longer being conducted under this name in the office building in Xiaobei. This development occurred in response to the crackdown by official authorities on unlicensed religious organizations across major Chinese cities. Meanwhile, African migrants faced stricter policing and racial discrimination, leading the size of the Xiaobei community to decrease dramatically. While some migrant entrepreneurs returned to their home countries to rethink their business plans, others moved to cities farther north—such as Xian, Chengdu, and Yiwu—where they could seek other economic opportunities. Indeed, as Pentecostal migrant entrepreneurs, mobility and economic struggle were key narratives in their interpretation of the prosperity doctrine. Though a number of scholars argue that this gospel offered believers a sense of hope in sustaining their lifelong search for health and wealth, I have demonstrated that, for some West African migrants in Guangzhou, their understanding of the prosperity doctrine exceeds a mere functionalist approach. Rather, their life histories of transnational migration, cross-cultural encounters, and economic successes and failures are interwoven in their accounts of geographical journeys and self-transformation. While pastors and congregants at the GPLFF believed that they were divinely chosen by God to leave their native places in West Africa, their search for health, wealth, and eternal salvation in the face of violence, racism, and poverty remained a continuous process of spiritual and entrepreneurial transformation that was extremely risky and uncertain.

NELLIE CHU

SOY MAKES US FRIENDS ... OR NOT

Negotiating the "Chinese Landing"
in Argentina's Contact Zone

In this chapter we address China's investments in one corner of Latin America: Argentina. Our main argument is that to understand the so-called rise of China in the Global South, we must examine how people located in a particular place in the Global South interpret this phenomenon and, moreover, how they do so by bringing in their understandings of their own country's history and relationships with past hegemonic powers. Echoing the introduction to this volume, we do not adjudicate whether China's presence in Argentina is an extension of the nonaligned alternative that China once represented to the Cold War–induced new world order. Nor do we claim that China's presence is an embrace of the post–Cold War neoliberal world order. We also eschew the US-based media rhetoric about the rise of China, underlined by anxiety about China surpassing the United States, that often portrays the deleterious effects of China's investments supposedly not found in other countries' investments. Instead, our approach in this chapter is to turn around the focus to discuss how Argentines view the presence of Chinese companies and Chinese people in their midst. We write about Argentine-Chinese relations from the position of Argentines, what we call a bottom-up worlding endeavor.[1]

Such an approach emerges from our own political and research positions. Cypher's dissertation research on the soy industry led her to the soy supply chain from the Argentine pampas to China's food consumer market. Rofel began by following Chinese investors from China outward. Because we collaborated, we were afforded a perspective that we would not have arrived at alone. Together, we interviewed and spent time with academic scholars, journalists, soy farmers, representatives of government agencies, environmental activists, and ordinary residents of small towns. They did not always agree with one another, nor did they converge into a unified "Argentine" viewpoint on the Chinese presence in their country. Some embraced the idea of the Beijing Consensus, per Luciano Bolinaga's argument in this volume, while others blamed their own government for any inequities in the relationship. Some were proactive about trying to educate the Argentine public about Chinese culture and contemporary Chinese politics and economy while others only knew the one Chinese family who ran their local supermarket.

In this volume, T. Tu Huynh's incisive argument about the intersections of neoliberal ideologies with changes in gendered labor among African traders in Guangzhou, China, Nellie Chu's examination of small-scale traders from West Africa and South Korea who double as preachers of the prosperity gospel, and Mingwei Huang's comparison of two historically distinct waves of Chinese migration to Johannesburg, South Africa, with their distinctive beliefs and experiences of race and development, similarly engage with bottom-up perspectives. Sharing their ethnographic approaches, we center the grounded, embodied experiences and perceptions of Argentines, but in this case in the country they call their own. Rather than discussing only the Chinese "wave" crashing down on the Global South, or assuming a dominant Chinese neo-imperialism, we seek to highlight the density and diversity of Chinese-Argentine social relations through everyday negotiations in the contact zone where multiple ideas, desires, and dreams are worked out.[2]

One striking feature of the Chinese-Argentine relationship is that very few Argentines have interacted with any Chinese. Conversely, that is because very few Chinese come to live long-term in Argentina. We argue that Argentines interact more with an abstraction called "Chinese capital" rather than with actual Chinese people. We posit that this relationship with an abstraction is undoubtedly a key feature of contemporary transnational capitalism. Depending on where one is situated in Argentina, the effects of Chinese capital might be keenly felt or completely invisible, with only indirect effects that are difficult to pinpoint or trace. Much of this interaction, therefore, happens not only on a material level but also on an imaginary one. Our chapter thus echoes the volume's introduction, emphasizing history, culture, and imaginative processes as central to constructing worlds of intercultural and geopolitical articulation, albeit unequal ones. Our chapter further reflects the introduction's discussion of communication as enabling a vision of a unified world order while simultaneously generating difference. In the situations we discuss, the idea of communication enables us to see how worldmaking can also be built as much on mis-communication or more aptly missed communication.

In this spirit, why, we ask, does the Chinese presence have such purchase on the national imagination despite the evidence that China's effects on Argentina's economy continue to be smaller than those of other countries, including Brazil and the United States? China's foreign direct investment (FDI) into Argentina is barely 0.7 percent of all FDI inflows to Argentina, while FDI from the United States is 23 percent, from Spain 18 percent, and from the Netherlands 12 percent—with the latter three nations accounting for more than half of FDI inflows in 2017 (Donaubauer, López, and Ramos 2017). We argue that a partial answer lies in the increasing imbalance of trade relations with China. But we also emphasize the imaginative investments that Argentines have in China's presence. While there are more Chinese companies in other countries of Latin America, such as Brazil and Ecuador, this interaction with an abstraction of Chinese capital also appears to be a feature of how local residents elsewhere in the Global South encounter much of neoliberal transnational capital.

We begin with an overview of the economic history of Argentina and a broad outline of Chinese investments in Argentina. We then turn to four heterogeneous interpretations by Argentines of China's presence: the Beijing Consensus, ecological imperialism, the Chinese as shadows, and racism. Finally, we offer a brief conclusion about local negotiations of and with contemporary transnational capitalism.

Economic History of Argentina

The past matters to Argentines. They often tell a history of decline about themselves, where Argentina topples from its previous wealth and world-standing to a marginalized third world country. It is a narrative that continues to motivate economic desires and informs how they interpret China's presence in Argentina. Indeed, it is true that the economic history of Argentina is one of the most infamous and most studied due to the perception that Argentina was once one of the wealthiest economies in the world in the early twentieth century but subsequently lapsed into a decline from which it still has not recovered to this day. Between 1880 and 1930, an influx of immigrants and British capital led to the expansion of agriculture as well as the creation of export markets. During what is known by Argentines as the belle époque, Argentina matched Australia and Canada in living standards, and by 1913 it was considered to be the tenth wealthiest nation per capita in the world. In 1914 it ranked as the largest exporter of wheat to Europe and was the largest producer of corn and linseed—leading some to dub it the breadbasket of the world. World War I dampened external private investment, but it was the Great Depression and World War II that brought a prolonged crisis in international relations, especially with the United States. Some economists pin the beginning of the end on the 1930s, when a conservative military government seized power, leading to years of political instability up to the election of Juan Perón to the presidency in 1946. Others pin the beginning of the end on Perón's protectionism, which inaugurated a strategy of import substitution in order to bolster the growth of the internal market but cut Argentina off from the international market. Industrial protectionism, the nationalization of railroad and gas industries, and high government spending sparked a period of inflation.

While other countries experienced a post–World War II boom, Argentina's economy stagnated. Political instability reigned, culminating in 1976 when a military dictatorship destroyed civic and intellectual society, driving thousands into exile and brutally murdering thousands more. This period of US-backed terrorism was part of a more general aggressive US military–led policy against Latin American countries seen as potential communist threats during the Cold War. Democracy was restored in 1983, but it is hard to overstate how this period of terror devastated the social conditions necessary for economic regimes to function, especially trust.

Between 1975 and 1990, inflation accelerated, averaging 300 percent per year. In an attempt to stop this runaway inflation, in the 1990s the economy minister Domingo Cavallo instituted free market reforms, open trade, and a currency board that pegged the peso to the dollar. Argentina was once again welcomed into international markets and became known as the darling of the Washington Consensus, a sweeping name for a unilateral process of trade reform that promoted trade liberalization and neoliberal policies. Although the 1990s were more stable, a sustained recession culminated in a default on foreign debt, the devaluation of the peso, and in 2001 one of the most terrible debt crises the world had ever seen. Overnight ordinary citizens' bank accounts devalued into dust. President Nestor Kirchner pulled Argentina out of the crisis by 2005, in part due to new export taxes on the booming soybean industry, but by 2014 the government had suffered a new default. This led to rising inflation, a local black market for dollars due to unofficial and official valuations, and an increasing grieta—or "crack"—between people who saw themselves as for or against the populism Kristina Kirchner had come to represent. In 2015 the Argentines elected President Mauricio Macri with the hope that he would open Argentina back up to the world, which he did, but with disastrous consequences, for inflation reached as high as 48 percent by November 2018.

This history of Argentina's rise and decline provides the context for the varied interpretations by Argentines of China's recent increased presence in their country. They ask: should the government turn to China to help them extract themselves from these economic woes, or will China's presence merely increase Argentina's dependency in the world economy? And in the gaps around these questions, some Argentines raise yet other questions about environmental degradation, inequality, and racial difference.

China's Presence in Argentina

So what does China's presence look like in Argentina? First, the Chinese state's investments in Argentina have a distinctly abstract quality in that Chinese state-owned firms have few Chinese people working on the ground in Argentina. Second, the Chinese presence is not homogeneous and includes several historical waves of migrants first from Taiwan and then more recently from the southern Chinese province of Fujian, something that we detail in the following section.

As is true of Latin America as a whole, China's presence in Argentina has grown significantly over the past decade, with Chinese firms focusing primarily on the search for oil, gas, and minerals such as iron and copper; the building of infrastructure to facilitate export; and purchasing soy. In Argentina, China has worked with local companies to build a nuclear power plant, a space station, and two hydroelectric dams, and they have also invested in projects on renewable energy, mining, and the electric car industry. Their primary focus, however, has been on purchasing soy and offering low-interest loans. In fact, China now purchases 95 percent of Argentina's whole soybeans and has contributed to an exponential growth in the nation's soy production.

China is currently Argentina's second-largest trading partner, after Brazil. Argentina exports natural resource–based products (mainly soybeans and soybean oil) to China while China exports manufactured goods to Argentina. This is the pattern with China's relationship with all Latin American countries (Bolinaga, this volume; Donaubauer, López, and Ramos 2017, 34). China's share of Argentina's exports increased from 1.4 percent in 1995 to 6.4 percent by 2012, with soybeans accounting for 56.2 percent of Argentina's exports to China in 2012. As for Argentina's imports, China's share of the total went from less than 2 percent in 1995 to around 22 percent in 2012. During this time, imports became increasingly diverse, and while they still consist mainly of consumer goods, they also now include capital goods and intermediate inputs (e.g., petrochemicals and steel). As a result, Argentina has developed a growing trade deficit with China (Donaubauer, López, and Ramos 2017, 35–37).[3]

By contrast, foreign direct investment from China into Argentina is rather low, around USD 500 million, a mere 0.7 percent of all FDI in Argentina between 2005 and 2012 (Donaubauer, López, and Ramos 2017, 38). While, in 2012, China's total foreign direct investments in oil, mining, and grains (including buying land) amounted to 30 percent, the bulk of China's FDI in Argentina (over 50 percent) was in banking. The Industrial and Commercial Bank of China, Ltd., a Chinese state-owned bank, acquired major shares in Standard Bank, which had already bought BankBoston Argentina.[4]

While China is certainly a strong player in the game of global capitalism, and has increased FDI and M&A in Latin America since 2005, it continues to be an emerging investment partner and has not replaced dominant trading partners such as the United States and Spain.[5] For those who are concerned about China's presence within global capitalist relations, however, these and other statistics could lead one to prognosticate. We will not do so here. Of more concern is that, given that China is a strong presence, it means China joins other investor countries in affecting social relations and environmental degradation in Argentina, as well as in other Latin American countries.

Debt is a significant aspect of China's relations with Argentina and other Latin American countries. As David Graeber (2011) has pointed out, debt is a flexible concept, built on the ability of the powerful to impose a moral justification for their exploitative relations with those they dominate.[6] They thereby ideologically make it appear as if groups and countries who have been colonized or, in contemporary times, made dependent through finance institutions, are the ones who have done something wrong and therefore "owe" funds to the wealthier nations. Thus, while in most cases lenders are supposed to accept a degree of risk—think of the stock market—in the case of loans from wealthier countries to poorer ones, the latter take on all the risk and must pay back loans ad infinitum through the scheme of compound interest. Graeber astutely notes that who really owes what to whom is often a matter of debate. Thus, the concept of debt is full of moral ambiguity while at the same time being a major means of structuring relations of inequality.[7]

Thus, as we learned in our interviews, the debt between Argentina and China plays a pivotal role in China's presence there. Argentina's debt defaults in relation to the United States provide the historical background to Argentina's current debt situation. Venezuela initially offered loans that would mean Argentina would no longer be indebted to US banks or under pressure from the International Monetary Fund to enact "structural adjustment." Venezuela did not create such onerous conditions. But the interest rate was 18 percent. China then came in and "rescued" Argentina from Venezuela, offering low-interest loans of 4 percent. China's loans generally come with commodities-backed guarantees, meaning that if Argentina cannot pay back the loan, China will have claims to its natural resources without needing to further pay for that access. As one person who is a cultural mediator between Argentines and Chinese—and who approves of China's presence—remarked, Argentina must continue the projects it has contracted with China, without changing the terms and whether the arrangements are favorable to Argentina or not. Otherwise, China will force Argentina to default on the repayment of these loans. Argentina already defaulted and cannot afford to do so again. "So now China is just like the US," he concluded.

Another person working in an Argentine labor institute emphasized the currency swap deals Argentina has made with China.[8] These currency swap deals have made China the largest noninstitutional lender in Argentina. While currency swaps are supposed to hedge against the risks of currency exchanges at different points in time, this person stated that Argentina's debt was increasing because the government was just holding on to the money instead of using it for investments. In two years, he said at the time, the external debt would double.

Yet there is also a moral aspect to these unequal financial relations, as Graeber has alerted us. China's trade with Argentina and the rest of Latin America was large enough to shield the region from the worst of the 2008 global economic crisis. There is thus a sense of gratitude on Argentina's part as well. And China has played up its history and location as a formerly colonized, third world nation that shares with Latin America a resistance to Western colonialism.

China's Presence Is Not the Same as Chinese Presence

Chinese presence is neither unified nor homogeneous. The Chinese Embassy estimates that about 180,000 Chinese immigrants live in Argentina, but some local scholars calculate that there must be more. Luciana Denardi, for instance, estimates that in 2015 there were 12,000 Taiwanese, 200,000 registered Chinese, and at least 100,000 nonregistered Chinese.[9] These immigrants arrived in three waves: the first came from China's coastal towns between 1914 and 1949, the second came from Taiwan in the 1980s, and the third came mostly from the southeast coastal province of Fujian in the 1990s. After their arrival, however, most Chinese immigrants, as Huang has noted in South Africa (this volume), have maintained very little formal connection with the PRC (Ellis 2014).

In addition to citing highly televised news reports about President Mauricio Macri's meeting with President Xi Jinping at the G-20 summit in September of 2016, most Argentines will cite their interaction with their local chino—their local supermarket—as the main way they interact with the Chinese presence. A chino is a second-tier grocery store that can be found in most neighborhoods in Buenos Aires and other medium-sized cities throughout Argentina and is popular in the urban imagination as the ubiquitous one-stop-shop owned by Chinese or Chinese Argentines. It is estimated that Buenos Aires has about 3,500 chinos—or about one every two or three blocks.

The other presence we heard cited as Chinese is the Barrio Chino, or Chinatown, although it is only four blocks long and until the 1990s wave of immigration from Fujian was simply known as Calle Taiwan, or Taiwan Street. Japanese, Korean, and Chinese markets and restaurants cluster near a Chinese community center and Buddhist temple, reflecting a diversity of immigrants. Compared to Chinatowns in North America, it feels small and, we conjecture, nascent.

The Beijing Consensus

Despite the fact that China's presence in Argentina, whether abstract or embodied, is not particularly large, there are anticipatory imaginations of the future, laced with anxieties as well as hopes, that shape Argentines' views.

Concerns about further decline in the country as a result of China's increased presence are prominent as well as hope that China will lead Argentina out from under American imperial interventions and toward greater development and autonomy.

The concept of the Beijing Consensus encapsulates left-leaning scholars' critique of China's presence as leading to increased inequality and economic dependency throughout the region. One of the leading voices that has developed this concept is the Argentina-based scholar Luciano Bolinaga. When Rofel met with Bolinaga in his university office in Rosario for the first time, he described how this concept helps highlight that consensus creates the same effects of dependency but through the appearance that governments of the Global South have consented to a continuation of relations that place them in a position of subordination. But, he made sure to emphasize, Argentina is not passive in this process. When we met with Ariel Slipak, Bolinaga's coauthor (Bolinaga and Slipak 2015), in a charming old tearoom in Buenos Aires, he confirmed what Bolinaga had described. While Latin American countries have rejected the policies once hailed by the Washington Consensus, they have simultaneously accepted a new system of asymmetrical relations with another world power, hoping for an alternative, inasmuch as China has declared a principle of respect for sovereignty and noninterference in the internal affairs of other countries.

The development of the concept of the Beijing Consensus both reflects and produces the abstraction of Chinese capital in Argentina and the region. It produces the abstraction in that this concept does not distinguish among the varied forms of Chinese presence nor the varied types of economic activity engaged in by various levels of Chinese companies. Nor does it distinguish between individuals who, as we point out above, have emigrated from different countries.

Ecological Imperialism

One generalized response toward Chinese presence among Argentines is to view this presence as a form of *ecological imperialism*. The environmental historian Alfred Crosby (2004) originally coined this term to describe the way Europeans accomplished their conquest of the New World with their animals, plants, and infectious pathogens. He showed that the European invasion was as much biological as it was social and ideological. For some Argentines who are critical of the Chinese presence, the soy boom of the past two decades is a stunning example of China's ecological reach into the region. Since 1996, when genetically modified soybeans were introduced into Argentina along with cheaper glyphosate and no-till farming, the area planted with soybeans skyrocketed from 300,000 to over 20 million hectares in 2016. Although Monsanto, a US-based company, was the initial inventor and disseminator of the genetically modified soybean technological package, soybeans are seen as emblematic of the imposition of Chinese tastes into the Argentine countryside. "We don't even eat soy" is a common refrain one hears on the streets, on farms, and in cafés in response to the question about how people feel about the recent soy boom.

One's occupation as well as proximity to farming seems to most influence the range of responses to these projects. From farmers to plant breeders, trading desks, and massive soybean crushing facilities, Argentines involved in the soybean supply chain are all clear about one thing: that they are inordinately dependent on the demands of the Chinese market. These demands have made them rich, but they have also left them scared. Farmers, for example, are concerned about their overreliance on one crop, which subjects them to the booms and busts of both the volatile commodities market and the supply-demand value chain of a single crop. They understand that if they do not diversify their output they put themselves at great risk. Yet because soybeans continue to be more profitable than corn, farmers who have the necessary capital tend to lease land and plant just one crop year after year: soy.

Social scientists studying the soy boom often frame their critiques within the paradigm of Eduardo Galeano's "open veins of Latin America" (1997). The gruesome image of sliced veins pulsing out the metaphorical blood of the continent—be it oil, sweat, gold, or soybeans—frames much of the scholarship on the region. These critiques offer a general and abstract approach to neo-extractivism that elides the more nuanced qualities of this relationship, one that, we argue, must also consider what we are calling "intractivism," that is, what gets put *into* the country, not only what is taken out.

More recently, some Argentine scholars have turned to a more nuanced examination of China's role in extractive and intractive regimes in the region. Maristella Svampa describes the shift from the Washington Consensus, with its emphasis on finance, to a "commodities consensus" based on the large-scale export of primary products, a "regressive dynamic aggravated by the new involvement of emerging powers such as China" (2015, 47). Amalia Leguizamón (2016) portrays the financialization of the Argentine food system as a form of "distancing." She focuses on the way financial capital enters agricultural production, examining land acquisitions made by Heilongjiang Beidahuang Nongken Group, China's largest farming company. Gastón Gordillo (2019) describes his surprise upon meeting Chinese businessmen from China Machinery Engineering Corporation (CMEC) in a small rural town, Las Lajitas, and examines what this means for the places he calls "zones of imperial extraction."

Criticism of the soybean complex as a Chinese ecological takeover, we found, could not be ideologically separated from what was seen as infrastructural imperialism: Chinese hydropower dams, the space station, the nuclear power plant, railcars, ports, and other foreign direct investments that were formally begun in 2009.[10] That year, for Argentina, was a particularly poignant moment due to financial vulnerability; the peso was fluctuating and inflation was starting to build after almost a decade of rebuilding after the 2001 crisis. Diego Guelar, Argentina's ambassador to China, described the way China lent money while at the same time making its own demands with a title that succinctly summed up how he and others felt about China's presence: *The Silent Invasion: The Chinese Landing in South America* (2013). By 2012 China had, according to him, "landed," striking a 10.2 billion USD currency swap, promising to invest another 10 billion USD to fix the railway system, and at the same time negotiating a deal for land in Patagonia for a Chinese military base. Critiques of "cheap" Chinese railcars and a secret military presence abounded (McCallum 2018). The ecological impact of the hydropower dams, in particular, had captured the popular imagination. For example, Sofia Nemenmann, cofounder of the activist group "Rio Santa Cruz Sin Represas" (Santa Cruz River without Dams), was particularly concerned about the fact that no environmental study had been conducted to examine the impact of the dams. The melting glaciers at the lake, the endangered Macá Tobiano, or Hooded Grebe (*Podiceps gallardoi*) bird, and the indigenous groups Mapuche-Tehuelche were sure to be impacted, although no official assessment had been made. "Most people working against this dam," another activist said without mincing words, "hate China."

Money Talks and Shadows Walk

The idea that "Argentina is open for business" pervades the general business community, where China's presence is seen as an opportunity as well as a "shadow." Whether it be the United States, Brazil, or China, one agribusinessman told us, "money talks." China has money, and therefore Argentines, the businessman implied, are listening. The fact that China has money and has entered the region is, for these businessmen, not imperialistic. It exists as a potential and possibility for business, even as the Chinese presence is recognized as being different from the United States. For most business-men we spoke with, Chinese ways of doing business are still *más extraño* (more foreign/strange) than the United States. "We have to learn," one high-powered executive of a dairy corporation told Cypher, emphasizing the fact that it was the responsibility of the Argentines to learn how to "conduct busi-ness" with a culture that was foreign to them in order to take advantage of potential opportunities for investment, trading, and technological exchange.

To that end, various groups have emerged that seek to open relationships and teach cultural competence. For example, the Cámara Argentino China (Argentina China Chamber of Commerce), directed by Ernesto Fernández Taboada, encourages bilateral trade through monthly meetings, export and import committees, seminars, a monthly journal, and courses on doing busi-ness with the Chinese. When we met with him, Taboada joked that Argen-tines hug and kiss each other on the cheek, chat over a coffee, then after half an hour cajole one another into signing a contract. The chamber teaches Argentine businessmen three main rules that, for him, summarized the dif-ference between Argentine and Chinese ways of doing business: (1) No fast decisions, (2) You must get to know the person over time, and (3) Don't pressure them to move quickly.

The chamber, in addition to teaching Argentines to be more formal and to respect status in a particular way, organizes exhibitions that are meant to create "opportunities" between the countries. The biannual exhibition of the China Chamber of Commerce for Import and Export of Machinery and Electronic Products (CCCME), for example, creates a space for Chinese manufacturers to come to Argentina and sell their products. When we visited this exhibition at a swanky hotel in downtown Buenos Aires, there was still a cultural tension that was evident throughout the meeting. The Argentines joked about how they were always late, and the Chinese businessmen were always punctual. The visiting Chinese manufacturers took seriously the busi-ness opening into Argentina and saw the meeting as an opportunity to make connections, even though only three Argentine businessmen showed up.

"Opportunity," Taboada told us at the meeting, "is culturally negotiated," in the sense that everyone is still learning. Another example of this desire to increase cultural competence was the first journal of cultural exchange between Argentina and China, *Dang Dai*. When we met with the editors of the magazine, Néstor Restivo and Gustavo Ng, they admitted to us that Argentina is open about immigration but can also be very xenophobic. To soften this xenophobic tendency, the magazine tried to provide a focus on language, calligraphy, Chinese medicine, film, and bilateral trade for Argentines to learn about China.

One of the most striking ways in which some Argentines expressed their interaction with the Chinese presence in their midst was through what were referred to as shadows. This concept was invoked by those professional employees who worked in the large Argentine companies that Chinese state-owned firms had bought or had a major share in through mergers and acquisitions. An executive at Nidera—which was bought by the Chinese state-owned COFCO (China National Cereals, Oils and Foodstuffs Corporation) in 2016—was shadowed by Chinese managers, and felt a simultaneous resentment and curiosity toward the men who shadowed him and toward the new Chinese managers above him.[11] There are only about a dozen wholly Chinese state-owned firms in Argentina, and their presence is mostly confined to commercial offices (Donaubauer, López, and Ramos 2017, 39). The Chinese state-owned firms that had bought or merged with Argentine companies send a small handful of employees to work in Argentina, mainly top managers and technical assistants. They literally follow the Argentines around the company as they work, to learn what they do. Hence the term *shadows*.

Alejandra Conconi (2016) has developed and analyzed this idiom of "shadows" in her research on Argentine-Chinese encounters. Conconi argues that the asymmetry in relations between Argentine employees and Chinese owners in companies in the petroleum industry is marked by "perceptions of race and ethnicity, corporeality and symbols, status, control over resources and the use of Chinese as the language of power" (2016, 25). Control over the finances, Conconi emphasizes, is exemplary of the inequalities. Decisions about the local situation in Argentina are made from Beijing. On the other hand, Argentine local unions have managed to press for wages that are six times higher than those paid to top Chinese executives. And while Chinese is the language of power, Spanish is the quotidian language of operations on the ground. Conconi concludes that in many of these contexts, a "contact zone" exists but with no "encounters." By this she means no transcultural relations or spaces are created. Both Argentines and Chinese, Conconi contends, are "in a physical contact zone but they do not inhabit the same reality or observe the same things" (2016, 29). Chinese managers shadow their counterparts and ask many questions but, according to the Argentine employees, do not

143

share their observations or views, nor their recommendations for future reorganization.

The concept of shadows evokes the sense of something that is attached to oneself but that one cannot grasp in one's hand. Nor can one fully communicate with a shadow. It does not seem to have substance. Nor can one get rid of it. It implies an ethereal or ghostly quality, a haunting. Of all the descriptions that arose in the conversations we had with an array of Argentines, and as Conconi's research also bears out, this concept of shadows most vividly evokes the abstract quality that Argentines feel they interact with in relation to China's presence, or more precisely Chinese capital in their midst.

Argenchinos?

While Argentines crafted various narratives of Chinese presence in Argentina as abstracted capital, ecological imperialism, and the evocative image of shadows, they equally engaged in—and were accused of engaging in—racism toward Chinese people in Argentina. In a small town in the pampas of Santa Fe Province, residents were bemused when a Chinese family opened a grocery store, the first such Chinese family in their town to do so. As narrated to Rofel by one older woman who had lived in the town all of her life (as had almost all of its residents), people in the town went from outright hostility to exoticized curiosity and, finally, to friendly acceptance. At first, almost everyone categorically refused to shop at that store or interact with its owners in any way. They assumed, the woman said, that these Chinese would be selling strange food products and that they most certainly would be overcharging them—in a word, cheating them. As people gradually came to realize that the prices were fair, they slowly began to shop there. Then came curiosity. This woman, for example, learned through the woman who cleaned their house, how they ate strange foods and with strange utensils. This was not spoken with hostility but with an amicable construction of essential cultural difference. After the son of the Chinese family adopted a Spanish name—Antonio—and began to play fútbol (soccer), the town residents relaxed even more. In other words, as this Chinese family came to appear more Argentine, the town was willing to accept their exotic difference. This woman then emphasized the coup de grâce of acceptance: the Chinese family had taken one of their Argentine customers back to their hometown in China for a vacation! Thus, this woman saw the transformation in the town as a linear movement from categorical racism to curiosity to willingness to engage in social relations of reciprocity. Of course, one could also see it as gradations of different types of racialization, if not racism. As Andrea Bachner points out in her chapter in this volume, there is continual slippage in representations of Chinese people in Argentine literature and film, from Chinese to "Argenchinos."

In addition to the chino being a symbol in the popular imagination for Chinese presence, another common idiom concerns the mafia chino, or Chinese mafia. Like other immigrant groups in the Americas subject to discrimination during the early twentieth century, those perceived as Chinese are often subjected to particular kinds of rumor-circulations. Even if there is institutionalized group violence, we found that because it is seen as Chinese it makes headlines in local newspapers in a way that other kinds of everyday urban violence do not. Either way, the ubiquity of the chino and the mafia are not separate. For example, a union of truck drivers boycotted chinos after a violent incident involving one of the drivers and the owner of the store. The director of the Association of Chinese Supermarkets for Argentina, Yolanda Durán, has decried such boycotts as a form of discrimination, saying "We are Argentines, not Chinese, this is discrimination" (Lopez 2018). When we met with her, it was clear that she was passionate about supporting Chinese supermarkets in Argentina, and had been working with the Taiwanese, Korean, and Chinese business community for twenty-five years. She dismissed gang violence at the same time that she emphasized mutual protection and group cohesion.

We end this section with a short musing on *Un cuento chino*, which Andrea Bachner has incisively analyzed in her chapter in this volume. We add only that Borensztein, the director, intends with this film to challenge Argentines to rethink their racism toward immigrants, specifically Chinese immigrants. Borensztein uses two framings to offer that challenge. One framing is the classic homosocial dynamic so well analyzed by Eve Sedgwick (1985), between the two lead characters, Jun and Roberto. The second framing examines the intersection of homosociality with racism. As Bachner points out, the Chinese man is portrayed as unintelligible to the Argentine man and to the viewers. The presumed opaqueness of Jun to a viewing audience recalls Gayatri Spivak's complex answer to her question, "Can the subaltern speak?" Spivak argued that those who write about third world subalterns erase the subjectivity of these subalterns in the very act of attempting to represent them, by making them stand in for the self-same other of the Western author (1999). Is Borensztein using exoticism of the Chinese in order to challenge his imagined white, monolingual Argentine audience? Or is he challenging the very exoticism he would like to undermine in order to foster acceptance? At the very least, it is hard for viewers who speak Chinese to be interpellated into the exoticism, instead moving us to ponder how difficult it is to represent and challenge white racism through art from a white perspective.

Conclusion

In this chapter we have juxtaposed four different imaginative contexts for evaluating China's presence in Argentina. None is singular. The imaginative context that shapes many reports explicitly belies a US bias that reflects US anxiety about China's rise. While much of the interaction has been with a form of abstract capital and foreign direct investments, many responses have pointed to on-the-ground effects. We have suggested that these revolve around the Beijing Consensus, ecological imperialism, Chinese presence in business both as a form of money and as a shadow and, finally, forms of racism. Of course, there are many more, and we hope that these might serve as a starting point for future research.

The evocative image promulgated by some Argentines of a Chinese landing in a new territory captures the simultaneous fear of imperialism and acknowledgment of a new and powerful presence. Joining other decolonial scholars who have argued that imperialism is not simply a one-way form of domination but a dynamic process in which both parties are changed, we have described the current and ongoing negotiations of the contact zone.

By shifting the focus to ask about Argentine perspectives on Chinese presence, we have explicitly reframed the terms of the debate. Rather than depicting a wave of Chinese imperialism crashing down over Argentina and Latin America, we have shown that to understand what has been called neo-imperialism or neocolonialism it is imperative to examine and analyze local, or rather, located, perspectives. The response to China and Chinese presence in Argentina has been heterogeneous, with multiple abstract, symbolic, and on-the-ground effects. And we have shown that, rather than being passive receivers of a Chinese landing, Argentines have a heterogeneity of perspectives: active, thoughtful, receptive, and resistant. They actively change the terms of the debate through their participation in and negotiation with their local chinos, foreign direct investments, the soybean supply chain, the space station, and films like *Un cuento chino*. At the same time that some businessmen learn to be better cultural translators, their perceptions and racisms shift in an ever-constant process that, we found, works both ways.

This constant and ongoing negotiation in the contact zone also exemplifies, we argue, a transnationalist capitalism that we will be seeing more of in the coming decades as finance continues to shift what we imagine as moral responsibilities for inequality. As anthropologists we have highlighted how important it is to examine located perspectives in order to avoid the trap of both US imperialistic rhetoric as well as that of assuming homogeneity. With the rise of transnationalist capitalism, we can only point to how important this work will continue to be in understanding these negotiations, responses, and the rich variety of ways to think about the power of capital as well as shifting understandings of states and nations.

Notes

1 Thanks to one of the anonymous reviewers for this phrasing. It also echoes Arjun Appadurai's notion of grassroots globalization, though we do not embrace the term *globalization*. See Appadurai 2000.

2 Pratt 1992; see also Ching Kwan Lee 2018. Lee has recently offered a much-needed corrective to what she calls the specter of global China, emphasizing the differentiations among different kinds of Chinese capital investment and how they have varied effects by sector.

3 Note also that they emphasize that Argentina's exports have always been predominantly in natural resources and their oil industry dates from over one hundred years ago, predating China's emergence as a major trading partner.

4 By comparison, the United States (23 percent), Spain (18 percent), and the Netherlands (12 percent) represent more than half of FDI inflows in 2017. Other main investing countries are Brazil, Chile, Switzerland, Uruguay, France, Germany, and Canada. These investments are mainly oriented toward manufacturing, mine and oil extraction, trade, banking and other financial entities, information and communication, and agriculture.

5 The United States and Spain continue to be the largest sources of FDI in the region, and even though China's largest average growth in FDI and M&A increased between 2005 and 2014 (FDI from 4.0% to 6.8% and M&A from 2.4% to 10.5%), it still has not displaced the United States, which during that period maintained trading dominance in FDI (23.5% to 22.9%) and M&A (17.0% to 18.5%). In addition, between 2015 and 2019 this marked growth slowed and FDI decreased to 5.6%. China is, in sum, an emerging investment partner. See Ching 2021 for an excellent analysis of investment diversification.

6 Note that the anthropologist Marcel Mauss (Mauss and Evans-Pritchard 2011) argued that in many precapitalist societies the wealthy lender was

obligated to the person they lent to, not the other way around, that is, they had a sense of obligation to that person.

7 Graeber incisively points out that when the debtor is a wealthy nation, like the United States, then the "loans" to the United States—in the form of institutional investors from foreign countries buying up treasury bonds—are really more like "tribute" (2011, 6).

8 A currency swap is a transaction in which two institutions or companies exchange principal and interest in different currencies. It is supposed to hedge against exchange rate risk or reduce the cost of borrowing a foreign currency. See https://www.investopedia.com/ask/answers/042315/how-do-currency-swaps-work.asp, accessed February 26, 2019.

9 Denardi 2015; see page 84 for statistics on immigration.

10 For a fascinating exploration of heterogeneous legislative responses to the space station, see Urdinez, Knoerich, and Feliú Ribeiro 2018.

11 Donaubauer, López, and Ramos 2017, 39. "Two large Chinese takeovers in Argentina's petroleum industry (including the purchase of 50 percent of local oil firm Bridas by CNOOC, China National Off Shore Oil Corporation, and the purchase of the Argentine assets of Occidental Petroleum by Sinopec, China Petroleum and Chemical Corporation)."

DISPLACING LABOR

China, Argentina, and

the Work of Globalization

What would a world without Chinese labor look like? In his 2007 novel *Chinese on a Bicycle* (*Un chino en bicicleta*), the Argentine writer Ariel Magnus has his protagonist fantasize about the global repercussions if all Chinese went on strike:

> I'd really have loved to know what would happen if suddenly all that is Chinese went on strike—and I didn't only think of Buenos Aires but the world as such. My sense was that our life would instantly descend into chaos. Certainly most of the things that we use on a daily basis either come from China or have some part of Made in. If the gringos went on strike we'd have some communication problems for lack of satellites, and if the strikers were the Europeans, we would go without auteur cinema for a time, but if the Chinese went on strike, the world would stop. Thinking in such a way, there was no doubt about who was the real global power. (244)[1]

Even though this reflection is steeped in humor, the protagonist's thought experiment leaves no doubt about the importance of China for Buenos Aires, Argentina, Latin America, and the world as a whole. In comparison to Chinese labor power the US-American and the European contributions to the functioning of the world pale. After all, what is communication technology, let alone cultural production, in the face of the overwhelming number of products made in China? Of course, a lot is wrong with this scenario, even if we bracket, for now, that its map of the world has major lacunae. For one, this reflection stereotypes economic structures along national and regional boundaries—as if Europeans contributed only to "high" culture productions such as auteur cinema but to nothing else, as if the United States was only capable of satellite technology but negligible in other economic fields, as if China was responsible for most everyday commodities in global use but capable of little else. China is the foremost economic power as producer of commodities "made in China," and as a reservoir of labor whose inexpensive products flood the world market.[2]

Of course, Magnus's vision of China's dominance does take stock of globally redistributed power, especially the frequently invoked "rise of China." It certainly reflects the changing position of Argentina as global economic dynamics in Latin America begin to be re*oriented* and turn from North-South axes or transatlantic fixations toward East Asia. More precisely, the novel responds to Argentina's turn to China after the country's economic crisis of 1998–2002, epitomized in the mutual visits of presidents Néstor Kirchner and Hu Jintao in 2004. The economic rapprochement between China and Argentina, however, has had ambivalent consequences. An initial export surplus has long since turned into an import deficit. And as China has become Argentina's second-largest trading partner (after Brazil), their relationship is unequal. Whereas imports from China to Argentina are of mainly manufactured goods, China's demand for Argentina's export goods focuses on agricultural products and natural resources. China's needs have pushed large sectors of Argentine agriculture into soybean production and have thus created an unhealthy reliance on a single product and a single buyer. At the same time, increasing Chinese competition in Latin American markets has made Argentina lose its edge there. The potential of new trade relations has turned into the threat of economic dependency.[3] This makes for an ambivalent relationship vis-à-vis China that also expresses itself on the level of culture. China's focus on the soft power of cultural exchange has made Chinese culture more present and available in Argentina.[4] And a heretofore unparalleled interest in Chinese culture has prompted Argentine authors, filmmakers, and critics to turn to "Chinese" topics and produce a variety of texts about Argentina's Chinatown, Chinese-Argentine relations, or China itself. Apart from the texts discussed here, works such as Marcos Rodríguez's documentary *Arribeños* (2015), Federico Jeanmaire's novel *High*

Heels (*Tacos altos*, 2016), or Florencia Davidzon's short *ArgenChina* (2012) speak to this trend.[5]

This trend is not limited to Argentina, but represents contemporary relationships between Latin America and China in general. But for countries like Argentina that do not have a long-standing history of Chinese immigration—unlike Cuba, Peru, or Mexico—this reorientation toward China marks a particularly interesting cultural change. Even though a smaller first wave of immigration dates from the first decades of the twentieth century, most of the Chinese diaspora in Argentina results from more recent migrations of immigrants from Taiwan and Hong Kong in the 1980s and immigrants from mainland China (mostly from the south) since the 1990s because of legal restrictions mostly in a pattern of following family members with established businesses—often supermarkets and restaurants—in Argentina. As in other Latin American countries, earlier references to China in Argentine literature and culture were mainly of the orientalist type—framing China as a remote, mysterious culture—from Jorge Luis Borges's "Chinese" inspirations in his 1941 story "The Garden of Forking Paths" ("El jardín de senderos que se bifurcan") to *A Chinese Novel* by César Aira (*Una novela china*, 1987).[6] While orientalist tropes persist, many of the recent China-themed texts from Latin America grapple with new global constellations in which China has become part of their everyday reality at home, no longer to be easily relegated to the distant other. In Argentina the coincidence of more recent immigration and global pressure has led to an imaginary increasingly attuned to economic relations. And this is particularly true for the texts on which I will focus here, such as Magnus's *Chinese on a Bicycle*, César Aira's novel *Marble* (*El mármol*, 2011), and Sebastian Borensztein's film *A Chinese Tale* (*Un cuento chino*, 2011). In these texts, the acknowledgment and disavowal of Argentina's precarious position and China's power go hand in hand as their representation of Sino-Argentine relations is itself ambivalent, strategically slanted. As they fantasize about global relationships—they reflect on global economic structures even though their plots have strong fantastical or incongruous elements—they also allow us to think about the possibilities and limits for imagining our globalized world.

The fantasy of a world without Chinese labor in Magnus's *Chinese on a Bicycle* embodies in miniature some of the prevalent ways in which Argentine culture confronts the rise of China. In spite of underlining China's importance by painting a global scene of chaos and standstill, the hypothetical world crisis caused by China's nonparticipation invoked in Magnus's novel frames

151

non-Chinese countries (such as Argentina) still as consumers of products made in China. This safely relegates China to a power of production, a reservoir of labor, and ties it to international consumer power, hence a double abstraction of labor. Such scenarios shift attention from labor as such to commodities. *Chinese on a Bicycle* and other contemporary Argentine novels and films replace a mode of *chinoiserie* with a "Made in China" paradigm in which "China is [still] the stuff it produces" (Hoyos 2010, 166). One could call this a culturally specific (or rather clichéd) version of commodity fetishism: labor is erased because the stereotype "made in China" does not focus on the process of making and its conditions, but merely ethnicizes the products, the outcome of labor. As such, superficial critiques read the ubiquity of products "made in China" as alien invasions of national economies but largely omit that the enjoyment of cheap consumer goods at home relies on the exploitation of labor elsewhere or that this is one of the consequences of the forces of globalization with which we are complicit. Such a fragmentation and displacement of labor is not just the stuff of fiction. In fact, as Sandro Mezzadra and Brett Neilson show, the "global commodity chain approach, like the debates about the new international division of labor . . . tends to assume stable geographical divides that cross the world of labor and production" (2013, 166). In fact, as the reality of economic networks and their strategic representations are often at odds, fictional texts provide us with ways of scrutinizing how global imaginaries work, helping us to take into consideration—as this volume's introduction suggests—the complex making of global scenarios as world orderings.[7]

Whereas a first displacement brackets labor and ethnicizes commodities, in a second, related shift the labor of production (in China) is commuted into the labor of selling (by Chinese in Argentina). After all, in texts such as *Chinese on a Bicycle*, "China" is mostly represented by the Chinese diaspora in Argentina, often referred to as Argenchinos. Of course, the service sector is not exempt from conditions of labor precariat. But the point of this maneuver of displacement is not primarily to cover up global structures of exploitative labor. Instead, it translates the global labor of production out there in China into domestic, yet still alien (since "Chinese") labor at home in Argentina. The concomitant focus on Argenchinos with their (stereo)typical restaurants and minimarts colors the way Chinese labor is viewed: Argentines as consumers of things made in China brokered by the Chinese (in Argentina). A displaced imaginary of Chinese labor allows for a strategic misreading of global economic constellations. The resulting tropes of Chinese labor are based on culturally and ethnically fixed laborscapes, whose boundaries are then subject to strategic manipulation. This allows for warped imaginaries of economic and affective circulations that symbolically recenter Argentina vis-à-vis the world while deemphasizing the transnationally shared consequences of globalized labor.

Alien Hallucinations

Between China and Argentina, laborscapes appear in the guise of racial forms. Like the racialized economic imaginaries that Colleen Lye (2005) describes for US literature from the late nineteenth to the mid-twentieth century, these come in paradoxical shapes. In the case of Argentina's China, the economic tropes of racial form are further complicated by intersecting imaginaries, cultural influences, and global positionalities: between the sway of European orientalist tropes and the model of US-American exclusionism, between racial superiority and economic inferiority, between the fear of neocolonial pressure in new (Chinese) form and the hope of different alliances beyond the usual inequalities along the North-South axis, between older imaginaries of the Chinese immigrant plight and newer specters of China as an invisible, infiltrating force.

Far from destabilizing racial stereotypes, however, such contradictions remain operative and useful, especially because they can be deployed flexibly—to stoke fear of a Chinese takeover or to allay just such anxieties, for instance. Much of this manipulation depends on a strategic location of "China" in relation to Argentina: either as the dyad of China and Argentina or in the form of "China" in Argentina. The Chinese diaspora in Argentina— often synecdochically represented by Buenos Aires's Chinatown Belgrano— brokers the flexibility of this link. As Argenchinos can become a stand-in for China, they can be represented as a kind of tamed unknown, as a difference at the heart of and thus subsumed under Argentine culture, or framed as alien other. Most literary and filmic texts treat the Chinese diaspora in Argentina not as Argentine, not even as Argenchinos, but label them outright as "Chinese." Ethnic difference trumps everyday cohabitation, local integration, and citizenship. Local histories and strata of immigration disappear as the Chinese in Argentina can become a *pars pro toto* for China. In this scenario, the multidirectional circulations between different Chinese places and the Chinese diaspora in Argentina—circulations of people, objects, money, information, and affects—are eclipsed. This connection, metonymical, but deployed

153

in a metaphorical guise, cuts both ways. Precisely because the Argenchinos are perceived as Chinese (irrespective of whether they hail originally from the PRC, Hong Kong, or Taiwan, or how long they have lived in Argentina), they are read as part of what constitutes China. In a complementary move, knowledge (or presumed knowledge) about the Chinese in Argentina can also be projected onto China. And while the "rise of China" potentially shows diasporic Chinese groups in a different light, older notions about Chinese immigrants—for instance, as hardworking refugees dependent on their host's goodwill—can still tint the picture of China, despite its newly powerful status.[8]

The "Chinese" in César Aira's 2011 *Marble* mirror this logic. The novel's first-person narrator, an older Argentine, teams up with a Chinese teen, Jonathan, to solve a riddle that leads them to discover Chinese-looking extraterrestrials and help them return to their home planet. To present some of the Chinese characters in the novel as extraterrestrials pushes difference to a new extreme, in that they are not "aliens" from the other side of the globe, but aliens from another galaxy. But, except for differences in class, wealth, and education, the "Chinese" extraterrestrials look exactly like the Chinese-Argentines of the novel. The total alterity of extraterrestrials collapses into similarity. The extraterrestrials come from another world that is an exact copy of the one to which they have traveled, down to the last atom. As the novel quips in the protagonist's voice, the extraterrestrials did not adopt the "format of Chinese counting on the fact that all Chinese look the same to Occidentals and thus blend in. No, they had no need to assume any other format, they just came as they were" (107). In other words, these "Chinese" really are Chinese, their Chineseness is not a mere facade that uses the non-Chinese inability to distinguish between Chinese individuals. And as they are identical to Chinese, their difference (with respect to the non-Chinese) remains intact.

The logical conundrum of complete similarity on a planetary level—all possible worlds are identical—leaves ethnic difference and national identities untouched because other worlds are imagined here as perfect replicas. The transition from Argenchinos to Chinese aliens eliminates, and thus underlines, the gray zone between the local and the global as a complex network of multidirectional interactions rather than clear-cut categories. As the Chinese extraterrestrials are sent home in a violent, cacophonous stream of images, the global is ironically blown up to a planetary scale. The alien Chinese are sent back home but, according to the logic of the sameness of all possible worlds that the novel proposes, "home" would be a Chinese supermarket in the same neighborhood of Buenos Aires—just on a different planet. The planetary has just collapsed back into the local. From the vantage point of this hallucinatory slippage between difference and sameness that sets up the local, the global, and the planetary as a vicious circle, the logic of racial form is destabilized only to be ironically reaffirmed yet again.

Racial form intersects with economic form in *Marble* with its focus on products made in China—on Chinese stuff, or China as stuff. Chinese products are present as the seemingly useless trifles at the checkout counter of a Chinese-owned supermarket:

> Seemingly a whole industry of small things of little or minimal value had sprung up.
>
> In fact, there was too much. A hanging forest in miniature assaulted one's eye with the commodities from Liliput, difficult to make out even though, or precisely because of, their gaudy colors and the letters and pictures of their wrappings. (Aira 2011, 18)

These Chinese trifles play a central role in *Marble*. For one, a series of trivial items, acquired by the protagonist in a Chinese supermarket in lieu of small change, becomes the driving force of the novel's action. A plastic eye, a mini camera, a hairclip, vitamin tablets, and batteries all have their function in the narrative. Or rather, one can surmise that the course of the narrative was inspired by a random handful of objects. More importantly, however, these objects lead to a reflection on value and equivalence. The only use value of these items, or so it seems, is in their excessively low value. As such, they can be used as small change since the Argentine monetary system does not provide currency below a certain value. Their exchangeability and their uselessness (except for their very exchangeability) rub off on the units of money they are supposed to supplement. In fact, the scene in the supermarket at the beginning of the novel engages in a somewhat tedious series of calculations of leftover value, as if the whole interaction had profound meaning, rather than simply taking up time and textual space. The function of these commodities is phatic, that is, they merely keep economic circulation and value calculi going. What looks like frivolous objects (marked as Chinese) is really at the heart of a whole system of economic flows, as Chinese stuff serves as a metonymy of economic circulation itself.

In this array of the trivial, small marble globules play a particularly important role, even as they do not contribute to the solution of the riddle, unlike

155

all the other small gadgets. As it turns out, these globules are not of Chinese importation, unlike the trifles made in China, but are an Argentine "national product" (Aira 2011, 33). Instead of the prestige of marble, however, these minuscule marble balls are a form of disaggregated premarble, used only as a form of nearly worthless pseudocurrency in Chinese supermarkets. The discovery that the mining site of the marble globules—referred to in the media as "zones of extreme poverty" (33)—is close to Buenos Aires comes as a shock for the protagonist, who muses that our imaginary constantly reads images of underdevelopment as a trait of remote places: "My mistake had probably been due to the term 'economically underdeveloped zones,' where, according to the media, [the marble globules] had been discovered. One always thinks of these places as very far away, and one does not want to know how far away or where exactly they are, because of a superstitious fear of poverty" (68). The proximity of underdevelopment, the specter of economic precarity at home—both *Marble* and *Chinese on a Bicycle* feature unemployed protagonists—present an Argentina in crisis. Globalization (or so the resonance with the novel's "globules" suggests) affects Argentina (see Hoyos 2015, 121). Rather than empowered customers on which the flourishing of Chinese businesses depend, Argentines are shown to covet Chinese riches. The Argentine protagonist, for instance, indulges in the fantasy of winning a Chinese supermarket after solving the riddle—albeit accompanied with the expectation of an unequal distribution of labor; his Chinese "partner" Jonathan would do all the work, buttressed by the protagonist's symbolic role to project respectability and inspire confidence (see Aira 2011, 87). Rather than complacent consumers of objects made in China, Argentines are shown to be part of an economy reduced to mining relatively worthless resources for Chinese uses. The juxtaposition of worthless Chinese goods and worthless Argentine marble globules, used for the same pseudomonetary purpose, provides glimpses of the extremes of economic networks: worthless raw materials, useless manufactured goods, monetary equivalents, engines of economy's churning.

But the economic short circuit of marble globules and trifles made in China that hints at the complexity of economic connections between China and Argentina (the exportation of raw material, the importation of manufactured goods) and, potentially, at the equivalence of precarious labor (the mining of natural resources in Argentina, the working conditions in Chinese factories) remains of secondary importance in *Marble*. The subtext of global economics in Aira's novel is muted by the absurd story of Chinese-looking extraterrestrials—itself a hint at a reflection on globalization that quickly defaults back into a stable constellation of racial difference. Even if much of *Marble* has to be read as ironic, in the end, racial form overrides economic patterns as global connections and shared conditions fracture yet again into ethnic difference.

Texts such as *Chinese on a Bicycle* and *Marble* use tropes of Chinese labor to symbolically recenter Argentina vis-à-vis the world. They reimagine Argentina (mostly through its capital Buenos Aires) in global or even planetary terms, but make globalization conform to an Argentine scenario. This does not result in a defamiliarized version of the known, but in a strategic perspectival displacement to have the world fit Buenos Aires. This has a double effect. It allays Argentine insecurity in the face of China's global position and its own vulnerability, for instance, vis-à-vis China's role as agricultural competitor or China's creation of economic influence zones in non-Western countries—especially those of Africa, the Caribbean, and Latin America—through a mixture of infrastructural investment and extractive economic relations. After all, in comparison, China's power as producer of cheap commodities is much less threatening. In addition, this allows Argentine culture to disregard laborscapes that span the globe and precarious conditions that exist as much in China as in Latin America. The cliché of "Chinese on strike" in Magnus's novel (reminiscent of, and yet fundamentally different from such initiatives as "A Day without Latinos"), for instance, does nothing to protest oppression, nor is it a move toward solidarity across different countries, cultures, and regions by way of a global connectivity rooted in shared conditions of neoliberal globalization and exploited labor. Instead, such representations strategically obfuscate global power structures. Even though they might show a glimpse of global economic circulations and shared structures of exploitation, they overwrite them with ethnicized imaginaries of laborscapes: production is isolated from consumption, labor from commodity, and each is coded in terms of cultural, national, and ethnic boundaries.

Arbitrary Affinities

The displacement of labor through alignments of racial and economic forms, brokered by maneuvers that either equate or separate the Chinese diaspora in Argentina and China, however, cannot do without reflections on global connectivity. But these thrive often on yet another displacement of economic structures. For instance, Sebastian Borensztein's 2011 film *Chinese Take-Out* (*Un cuento chino*, literally *A Chinese Tale*) paints a reassuring picture of global connectivity between China and Argentina for an Argentine audience precisely because it replaces geopolitical and economic relations with a narrative of chance encounters.[9] Proximity is here wrought from arbitrary links rather than being rooted in structures of solidarity. The film's Argentine protagonist, Roberto (played by Ricardo Darín), an owner of a hardware store in Buenos Aires who leads a secluded existence after having suffered through the trauma of the Falklands War as a young man, learns to believe in the meaning of life after an encounter with a displaced Chinese, Jun (played by the Chinese Argentine actor Huang Sheng Huang). Both men, separated by cultural differences, unable to communicate throughout most of the film, are united by chance—or, to quote the film's tagline on the DVD cover: "An Argentine and a Chinese united by a cow that fell from the sky."

The film's opening scene—a more detailed version of which reappears toward the end of *A Chinese Tale*—is set in China, albeit in a China that, in spite of the toponym "Fucheng, China" provided on screen, is full of caricature and orientalist stereotypes. We see the film's Chinese protagonist, Jun, prepare to propose to his fiancée in a sequence of timeless orientalist kitsch. A Chinese couple in traditional clothes frolics on a sampan adorned with red lanterns, making trite dialogue in Chinese and singing a love song. The idyllic scene is interrupted as a cow falls out of the sky onto the sampan—anticipated for the audience by crosscut frames that show the falling cow. An extreme wide shot shows us the male protagonist, reduced to a tiny figure, desperately looking for his fiancée in the lake waters before the scene switches from China to Argentina.

The unreal flavor of the "Chinese" scene gives way to the unremarkable everyday: Roberto's hardware store, placed on a global map by way of the onscreen label "Buenos Aires, Argentina"—a place that the film does not cast as a spectacular city, but rather as a gray, normal, everyday space. The contrast between the exotic Chinese scene and the trite Argentine setting of the film is underlined by the cinematic sleight of hand of an upside-down image: the frame that shows Ricardo's storefront turns slowly downside-up before the Argentine plot can unfold. As the film points out formally, China and Argentina are geographical and cultural antipodes positioned at opposite ends of the globe. Of course, Jun, the young Chinese of the opening scene, will end up in the hardware shop in Buenos Aires, begrudgingly accepted and assisted by its owner Roberto.

The contrast between the film's representation of China and of Argentina sets up the two protagonists as opposites. Throughout most of the film,

Roberto and Jun fail to communicate beyond the most basic level of food to be eaten or work to be done. Much of the film's humor is based on a fundamental structure of misunderstanding as the (intended) filmic audience participates in Roberto's perspective of ignorance. Throughout most of the film, it is assumed that Chinese is as unintelligible to the target audience as it is to the Argentine characters, with the exception of the few scenes in which Chinese Argentine characters serve as translators.[10] The language barrier between Jun and Roberto serves to maintain suspense throughout the film. Only toward its end, through the translation of an Argenchino takeout delivery boy, do both protagonists start to understand the other's situation.

As the film progresses, Chinese culture gradually surfaces as an element of Argentine culture: from the Chinese Embassy to Chinese supermarkets and restaurants in Buenos Aires's Chinatown. The film shows glimpses of Chinese-Argentine connections based on histories of migration and economic relations, but it does so in a nostalgic mode. Roberto's initial treatment of Jun—a mixture of superiority, condescending support, and labor exploitation—is reminiscent of older diasporic structures premised on the inferior position of Chinese immigrants in Argentine society and in Latin American contexts in general, pointing to a history of displacement and exploitation, from the coolie trade to the stereotype of Asian immigrants as cheap labor and shop owners. Jun helps Roberto with menial tasks, such as cleaning up his house and yard, and is read by Roberto's acquaintances as hired help—at some point, Roberto is even advised to get Jun's papers in order, to "whitewash him" (blanquearlo), in the face of increased scrutiny of illegal immigration by officials. Jun, the stereotype of the displaced refugee—fresh off the boat, destitute and disoriented, with the address of his uncle tattooed on one arm—has to rely on Roberto's grudging help. The supposedly humorous scenes of the unlikely cohabitation of grumpy Roberto and displaced Jun border on scenarios rife with dependency. Roberto provides for "his" Chinese, but does not seem capable of treating him quite like a fellow human being—throughout, Roberto (and the film) infantilize Jun. China's global success story is metonymically (and metaphorically) rewritten with reversed roles through the destitute Chinese immigrant and his Argentine benefactor. Jun and Roberto's relation, as an unequal host-guest dyad, presents a reverse mirror image of Chinese-Argentine relations on a macroeconomic level—reminiscent of older figures of Chinese displacement and disempowerment in Latin America. The issue here is not that figures such as Jun (less stereotypical maybe, and less suffused with romantic tragedy)

159

do not exist. Of course, there are still Chinese migrants who seek a new life in Latin America, often following the past trajectories of family members. Rather, the problem lies in the film's suggested slippage between metonymy and metaphor: Jun is not simply one of many possible figures of Chineseness in Argentina. Instead, for the duration of the film at least, he comes to embody Chinese-Argentine interactions as such.

But, apart from the uncanny echoes of the displacement of Chinese labor to Latin America, *A Chinese Tale* downplays the economic components of global entanglement. Or rather, much of the film sports economic subtexts that remain latent or are strategically displaced. Jun has come to Argentina to find his uncle and only surviving relative after the tragic death of his fiancée, but his potential economic reasons remain implicitly assumed, yet unaddressed. Roberto's curiosity about Jun's life in China expresses itself as a question about his occupation: labor as identity. But Jun's labor expertise—he hand-painted toys in a factory—is translated from labor precariat to craftsmanship. As we see Jun's sophisticated sketches of Roberto as a tiger-fighting hero and Roberto's love interest Mari as a bodhisattva, nothing invokes the potentially precarious context of hand-painting parts of toys made-in-China in a conveyor-belt mode that makes human labor part of an integrated semiautomated production circuit. By the same token, Roberto's economic position as a small store owner remains anecdotal. The film represents his business and way of life as anachronistic: his insistence on quality and personalized advice against shoddy products and chain stores, his obsession with the inexactitude of mechanized distribution and supply chains. But his incessant recounting of boxes of nuts and screws that always contain fewer items than specified results in frictions with local suppliers rather than leading to a reflection on the local impacts of global manufacturing. What could lend itself to an allegorical reading—Roberto as a tiny, powerless part in brokering globally produced commodities (many smaller hardware products are indeed made in China)—merely contributes to his characterization as a misunderstood outsider. In other words, the film toys with unnecessary details related to economic structures, then leaves them dangling—loose ends that point to a global scenario that the film bypasses without being able to silence it completely.

When Roberto finally acknowledges his link with Jun, his epiphany is based on a chance connection. The Argentine store owner, an avid collector of odd news reports, had read and singled out for his collection the sad and somewhat surreal story of his Chinese guest before meeting him in person.

ANDREA BACHNER

Roberto shows Jun a newspaper clipping, part of his collection of absurd tales, but the "Chinese tale" turns out to be Jun's own story: the impossible coincidence of a cow falling from a cargo plane onto the sampan on which Jun is about to propose to his beloved. For Roberto, his collection of newspaper clippings is daily proof of the absurdity of human existence, a list of stories that trigger grim humor precisely because they do not make sense and thus underline life's lack of meaning. But Roberto is deeply impacted when he realizes that Jun is the protagonist of one of the absurd stories of his collection. He sees Jun's reaction of sadness when he is confronted with his own story as a newspaper clipping brings Roberto's own tragic past back to the surface. Roberto returned from the Falklands War after Argentina's defeat at the hands of Great Britain, only to find out that his father had died—an article on the Falklands War in an Italian newspaper, including a photo of Roberto as defeated combatant, one of the last things he must have seen before his death.

Jun concretizes and humanizes an absurd tale for Roberto, confronting him with the proximity of a trauma heretofore safely confined to the other side of the world and to the flat representation of newsprint. Instead of an indicator of the meaningless absurdity of life, chance here is reread as a force that can connect individuals across different places and cultures. It seems to harbor the possibility of making us understand loss and trauma as a shared condition—Jun's loss of his fiancée or Roberto's traumatic experience during the Falklands War and the sudden death of his father. In fact, the multilingual play with the titles of the film underlines the importance of chance as an engine of relationality, as the first title to appear on screen, in Chinese, is "*yisi ouran*" (一丝偶然: "a thread of chance" or maybe "a chance connection").

Throughout, *A Chinese Tale* hints at economic realities and laborscapes between Argentina and China, only to overwrite them by a facile gesture toward a shared humanity thrown into high relief by chance. Even as the film needs the scenario of global information brokerage for its big reveal, it also downplays the implications of global circulation—the complexity of economic networks reduced to global mediascapes. Especially in the flood of incessantly reposted news tidbits, access to images of another's pain are mainly ineffective. If they succeed in moving us, against all odds, this is mostly due to mechanisms of emotional projection, to individualized empathy disconnected from sociopolitical solidarity. Media circulations are part and parcel of global economic networks and their unequal distribution of resources—

allocations of grievability negatively proportionate with precarity.[11] While the context of globalized news coverage in the film creates an unlikely link between two individuals at opposite sides of the Pacific, this connection remains tenuous at best. What seems like a connection is, in reality, just another pattern of displacement; the tragic story of a Chinese is ultimately reenacted as a happy ending for his Argentine host.

The displacement of trauma continues on a para-filmic level. As highlighted on screen at the film's beginning, the story that is rewritten in *A Chinese Tale* as Jun's is based on real events. After the film credits, we are shown a subtitled clip from a Russian newsreel that recounts a similar anecdote as one between a Russian aircraft transporting cattle (not Chinese cattle raiders as in the film) that had to release its cargo, resulting in the foundering of a Japanese fishing boat (not the sampan on which Jun is proposing to his beloved). The real story that inspired *A Chinese Tale* has nothing to do with either China or Argentina. Instead, it is a testament to the facile replicability and superficial sensationalism of anecdotes happening elsewhere that come to us via the arbitrary network effects of social media. After all, the "Chinese tale" is "Chinese" only figuratively in that the Spanish expression "un cuento chino" designates an unlikely, untrustworthy story—one of many, mostly derogatory figurative uses of "Chinese" or "chino" in Spanish. At first glance, this suggests that the choice to portray such a link between an Argentine and a Chinese is arbitrary and that the film could have portrayed any number of transcultural encounters (or at least, displaced individuals in Argentina from any number of countries). At a second glance, however, the fact that this Russian-Japanese story gets rewritten as Chinese, and then transplanted to Argentina, is anything but arbitrary. After all, the global connection between Argentina and China is clearly a motor of anxiety for Argentine society. Displacement functions on different interrelated levels in Borensztein's film. The film has to underline as well as disavow its reference to China—especially in the form of Chinese economic power and Chinese labor. Chance relationality overrides global patterns of unequal connection, as the film invests in arbitrary, and thus depoliticized, structures of sympathy. But the very emphasis on its arbitrariness protests too much. And the contrived actualization of a random story through an Argentine and a Chinese gives the lie to the structure of blind chance that motivates their encounter in *A Chinese Tale*. The film's logic of displacement functions precisely because of this oscillation: the fact that its content is "Chinese" is presented as arbitrary, but, given the underlying anxiety about China's and Argentina's geopolitical entanglement,

ANDREA BACHNER

this is actually a necessary and strategic choice. In order to allay Argentine anxieties around globalization and the rise of China, *A Chinese Tale* has to thematize Chinese-Argentine relations while also insisting on the potential replaceability of its "Chinese" content.

Unhappy Together

There is one more "Chinese" connection at work in *A Chinese Tale*. The formal sleight of hand of the world upside down as the film "turns over" from China to its Argentine setting unmistakably references the 1997 film *Happy Together* by the Hong Kong filmmaker Wong Kar-wai. Wong's film uses Argentina as an exotic backdrop for the relationship woes of two gay Hong Kongers who break up and start over, never able to be happy together for more than a short stretch of time. The sequence in *Happy Together* that *A Chinese Tale* cites cinematographically is motivated by the reflection of one of the protagonists, Yiu-Fai, on the distance between Hong Kong and Buenos Aires when he is on "Hong Kong" time in the Argentine capital, working night shifts in an abattoir. A series of shots in which the camera captures drab, nondescript images of a Hong Kong upside down simulates the protagonist's musings by way of the filmic medium. *A Chinese Tale*, in contrast, pits exotic images of China against an unspectacular everyday Buenos Aires. However, whereas *A Chinese Tale* effectively tells an Argentine tale, *Happy Together* is arguably more about Hong Kong in the face of its 1997 return to China than about Buenos Aires. In his shooting diary, "Don't Try for Me Argentina," cinematographer Christopher Doyle explains the choice of setting as a strategy of defamiliarization, a means of reflecting on Hong Kong from a different vantage point. Wong's exoticization of Buenos Aires also displaces a different Chinese reality—that of its Chinese diaspora. The focus on the film's Hong Kong protagonists, who are merely temporary sojourners in Buenos Aires, relegates examples of the Chinese diaspora in Argentina to an afterthought. To frame Buenos Aires and Hong Kong as antipodes, the presence of the in-between category of Sino-Argentine elements and the labor of Argenchinos has to be downplayed: that of the interculturally savvy go-between figures who assist the film crew in Argentina (visible only in *Buenos Aires Zero Degree*, a documentary about the making of *Happy Together*), or that of the perfectly bilingual owners of the Central Restaurant (where one of the film's protagonists is shown to work for a while) who are Argentines as well as integral members of the Chinese community in Buenos Aires. Wong's

Hong Kong film (also partly) made in Argentina thus engages in its own mechanisms of displacement as it strategically underlines some experiences of displacement and downplays others, as it displaces some laborscapes and engages itself in the work of dislocation.

Happy Together's projection of a phantasmic Argentina shows, especially in its Argentine reception, that fantasies are fungible, prone to being reframed, yet also susceptible to triggering other displacements. For instance, the Argentine critic Francine Masiello reads *Happy Together* as a film about the Chinese diaspora in Argentina, and, through the "diasporic" bridge between China and Argentina, relates the disorientation of the film's protagonists to a shared condition of globalized displacement, especially as an alternative to the "geopolitics of Western privilege": "Although Wong Karwai was primarily concerned with the plight of Hong Kongers, his routing through Buenos Aires is paradoxically important insofar as local Argentine poets and novelists also struggle with this sense of the foreign even in that place they call home" (2001, 143). This Argentine phantasmic attachment solicited by a film that fantasizes from a different positionality, that of Hong Kong, speaks to the fungibility of identifications and fantasies in relation to cultural texts, to their ability to be displaced across languages, nations, cultures, and regions. At times such fantasies erase social context completely, for instance when Argentine writers and intellectuals fantasize about their own displacement at home as if it were equivalent to the experiences of diasporic subjects. But the network of different displacements across the boundaries of cultural, ethnic, and national imaginaries also makes the complete erasure of a given context impossible.

The laborscapes and global networks constructed by recent China-themed novels and films in Argentina are phantasmic. They pair apparently realist modes with fantastic elements, such as the absurd news stories of *A Chinese Tale*, the "Chinese" aliens in *Marble*, or the harebrained complot that drives the plot of *Chinese on a Bicycle*. They shelter ethnic prejudice by presenting it as the perspective of their stereotypical Argentine characters and by infusing their texts with humor and irony. However, as they attempt to work through Argentina's global position, especially with regard to the "rise of China," by way of confabulation, the scope of their fantasies is often limited. Anxieties about new global imbalances surface in the economic structures that pervade their fictions, but give way to consolatory narratives as specific Argentine and Argenchino/Chinese characters and their unequal relationships come to embody Chinese-Argentine interactions as if in reverse mirror images. Strategic slippages between the Chinese other out there and the Chinese other at home in Argentina buttress global frameworks in which the national can be safely integrated into the global, as well as anchored in local characteristics. Thus, displaced and fragmented along ethnic and national lines, global laborscapes and their national and local repercussions can be safely contained.

As they strategically displace labor, these narratives engage in a labor of displacement. Yet the work of globalization in these narratives constantly threatens to undo their efforts of displacing labor. After all, it has to construct laborscapes with recognizable real-world referents as a basis for its phantasmic slippages. What these texts really fictionalize, then, is no longer a drama that unfolds either at home or effectively at the other end of the world (i.e., on the other side of the Pacific). To pit the local against the global or to reduce the global to yet another version of the local is no longer sufficient. Instead, relation and division, entanglement and fragmentation lie too close to one another. If we are called on to understand today's world through patterns of relationality (as Shu-mei Shih [2013d] suggests) and excavated intimacies (as Lisa Lowe [2015] argues), we also need to take stock of a proliferation of borders and a fragmentation of labor and political solidarities (pace Mezzadra and Neilson [2013]). Fictions—in literature and film, but also those of cultural and socioeconomic discourses—play an important role in the work of globalization. But rather than accepting the blinders of representation and equivalence apparently imposed by the global status quo (even and especially when they engage in the construction of fantasies), they need to reclaim the power of fiction: the power to help us imagine otherwise, even if this "otherwise" remains a precariously elusive thing.

Notes

1 All translations are my own.
2 For a paranoid version of the made-in-China paradigm, see Bongiorni (2007).
3 For an in-depth perspective on economic relations between China and Latin America, see Luciano Bolinaga's chapter in this volume.
4 See the culture section of the online journal *Dangdai: Primera Revista de Intercambio Cultural Argentina-China* as one example of cultural activities focused on Argentine-Chinese exchange.
5 This also accounts for the growing interest of literary and cultural critics whose work involves Argentina in transpacific exchange and Asian–Latin American cultural production.

6   In "The Garden of Forking Paths," the ideal, yet impossible narrative, one that would include all possible choices, is presented as Chinese—Chinese form as epitome of complexity and difference. For an overview of Latin American orientalism, especially in modernismo, see Tinajero 2004.

7   The chapter by Rachel Cypher and Lisa Rofel in this volume provides an intriguing insight into the diversity of representations and imaginaries specifically with regard to Argentine-Chinese relationships. Their focus on the perspectives of local residents embodies a useful supplement and counterpoint to my discussion of fictional representations.

8   See Kuehn, Louie, and Pomfret 2014. Their volume is mainly concerned with the renegotiation of Chinese diasporic identities after the "rise of China." But this renegotiation is also at work in the imaginaries of the host cultures.

9   I will refer to the film by a literal translation of its Spanish title, namely *A Chinese Tale*, in what follows.

10 Judging from Chinese websites and blog comments, the film has developed a following among Chinese audiences, too. Unlike non-Chinese-speaking viewers, they do not share the lack of understanding of the Argentine protagonists (after all, dialogue in Spanish is subtitled). Yet most commenters appreciate the film's humor and its appeal to a shared human experience of chance encounters. See for instance, https://movie.douban.com/subject /6284748/reviews.

11 For a discussion of visual culture and empathy, via a critique of Susan Sontag, see Judith Butler 2009, especially the chapter "Torture and the Ethics of Photography: Thinking with Susan Sontag."

MOBILITY AND DISPLACEMENT

Part III

GLOBAL SOUTH
FRONTIERS

Chinese Worldmaking and Racial
Imaginaries of Johannesburg

The South African megacity Johannesburg is home to the continent's largest and oldest Chinese population. With the strengthening of geopolitical and economic ties since the late 1990s, the People's Republic of China has reigned as South Africa's largest trading partner since 2010. Johannesburg has also been a key site of the unfolding China-Africa story; it frequently hosts meetings for the leaders of the BRICS states (Brazil, Russia, India, China, and South Africa) and the Forum on China-Africa Cooperation (FOCAC), as President Xi Jinping describes, for the "shared development and prosperity for all emerging markets and developing countries" (Ministry of Foreign Affairs 2018). Concurrent with these developments has been a wave of new Chinese migration beginning in the late 1990s and increasing in earnest after 2000. In Cyrildene Chinatown, in Johannesburg's eastern suburbs, the Chinatown Gateway—two arches proclaimed to be the largest of their kind in Africa—symbolizes China's stature in South Africa and the arrival of new Chinese migrants.[1] At the ribbon-cutting ceremony in 2013, not the mayor of Johannesburg, but President Jacob Zuma himself was present, recognizing the "Chinese community" as "an important bond between South Africa and China." He proclaimed, "The establishment of Chinese Gateway embodies the Chinese spirit of pioneering and striving, as well as their willingness and determination for long-term developments in South Africa." Ambassador Zu Qin similarly spoke of "arduous pioneering" and integrating the "Chinese Dream" and "South African Dream" (African Program 2013). Absent were Chinatown's residents, small-scale traders and workers at their shops, who are worlds apart from the engagements of which state and elite actors speak.

Ordinary Chinese migrants are often invoked in China-Africa narratives to various political ends. In Chinese and African state discourses, migrants are figured as ambassadors of "China-Africa friendship," engaging in "people-to-people exchange." Alternatively, in Western narratives of the Chinese empire, Africa has emerged as a frontier market for daring Chinese entrepreneurs, invoking the American Wild West and the African Dark Continent. Howard French puts it bluntly in *China's Second Continent: How a Million Migrants Are Building a New Empire in Africa*: "The continent's rapidly rising population means lots of new mouths to be fed, lots more people to be clothed, devices and appliances and goods of all kinds to be sold. . . . No other big outside players in the world besides the Chinese have fully understood the opportunity this represents" (2014, 44). As the photojournalist Paolo Woods similarly articulates, "For the over 500,000 Chinese who have emigrated in the last decade, Africa holds the promise of a twenty-first century frontier." Ordinary traders are figured as part of a state project as "the government in Beijing is sending Chinese state companies and adventurous entrepreneurs to Africa" (Michal, Beuret, and Woods 2012). Writing with cautionary optimism about what China represents for African futures, Achille Mbembe looks to China, India, and Brazil as key actors in a new global order. Mbembe remarks, "Africa does indeed represent the last frontier of capitalism. The question is under what conditions will these new forms of exploitation be conducted, by whom, and for whose benefit" (Blaser 2013).

With these narratives about Chinese migration and African frontiers in mind, I tell a story of the aspirations, experiences, mobilities, and "imaginative processes," as Carlos Rojas and Lisa Rofel discuss in the introduction to this volume, of Chinese migrants and the worlds they make in South Africa. Following Mei Zhan's approach to worlding, I explore the "emergent socialities entangled in dynamic imaginaries of pasts, futures, and presents" and "specific ways in which multiple worlds are envisioned, constituted, and experienced in everyday life on the ground" (2009, 6–7). This particular approach enables rethinking China-Africa in two ways. First, Chinese worlds in South Africa are multiple and intersect and diverge across scales, histories, and locales. As migrants are often subsumed within bilateral trade and diplomacy "from above,"

I focus on the world of ordinary Chinese migrants "from below" and their entanglements and disconnects with other worlds. Second, race is often absent but looms as a specter in the racial imagery and implicit assumptions about "Chinese in Africa." I foreground the racial dimensions of Chinese worldmaking in South Africa, exploring the racial discourses and imaginaries that shape how migrants envision and experience South Africa. South Africa is imagined as an emerging market and racialized place of crime and disorder, complementary imaginaries that cohere around ideas about race and development.

Between 2014 and 2015, I resided in Cyrildene Chinatown, following the lives of Chinese migrant traders at China Malls, popular wholesale centers for low-cost Chinese goods of which there are over a dozen in Johannesburg.[2] I lived with Mr. Zheng, Chinatown's "big boss" who managed its daily affairs for over a decade. Mr. Zheng was an early arrival, leaving Fujian Province for South Africa in the 1990s. Integral to the making of this migration wave, he was one of the main snakeheads, the name for a human smuggler, from China to South Africa. Present at the Gateway opening, he was one of the few intermediaries between Chinese and South African state actors and ordinary migrants. I also worked at one of Johannesburg's busiest China Malls, a microcosm of China–South Africa flows and immersion in fields of power and difference.

In what follows, I situate contemporary Chinese migration within the history of the Chinese diaspora in South Africa to illustrate how new migrants enter a fragmented, layered diasporic world and racial terrain. Next, I give a snapshot of migrant trajectories, subjectivities, and aspirations shaped by globalizing China's market economy. This is a reflection on Johannesburg but also on the wider phenomenon of Chinese migration to the Global South, of which Johannesburg is only one destination among many. I map migrants' itineraries to emerging markets across Africa, Asia, and Latin America. Finally, I explore Chinese worldmaking as a racial project and imaginative process. Through the language of blackness, crime, and disorder, migrants envisaged Johannesburg not through a universal globality of capitalist markets, but through the politics of location and racial difference.

Historical Entanglements

The history of the Chinese diaspora in South Africa has undergone distinct moments under the colonial and apartheid-era anti-Asian exclusion and the postapartheid welcoming of China. The forefathers of the Chinese diaspora in South Africa began arriving in the 1870s as independent migrants. Of

Cantonese and Moiyeanese (Hakka) descent, most were from Canton, today known as Guangzhou. This early wave of migrants fled natural disasters and war for the fortune of the "gold mountain" in South Africa, Australia, and California, coming to South Africa by way of imperial routes via Hong Kong, Macau, and Mauritius. These forefathers were not the sixty-four thousand indentured laborers on the Witwatersrand's gold mines in 1904 who were repatriated by 1910. During the late nineteenth and early twentieth centuries, a flurry of anti-Asian laws in Johannesburg were implemented to curtail the rights of Chinese and Indian migrants racialized as "Asiatic." Chinese were barred from citizenship and forced to trade in designated multiracial areas. Immigration continued covertly as new arrivals assumed the identities of family members of established Chinese, becoming "paper sons and daughters" (U. Ho 2011). By the 1890s, a "Chinese quarter" or "Cantonese quarter" of small Chinese shops was formed, which later became First Chinatown. Social clubs, schools, a language press, and social organizations in First Chinatown organized the social fabric of Chinese, who were classified as Coloured under apartheid (Yap and Man 1996). The designation of First Chinatown as a heritage site commemorates this history and recognizes Chinese as part of the multiracial citizenry. Generational upward economic mobility and urban crime led to Chinese leaving the inner city in the early 1990s (Harrison, Moyo, and Yang 2012, 917).

Following the halcyon era of China's socialist internationalism, in the 1970s and 1980s the internationally isolated apartheid state recruited Taiwanese industrialists to spur development (Hart 2002). In the 1980s and 1990s, entrepreneurs and investors from Hong Kong, Taiwan, and mainland China began coming to South Africa as Taiwanese industrialists left. After diplomatic normalization with mainland China in 1998, the year 2000 marked the largest influx of Chinese migrants—mostly aspiring small-scale traders from coastal Fujian and Guangdong—which led to the creation of Cyrildene Chinatown in the late 1990s and the establishment of China Malls in the early 2000s. Estimated in total from 200,000 to 350,000, the post-2000 migration wave of mainland Chinese constitutes the largest group within the Chinese diasporic community in South Africa (Huynh, Park, and Chen 2010, 289–90). From the new wave, my interlocutors fell into two categories: traders who had arrived with small amounts of private capital to set up family wholesale businesses, and workers who were trying to save up to become traders. Although Chinese entrepreneurial migration has coincided with bilateral relations, my interlocutors did not identify with Chinese investments and firms involved with infrastructure, agriculture, finance, and manufacturing. Ordinary traders rely on their own robust informal networks: community associations for governance, snakeheads for migration, and underground banks for remittances. These relationships are distinct from official channels connected to the Chinese Embassy, South African government, and Chinese banks operating in South Africa. Chinatown and China Malls are not sites where state-level diplomacy and trade "scale down," but rather instances of worldmaking orthogonal to geopolitical orders.

Even as Chinese migrants have a weak connection to the Chinese state in South Africa, to South Africans they still represent "China." For most South Africans, diplomacy and investment are out of sight, appearing only in business headlines. Given the ubiquity of Chinese goods and China Malls, traders have become the most visible face of China. For example, in 2012 the South African magazine *Noseweek* ran a cover story titled "Howzit China?" on Chinese migrant shopkeepers. Deploying Yellow Peril tropes about China's rise in South Africa, the unnamed author describes a "mass of illegal immigrants from China" and a "mass of non-essential imports flooding the South African market." While Chinese traders have been orientalized as the perilous embodiment of China's rise, they have also been embraced for the goods they make accessible to multiracial middle-class consumers. Black and Coloured South Africans often nostalgically viewed Chinese traders through memories of bartering with Chinese and Taiwanese shopkeepers in townships during apartheid. While they are bound together by other South Africans through processes of racialization, Chinese migrants, Taiwanese migrants, and South African–born Chinese rarely interact. Established generations of South African–born Chinese who fought for citizenship have distanced themselves from newcomers, citing illegal immigration, poor business practices, and organized crime (Yap and Man 1996; U. Ho 2011). One Taiwanese South African complained, "The newcomers have been in gold-rush mode and they don't have roots here. . . . They just want to make their money."[3] My Chinese interlocutors saw themselves primarily as ethnically and nationally "Chinese people" (huaren or zhongguoren), in contradistinction to South African–born Chinese, known as "overseas Chinese" (huaqiao or laoqiao), who had lost their connection to China over generations. The relationship between new migrants and Chinese born in the region disrupts assumptions of sameness, continuity, diasporic belonging, and coethnic solidarity. Distinct from state-driven projects and previous waves of migration, new Chinese migrants constitute one of the many Chinese worldmaking projects in South Africa across histories of racial citizenship and geopolitical alliance.

173

As migrants have traditionally sought out locations in North America, Europe, and Australia, the Chinese migrant in Africa is commonly figured in terms of failure. In the first survey of Chinese migrants in southern Africa, researchers funded by the Brenthurst Foundation make this judgment clear, stating, "Africa is the bottom-rung destination for China's migrants. The continent draws the poorest and least educated of the Chinese diaspora. . . . If they don't make it in Africa, they have nowhere else to go" (McNamee et al. 2012, 4, 6). Starting around 2015, the booming business I had previously witnessed was waning, and migrants began to plan where they would go next. All year, I listened to Chinese traders, many of whom had resided in South Africa for a decade, lament the worsening of crime, the weakening exchange rate, and the economic recession. I constantly heard chatter of *huiguo*, which refers to returning to China, either temporarily or permanently. Chinese migrants at China Malls and Chinatown slowly began to leave. Chinese workers with few financial or family ties were the first to go. Traders downsized, liquidated, and left. However, many stayed in a state of suspension (Xiang 2017), wanting to leave but stuck with assets, or unsure what returning to China would hold. By 2020 Mr. Zheng estimated that over 100,000 of 300,000 Chinese had left Johannesburg, and even he felt stuck there. After so many years away, he concluded, "Everything had become derailed."

Yet what intrigued me most is that while many returned to China, others moved to different destinations in Africa and Latin America. The pioneering spirit that brought them to South Africa was pushing them onward to new places. As Heidi Haugen and Jørgen Carling argue, Chinese entrepreneurial migrants "see the Chinese diaspora as an expanding social field that gradually covers virgin territory. It is on the ever-shifting edge of the diaspora that courageous pioneers make large profits" (2008, 660). Johannesburg was only one node within a constellation of locations in the Global South. Migrants were positioned on the edge of the rise of China and sought opportunities on the overlooked or undiscovered fringes of the global economy in the Global South. These transient mobilities form a distinct worlding project of Chinese migration "from below" in multiple senses: with respect to being "above" or "below" the state, and also insofar as mobility for the marginal is lateral or even downward, found near the bottom tiers of global capitalist orders.

The historic making of contemporary Chinese entrepreneurial migration in South Africa is thus the product of the social and economic transformations underway in post-Mao China as well as new frontiers of capital in the Global South. Chinese migrants' paths were congruent with, but not necessarily directly determined by, economic reforms, including the first stage of Reform and Opening Up in 1978, which allowed some to "get rich first," and the second stage of the intertwined policies of Going West and Going Out in 1999, which responded to the uneven development of the first stage. In addition to the relaxation of emigration policy in the 1980s, as Emily Yeh and Elizabeth Wharton observe, Going Out encouraged Chinese firms to open up new markets overseas and functioned as a spatial fix to "cool off China's overheating, investment-driven economy" (2006, 287). Trajectories of Chinese traders to Johannesburg, however, are not a direct effect of state policies encouraging overseas trade and investment. Rather, they result from the widening of socioeconomic inequality, the cultivation of entrepreneurialism, and the desire for class mobility in China. Chinese migration to African countries has coincided with the continent-wide economic growth since 2000, dubbed "Africa Rising." African markets provide a high demand for low-end Chinese goods, business regulations are lax, and little start-up capital and expert knowledge are required to launch a business (Haugen and Carling 2008, 642). In South Africa, a newly enfranchised Black middle class has provided a large consumer market for low-cost Chinese goods, and corrupt state officials allow informal commerce to flourish.

The Chinese men and women I met were incredibly diverse with respect to age and generation, hailing from the southern coastal villages and cities in Fujian, Zhejiang, Jiangsu, and Guangdong, to northeast Dongbei and western Xinjiang. The economic dislocations and novel class formations of the globalizing market economy manifested in gendered and regional ways and produced differentiated trajectories to South Africa. Many of my male interlocutors from Fujian had been construction workers, building the mansions that overseas remittances funded; others had been farmers, watching the countryside empty out as a result of rural reform and urbanization. I encountered two different generations of women in their twenties and forties: some of the older generation were "factory girls" who had produced exports for world markets in the early days of multinational corporations in the 1990s; the younger generation, instead of working in factories, juggled multiple jobs in the booming service economy. Most of my informants were precariously employed in the low-wage service sector. Most had limited formal education. Researchers for the Brenthurst Foundation explain that Chinese traders are in southern Africa because "they could not make a living in

175

the pressure-cooker that has become China's job market" (McNamee et al. 2012, 4). Compared to labor markets in China, migrants could earn higher wages based on the favorable exchange rate from rand to yuan—that is, until the rate evened out. On the peripheries of China's spectacular growth, migrants explained they were in South Africa because China had become *too* developed (fada). Wages were too low, and in the age of Taobao Marketplace, business was too competitive.[4]

Historical forces converged with personal circumstances and chance— parents, boredom, divorce, and debt. One of my interlocutors of the Cultural Revolution generation spent two decades working in a governmental unit in Sanming, Fujian Province, until it was privatized. Laid off, he drove private taxis around the clock, but in his fifties he could not endure the long hours. In order to support his retired wife and son at university, he went to Johannesburg where he had a relative who helped him find work. Sojourning to South Africa was also shaped by how Chinese migrants experienced a globalizing China. A minority worked in multinational offices in Shanghai and Shenzhen or were English translators in Beijing. Most were embedded in mobile families and chain migration networks. One young woman from Jiangmen, Guangdong, told me her parents, domestic migrant workers in China, pushed her to go abroad to gain life experience and "toughen her character" after high school. She considered South Africa, Costa Rica, and Venezuela—places she knew little about but had a family member there.

South Africa came with the possibility for new freedoms and opportunities. I commonly heard the refrain *ziji zuo laoban*, meaning becoming one's own boss, and *facai*, meaning getting rich. I met a free-spirited former railway engineer who sought to escape the bureaucracy of working on a government project in rural Chongqing, and a former salesman for a state-owned company who wanted to directly reap the profits he generated. Working for themselves, they could unleash their full entrepreneurial potential. Johannesburg represented freedom, mobility, a new start, or a temporary layover.

Migrants' trajectories to South Africa were more uncertain and multisited than I had assumed. As much as traders joked about getting rich in South Africa, they did not always have concrete plans to do so upon leaving China, nor was South Africa the final or only possible destination. Oftentimes they seized an opportunity, such as an invitation to join an existing business, or came after a chance encounter with someone connected to a snakehead. South Africa was a stepping-stone to Italy, Russia, or the United States. I met traders who, prior to coming to South Africa, had worked or traded from South Korea, Cameroon, or in a remote South African town bordering Swaziland, a place whose name they did not remember but starred in a regional atlas. I heard of many migrants who were stranded in South Africa after their journeys to the US with snakeheads went awry. When business took a downturn in Johannesburg, some left for Mozambique, Ghana, Zambia, or the DRC. My downstairs neighbors, a married couple from Fujian who had been in Johannesburg for over ten years, suddenly sold their stock and shop and joined family in Buenos Aires. Even though they would be starting over, including learning a new language, the exchange rate and economy were perceived to be more stable than in South Africa. Giles Mohan and May Tan-Mullins describe a pioneering spirit in the ongoing search for undiscovered markets that manifests as "willing to move to greener pastures when the chance arises" (2009, 601). A variation on flexible citizenship, migrant entrepreneurs gravitate toward fringe markets and embrace conditions of uncertainty.

A product of class inequality and aspiration in post-Mao China, migrants chase after the mobility unattainable to them in China in the untapped consumer markets in South Africa and the Global South. This worldmaking project not only entails flexibility and risk-taking but also racial ways of mapping the world. As the Global South is often perceived as "emerging markets and developing countries," they are not abstract or nonracial places.

Imagining Yuebao

Global imaginaries of race and development shape how Chinese migrants view and experience Johannesburg as more than a market, transforming it into the socially and culturally meaningful place of Yuebao, short for *Yuehanneisibao* (Johannesburg). My usage of Yuebao refers to Chinese representations of Johannesburg. Tracing how migrants talk about Johannesburg and conduct daily life illuminates how they understand the city as a "place-in-the-world." As James Ferguson conceptualizes, within a world divided into hierarchical categories, a place-in-the-world refers to "both a location in space and a rank in a system of social categories (as in the expression 'knowing your place')" (2006, 6). Chinese migrants view South Africa, the premier economic power on the continent, as the most economically developed African country. However, it is a Black majority country on the African continent, and hence is perceived as a "backward country" (luohou guojia).[5] The standard Chinese term for South Africa (Nanfei) features a character from the Chinese term for Africa (Feizhou). *Fei* is used for its phonetic value but in other contexts indicates negation. If China's hyperdevelopment pushed migrants out, South Africa's imagined lack of development makes it a destination and undergirds the racialization of Yuebao as a place of crime and disorder.

One of the reasons that traders often cited for their departure was crime—a catchall category I use to describe the continuum of minor theft to armed robbery that preoccupied the Chinese. Crime was the stuff of everyday parlance. The number of Chinese killed in South Africa per year was a metric invoked as commonly as the weather forecast or exchange rate. My WeChat feed was filled with crime scenes, surveillance video footage, mugshots, and local warnings. The obsession with crime and security is not unique to Chinese. Since the early 1990s, residential burglaries and car hijackings have increased with rising economic inequality, leading to the securitization of public and private space through boundary walls, gated communities, and security patrols. As Lindsay Bremner has argued, since the end of apartheid, "Crime has replaced race in the ordering of the city," transforming Johannesburg into a "city of walls" (2004, 461, 64).

Chinese newcomers enter a city obsessed with crime and security and encounter scenarios unique to cash-based business. Chinatown and China Malls run nearly entirely on cash. Cash does not produce a paper trail and allows traders to circumvent paying full taxes, enabling them to turn a profit on low-cost goods within a hypercompetitive market. These profits come at a cost as traders are also hypervisible as a racial minority concentrated in a few parts of the city. As one China Mall security manager explained, "It's a cash-flow business. . . . That's the reason they've been targeted. . . . The situation is a lot of cash is going around." Consequently, "people see the Chinese community as an ATM. You know, why go in and rob a bank when you can pull a car over on the road and get 400,000 or 500,000 rand [30,000 to 40,000 USD]?"

In July 2014, the Beijing-based Chinese Central Television (CCTV) produced a series of short documentary videos about overseas Chinese in Johannesburg that circulated on the video-hosting website Youku. The story begins with an aerial shot of the Ponte building in the Central Business District (CBD) and opens with "There is a common saying, 'If a Chinese has lived in South Africa over a year and has not been robbed, then he has not truly lived in South Africa'" (CCTV 2014). The morning the camera crew and journalists arrived in Johannesburg, a professional heist happened to occur at a Chinese-owned blanket factory where ten gunmen critically injured one person and took hundreds of thousands in cash. The film reconstructs the events of the heist, documenting the failed safeguards of armed security guards, dogs, and razor wire. Interviews with representatives from Chinatown and the Chinese Embassy highlight the vulnerability of Chinese. The film does far more than chronicle a robbery. In attempting to "show what South Africa is really like" to domestic and international audiences, it visually re-creates the dominant racial imaginaries of Chinese migrants.

The film depicts the South African "world-class city" as a simultaneously developed and underdeveloped place, contrasting the CBD's skyscrapers with littered industrial yards and crowded informal settlements. As the reporters tour the city in the safety of a Mercedes Benz, a dramatic metal soundtrack creates a sense of harrowing adventure and chaos. Using the Black male body to signify danger, the film makes frequent use of original and stock images of Black men crowded on the street, sitting on street corners, holding weapons, or facing off with the police. Contrasting with these visualizations of crime and disorder are narratives of economic promise. Throughout the film, reporters refer to Johannesburg as a "big city like other big cities" and a "beautiful city" but also a "city that trembles with fear," a "crime city," and a "dangerous city." In its closing, against the backdrop of Cyrildene Chinatown, they comment that migrants have arrived in pursuit of mythical gold but pay a price. A reporter asks, "Is Johannesburg paradise?" before answering, "For them [criminals], it is, but for us newcomers, I think heaven and hell are one step away from each other." As one trader put it, "The opportunity to make money is great, but you pay with your life." Each day, migrants experience these two sides of Yuebao, the emerging market and the dangerous city.

Johannesburg remains a fragmented, racialized city. According to Martin Murray, city-building practices after apartheid created a "scattered assortment of island-like enclosures [that] has been laid on top of an already distorted urban landscape divided along racial lines" (2011, 3). In Johannesburg the most militarized crimes—such as hijackings and military-style cash heists on highways—involve vehicles. Bremner points out that the "transportation routes of the city have become high-risk zones" (2010, 226). Getting around the city entails understanding its racial terrain and taking defensive measures to conceal cash and bodies. In areas concentrated with China Malls, traffic lights and highway entrances are sites for hijackings, smash and grabs, and armed robberies. In these same places, corrupt police routinely set up roadblocks to check immigration papers of Chinese passing

179

through in hopes of scoring a bribe. Driving is a high-stakes everyday activity with a racial dimension as migrants seek to protect themselves from an imagined black criminality. While Chinese are targeted for robberies, this racial specter is overblown and imagined as larger-than-life. As the CCTV film dramatizes, the car and the street are where crime happens. When I asked a trader about her most vivid memory in the country, she recounted, "a black person [heiren] came to knock on our [car] window. It looked like he had a gun." Although nothing transpired, "I'm scared because I always hear of Chinese dying." Fear of crime forcefully imprints on experiences of place and race, permeating all aspects of everyday life. A young woman explained that while walking in Cyrildene Chinatown, "I will be very vigilant, I will definitely keep my distance . . . at least one meter away. . . . This is a street and you will often hear about robberies. I will protect myself. If I see a black person, I will go around [the long way] and not let them come too close."

Charting the points, routes, and itineraries of how migrants moved around Johannesburg elucidates the racial dimensions of everyday life. Chinese did not walk, they drove. Stepping outside the securitized perimeter of a mall or walking two blocks at night in Chinatown were deemed unsafe. From my daily commute, I learned the manifold defensive habits, routes, and rhythms for moving through the city. Traders avoided passing through town at all costs. On my commute, we rarely drove directly through the CBD; rather, we took the long way around through a wealthy white suburb. Chinese migrants adopted commonsense practices related to driving. To avoid being tailed home or held up at a traffic light, they preferred to drive when there were many cars on the road. Bright colors for cars were also avoided because they would make a vehicle easy to track in traffic. Dashboard cameras were popular in China for settling disputes in car accidents. After dashboard footage of an armed robbery on the highway went viral on WeChat, the local use of cameras surged. To conceal Chinese drivers and passengers, tinted windows were common.

Every day for most of a year, I took a fourteen-seat Toyota Quantum minibus from my home in Cyrildene to the China Mall where I worked. Although it took the same route every day, the minibus evaded detection from police and potential hijackers. The passengers were young women workers with no other means of transportation and traders who preferred the safety of this vehicle for commuting with cash. The Toyota Quantum is the ubiquitous South African minibus taxi, which Chinese traders and workers never took because of safety concerns. They referred to minibus taxis as *heiba*, a combination of black (hei) and minibus (zhongba), but often simply called it the "big vehicle" (da che). This vehicle had previously belonged to a security company, and the van's front, sides, and back were prominently marked with its logo. It operated under two guises: because of the expected absence of Chinese in minibus taxis, it concealed the presence of Chinese traders inside; as a private security vehicle, it suggested armed response and surveillance. Racially marked and geographically concentrated, Chinese migrants imagine and experience Johannesburg through vulnerability and risk. The ordinary acts of walking or driving signify how racial imaginaries of Yuebao are lived in daily practice.

As an imagined place, Yuebao coheres around race, crime, and development. Discourses of crime are fundamentally racial. Criminals were always already conceived of as Black, and Africans were viewed as always already criminal. At China Malls, African employees—mostly young undocumented men and women from Malawi and Zimbabwe—were keenly aware of racialized criminalization. As a Malawian worker articulated, "You know when one fish is rotten in the pond, all the fish are rotten. . . . When a Malawian person steals from the Chinese, they say all of them are thieves." Chinese employees also stole things but were treated as exceptions rather than representative of all Chinese.

The pejorative term *black devil* (heigui) circulates at China Malls and calcifies stereotypes of black criminality. Historically, the color black (hei) has shared linguistic associations with darkness, immorality, and illegality (Sautman 1994, 427–28; Hood 2013; Shih 2013c). In modern Chinese racial discourses, Africans have been constructed through blackness and othered as less than human, whether as slaves, beasts, animals, or devils (gui) (Dikötter 1992). More recently in China, the term *black devil* (heigui) has been used as a racial epithet in lieu of the term *black people* (heiren).[6] In coastal cities such as Guangzhou, increasing crime has been attributed to "triple illegal" (sanfei) foreigners who enter, work, and reside without legal authorization. Black African migrants, who are often referred to as sanfei heiren, are paradigmatic sanfei foreigners, reifying racial stereotypes of black criminality (Huang 2020; Lan 2017). A translocal process, Chinese discourses on blackness are refashioned as they circulate in new contexts in South Africa. As some traders used these terms interchangeably, I asked a Chinese employee, a woman from Guangdong in her thirties, about the difference between them, to which she answered: "They are the same, black people [heiren] is simply the same as black devil [heigui]. Because black

181

people [heiren] are sometimes very lazy, they like to steal things and rob. We call the annoying ones who steal black devils [heigui]."

In addition to the racialization of crime, imaginaries of Yuebao also center on "disorder" (luan). Like crime, the term *disorder* does not necessarily have a racial meaning, but its usage in Johannesburg does. In my numerous conversations with migrants, crime and disorder mediated their general impressions of Johannesburg. I frequently heard "Johannesburg is a city of disorder," "Johannesburg is not safe," "public security is poor," and "armed robbery is frequent." Disorder carries the meaning of backward, a lack of modernity, and also crime. To give an example of how crime, race, and disorder are intertwined in everyday racialization processes, my boss explained how she learned to profile African employees and visitors:

> This is a very disorderly country [luan guojia]. If you are not careful, you can run into trouble. Whoever comes in—anyone, black women, black workers, black devils [heipo, heigong, heigui]—I will look at their appearance, [listen to] what they say. If they are speaking in a black language [heihua] with our workers, I can tell if they are bad or good. For the most part, I can guess. . . . You have to be very careful. You aren't doing business; you won't feel these suspicions. But we are in the store every day doing business and are scared. . . . Many Black people are bad.

Disorder, crime, and blackness are closely associated. Crime is seen as inevitable in a "disorderly country," similar in meaning to an "underdeveloped country." Animated by fear, migrants' sense of victimhood legitimates racial ideologies and racist practices while obscuring them as such. Yinghong Chen's insights are apt here: "Chinese are racially supersensitive and superinsensitive at the same time. The paradox continues a history with China as a victim of foreign racism while denying its own racism" (2011, 575).

Representations of Yuebao as a disorderly place-in-the-world are grounded in Eurocentric narratives about development and colonialism in South Africa. Even as most Chinese migrants were not versed in South African history, a common strain of thought praised whites for their role in "developing" South Africa's governance, industry, and infrastructure, the hallmark of Chinese development projects in African countries past and present. Here are two examples of how ideas of development and race crystallize in dominant narratives of world history. One wholesaler of Chinese medicinal teas from Dongbei expounded: "A century of British colonialism was, in my mind, ultimately correct. It was right to have Western countries control with

Western ideology and culture. . . . Look at the black government, it's getting worse and worse. . . . It's best to have white people govern the country. You cannot leave South Africa to black people because they are not as smart as Western people." Chinese migrants in Johannesburg's ideas of race were shaped by social media about African migrants in Chinese cities. A Chinese netizen, commenting on African migrants in Guangzhou, makes a similar point: "Blacks are simply a low-level race. . . . When white people ruled South Africa and social resources were in the white people's hands, all various aspects of South Africa achieved great development! But after Mandela overthrew white rule . . . there's almost no social control development and the violence rate has increased daily!!"[7] These comments gesture toward emerging Chinese ideologies of race and changing world orders. Across these views are racist ideologies about white superiority and black inferiority, and a narrative of modernization under colonialism and postapartheid decline. Whereas white rule brought modern infrastructure, economic development, and social order, the transition from apartheid to democracy resulted in increasing violent crime, social disorder, and urban decay. When talking about disorder and poor public safety, migrants often lambasted the predominantly Black street-level police over the failure to protect them or investigate incidents. To them, the police were the everyday face of a dysfunctional government incapable of enacting law and order, reinforcing a narrative of disorder after 1994.

While these racial ideologies are dominant, Chinese racial beliefs are not monolithic. A more egalitarian-minded minority—often younger, more educated, and from urban backgrounds in China—distanced themselves from discourses of racial superiority. While also sharing concerns about crime, they acknowledged they were "making money from black people" (zhuan heiren de qian), which demanded a level of humility. A woman from Guanxi who had been wholesaling in Johannesburg for a decade explained: "Many bosses really like saying 'heigui,' but you are in a black country [heiren de guojia] and you cannot disrespect them. Black people will sometimes steal stuff, but there's no way to change that. . . . A lot of bosses act like they are savages [chusheng] because armed robberies [qiangjie] and stealing are often committed by black people." Even as racist beliefs about black criminality remained intact, they were not overtly expressed. As another woman from Hubei framed it, "For me, I thank South African people because these people let me earn money, so I must be very kind to this country, to this country's people. But only some Chinese people think this way."

183

To summarize, in South Africa, migrants bring with them racial ideologies and lexicons from China that take on new meaning in new contexts. The language of blackness and disorder, already freighted with historical ideologies of race and development, assemble with media representations and circulate in everyday conversations, subsequently producing new racial knowledge. Racialization processes and ideas about inferiority, superiority, colonialization, and modernity are heterogeneous and complex. Chinese migrants are both agents of racism and racialized. They are a racially marked entrepreneurial community. I grappled with reconciling my interlocutors' real sense of vulnerability to crime and homesickness with the harshness of racist perceptions and practices. Perhaps a steadfast belief in Chinese racial superiority became a way to make sense of a new social terrain, one that was already highly racialized, and to counter a feeling of victimhood. As most migrants continue to see the United States at the top of the global hierarchy, a sense of racial superiority reconciles their quest for upward mobility with a sense of downward mobility as migrant entrepreneurs and workers in South Africa.

Conclusion

In this chapter, I use worlding as an approach to underscore the multiplicity of Chinese worlds and the co-constitution of world- and race-making. "China" is far from being a single entity, constituted through heterogeneous flows, actors, spaces, and histories that intersect, run parallel to, and contradict one another at various scales. Economic growth throughout the Global South has created new consumer markets for Chinese goods, demand for infrastructure, and opportunities for investment. Johannesburg is a place that attracts a range of economic actors from private firms building factories to international delegations crafting trade policy to first-time entrepreneurs selling plastic goods. Even as they all variously symbolize the Rise of China in South Africa, rarely do they cross paths. Chinese trajectories of people and capital "from above" and "from below" in South Africa are more often parallel to one another rather than intersecting. Ironically, ordinary Chinese migrants take part in a new China-centric world order, even as they were pushed out of China's globalizing market economy back home.

Akin to earlier generations of Chinese sojourners in search of gold on the Witwatersrand, Chinese migrants search for an elusive fortune in the frontier of South Africa—and a frontier it is with its real and imagined promise and danger. Migrant mobilities are produced from the uneven modernization of China and its resulting class inequalities, aspirations for mobility, and flexible mobilities as well as the emergence of markets in the Global South to sell Chinese goods to working-class South Africans with their own aspirations of attaining the good life. For those with limited social, cultural, and economic capital, Johannesburg is an accessible destination when cities in North America, Europe, and Australia are out of reach. While framing China-Africa relations as "South-South" is contested, ordinary traders might be meaningfully and contingently framed within the rubric of "south-south" through their lateral trajectories from margin to margin, albeit margins of different scales.

Migrants' interactions with the city are entangled with racial discourses and imaginaries from China, which are remade through the racial processes of how everyday life is lived. As Chinese migrants go to Johannesburg, they do not merely imagine an emerging market but also a "developing" African country. Grounded in dominant Han Chinese discourses about race and development, imaginaries of crime and disorder transform Johannesburg into Yuebao, influencing the most banal aspects of everyday life and powerfully mediating experiences of place and difference. Chinese worldmaking in Johannesburg is more than a story of class or geopolitics; race is constitutive of Yuebao. Looking forward, as the Chinese state intensifies its engagements with African countries and the Global South, Chinese worlds will proliferate, and so will racial imaginaries, practices, and discourses.

Notes

1 Harrison, Moyo, and Yang 2012, 918–19; Ufrieda Ho, "The Arch Angel of Booming Chinatown," *Mail and Guardian*, July 12, 2013.
2 This chapter is based on sixteen months of fieldwork between 2013 and 2020 in South Africa. The names of people and most places have been changed. Translations are my own.
3 Ho, "Arch Angel."
4 When I returned in 2020, the turn to online commerce had made business even more competitive in China. I heard anecdotes of several traders who went back to China with their earnings from Johannesburg, only to return after being scammed or not being able to cut it in the new e-commerce environment.
5 See "South African Overseas Chinese Security Warning Video" (Chinese Embassy in South Africa 2015).
6 Scholars have noted, "There is no Chinese translation for the highly derogatory English ["N-word"]. However, 'black devil,' functions in Chinese in a

185

similar, intensely derogatory way" and is only used to describe men. In an analysis of online comments on Africans in China from Chinese netizens, African women were never referred to as "black devils" (Pfafman, Carpenter, and Tang 2015, 548, 551).

7 This quote is from "Africans in Guangzhou: Opportunities and Discrimination" (2011) on the online news aggregator ChinaSMACK (Pfafman, Carpenter, and Tang 2015, 547).

A CULTURAL CARTOGRAPHY OF THE SINOPHONE DIASPORA IN SOUTHEAST ASIA

The Cinema of Midi Z

As China continues to expand its economic, political, and even military influence in the East Asian region and the world, one witnesses a worlding process in which Chineseness undergoes a transformation through negotiations across differences. In this regard, the region of Southeast Asia becomes a perfect case for examining such a worlding process. The Sinophone diaspora in this region unfolded for a variety of reasons, though the wave of migration from the 1990s through the early 2020s, mostly driven by economic factors related to global capitalism, becomes even more evident. Here, the term *Sinophone diaspora*, despite controversies over its meaning and implications, is mainly used to indicate the migration of ethnic Chinese to Southeast Asia and its consequences. It thus suggests cultural, national, political, and even economic tensions between ethnic Chinese and local ethnic groups.

Before World War II, ethnic Chinese in Southeast Asia were commonly called Overseas Chinese (or Chinese overseas), implying that they were still "citizens" of China and hence tended to be oriented toward their ancestral land, both politically and culturally (Suryadinata 1997, 19). After the war, when most Southeast Asian countries achieved independence from their former colonizers and the concept of the nation became more consolidated, ethnic Chinese in the region were forced to make a choice among their multiple identities. Their identity has never been a clear-cut issue for these ethnic Chinese, however, and it varies greatly depending on when they migrated, where they live, which school they attend, as well as the various laws and policies that their host nation has imposed on them.

The growing influence of Chinese political and economic power in the region has no doubt intensified the conflicts and gaps that exist between ethnic Chinese and local ethnic groups. For example, Mya Than shows that the "new wave" of ethnic Chinese migrants in Burma (now known officially in English as the Republic of the Union of Myanmar) improved its economic condition and also transformed the landscape of the city of Rangoon. Yet it also brought change to their relationship with native Burmese due to their economic dominance in business (1997, 144). Nevertheless, not all ethnic Chinese have benefited from the wave of migration from the 1990s through the early 2020s driven by global capitalism. Many Chinese migratory workers in this region travel across borders of different nations, legally or illegally, seeking jobs for economic survival and better lives. Leaving their homeland, these workers face the challenges caused by barriers of language, culture, and ethnicity, even as their shared Chinese heritage provides them with hope and support. In this chapter, I will consider how this new phenomenon of the contemporary Sinophone diaspora—shaped by multiplicity and hybridity—should be understood, and how this paradigm should be reconsidered.

Originally from Burma, the Taiwanese film director Midi Z has drawn attention because of the way his films reveal a world rarely seen outside the country. More significantly, Midi Z's personal experiences provide a typical example of the contemporary Sinophone diaspora. Born in Loshio, a city with a large Chinese population located close to the Burma-China border, Midi Z migrated to Taiwan and later obtained Taiwanese citizenship. His cinematic works, largely based on his personal experience, depict the diasporic condition of the Chinese Burmese. His artistic form, which was influenced by Taiwan New Cinema, has also helped him win multiple prizes at international film festivals. This chapter will examine how Midi Z's cinema presents a cultural cartography of the Sinophone diaspora in Southeast Asia, in terms of its content and form.

Midi Z's films offer valuable information about the contemporary Sinophone diaspora. His family belongs to the Chinese Burmese community in Lashio, Burma, whose diasporic history can be traced back several generations to those who migrated from China for various reasons. Apparently, the Chinese Burmese in Lashio share the same language, historical memories, and cultural heritage. Beginning in 2010, Burma underwent a series of political upheavals, and despite political reforms and a process of opening to the world, violent conflicts between different ethnic groups continue to erupt in various regions in Southeast Asia.[1] In Burmese society, Chinese Burmese are a minority, and many suffer from both destitution and discrimination. It is these poor Chinese Burmese that are the subject of Midi Z's cinema.

Jayde Lin Roberts has characterized Chinese Burmese (or Sino-Burmese) in Rangoon as "in-between" people, pointing to their unique "unstable and unbounded" existence (2016, 6). However, this aspect of their existence is relevant not only in Burma but can also be extended to describe Chinese Burmese migratory workers in other regions of Southeast Asia. On one hand, the Chinese features of these populations distinguish them from native Burmese, but on the other hand, this simultaneously allows them to connect easily with Sinitic communities in countries like China, Taiwan, Thailand, and Malaysia. That is to say, their Chinese background not only helps them establish linguistic and cultural bonds in the Sinophone diaspora, but also provides a convenient outlet for their political escape and economic survival. As a result, a network of Sinophone diasporic communities came into being, not only in Burma but also throughout Southeast Asia. From this perspective, what Midi Z's cinema presents is a map of the formation of the Sinophone communities in Southeast Asia.

It is worth noting that this wave of Chinese Burmese migration is largely driven by global capitalism. Therefore, the Sinophone diasporic community in Southeast Asia is bound more by its economic relationship than cultural nostalgia. However, this emphasis on economic linkage does not just highlight the economic factors in an age of globalization; it also foregrounds its cofunctioning role for linguistic, cultural, and political issues.

This particular configuration of the Sinophone diaspora is perfectly illustrated in the form of Midi Z's cinema. Having studied in Taiwan and learned cinematic techniques from Taiwan New Cinema directors such as Hou Hsiao-hsien, Midi Z demonstrates an affinity for Taiwan New Cinema. However, his cinematic semiotics have undergone a transformation in order to depict the devastated condition of the migratory workers in Southeast Asia. Midi Z's films, accordingly, exemplify the development of Sinophone cinema in the sense that the term *Sinophone* suggests a continuous variation in form and style.

What follows is an exploration of various issues relating to the Sinophone diaspora in Midi Z's films. First, by focusing on poor migratory workers, I examine how their visibility illustrates their separation and compartmentalization while establishing their network of relationship in the Sinophone world in Southeast Asia. Second, turning the focus to its cinematic expression in relation to Taiwan New Cinema, I explore how Midi Z's cinema demonstrates the development and transformation of Sinophone cinema as he confronts new problems in the Sinophone world. Finally, drawing on Fredric Jameson's idea of cognitive mapping, I argue that Midi Z's cinema presents a cartography of the Sinophone world as configured through expressing the various viewpoints of these diasporic migratory workers. As a result, filmmaking becomes an "event" whereby Midi Z makes the condition of the Sinophone diaspora in Southeast Asia clearly visible through his cinematic production.

The Poor and Their Fragmented Visibilities

In a nostalgic tone, Midi Z's cinema functions in part as an autobiographical account of his personal experience and his homeland in Burma, as the activities of the Chinese Burmese become the primary focus of his films. His first feature film, *Return to Burma*, depicts a migrant laborer returning home after having spent years working in Taiwan, following the death of a coworker from his village. The camera follows the protagonist on his journey, presenting the contemporary economic conditions of his family, friends, village, and country. Considering the current social and economic conditions, the protagonist cannot decide whether he should stay or go back. The film anticipates the primary concerns of *The Poor* and *Ice Poison*, the other two works in Midi Z's so-called Homecoming trilogy, and his more recent work *The Road to Mandalay*. Each of these later works tells the story of migratory workers. In an interview Midi Z once described how the theme of *Return to Burma* is "universal, drifting, and migratory" (Midi Z 2012b). Highlighting these characters' separation from their homeland, he added that the film "is the epitome of all 'expatriates.'"

The term *expatriates*, in this context, refers to the Chinese Burmese who migrate across national borders, regardless of whether they intend to return to their homeland. The migrants' desire for home and their despair upon returning home preoccupy Midi Z's cinema—best illustrated by *The Road to Mandalay*, which depicts a group of young Chinese Burmese who stow away to Thailand to find jobs. The protagonist soon falls in love with a girl from his original village as the girl and the protagonist both strive in vain to obtain legal documents. However, since they disagree on whether they should return to Burma, the story ends with the protagonist committing suicide after killing his girlfriend. Ultimately, they both died in a foreign land, failing to realize their dreams. The Chinese title of the film, *Zaijian Wacheng* (literally, "goodbye to Mandalay"), reflects the desperate efforts of many migrants to return to Burma. The use of the word *zaijian* (goodbye) in the title suggests that there is only a one-way trip from home. This motif can be observed in nearly all of Midi Z's films, which depict transnational migratory workers victimized by a global capitalism that is further intensified by political turmoil in Burma. The workers find themselves unable to escape from this devastating reality and therefore continue to drift across national borders.

Their migratory routes produce a map of the contemporary Sinophone diaspora driven by the forces of globalization. Chinese Burmese migrate to Thailand, Malaysia, China, Taiwan, and elsewhere, to become construction workers, household help, or even sex workers. This wave of migration is the result of globalization, wherein the labor trade operates parallel to the flow of capital. However, their migration is also marked by a diasporic genealogy that can be traced back to previous generations who also left China for various reasons, including World War II and the Chinese Civil War. This explains why nostalgic yearnings for the Chinese homeland are always visible in Midi Z's films, and why cultural heritage plays a vital role in his work.

In this regard, the *Anlaoyi* (burial shroud) episode in *Ice Poison* is perhaps the clearest example.[2] This episode portrays a dying elderly man waiting for the arrival of his burial shroud, which had previously been prepared but had been left behind in China. The episode is intended to address the central sentiments of the Sinophone diaspora, in the sense that the shroud not only represents a genealogical link with the ancestors but also illustrates a strong nostalgic attachment to the homeland. Ironically, the shroud has disintegrated, so the elders pray to their ancestors to take the old man's spirit back to China upon his death.

That the spirit longs to return to the homeland after death is a belief shared throughout the Sinophone diaspora. In this sense, migrants remain tied to the homeland and do not engage significantly with the local people. Community life seems transient, and their stay in a far-off location is perceived as only temporary. However, this idea is maintained only by the older generations. The same film depicts a contrasting figure, a daughter named Sanmei, who was sold to China as a mail-order bride without her consent, but subsequently returns to Burma and attempts to stay there instead of returning to China. For Sanmei, China is no longer a genealogical or cultural place of origin, but simply a connecting point on the migratory network, like Thailand, Malaysia, Taiwan—any one of which could provide her with a better life and enable her to connect to the outside world.

Despite the fact that China has lost its genealogical and cultural connotations for the Sinophone diaspora, Chinese cultural features remain essential in the networking of the diasporic community. Among these features, language is the most prominent. With the help of Chinese subtitles, the language used by the characters in these films is rendered intelligible to Chinese-speaking viewers, despite the degree to which the language has become hybridized with the local Burmese language. That is to say, their language has extended to join a linguistic family that serves a broader community. This is the function of language in the Sinophone world. It consolidates an approximate community by creating a cultural intimacy and affective affinity in that world then further suggests a wide-ranging community with a similar intimacy and affinity.

Diasporic Chinese often tend to form communities in which they can maintain close ties through the use of Chinese language and customs, and this phenomenon is also evident in Burma. For example, the beginning of *Ice Poison* presents an old farmer and his son walking from the mountain field to the village to visit friends and relatives, and to ask for financial support. The dialogue between these characters vividly demonstrates the interwoven network of genealogical and affective relationships in the Chinese community in a small town in Burma.

It is not surprising that the same language and culture establish an affective and economic bond among those in the Sinophone diasporic community. It should also be noted that language functions to distinguish this group from others in actual living situations. Most of the Chinese Burmese characters in Midi Z's films primarily speak Chinese in their daily lives; they only speak other languages, such as Burmese and Thai, when the situation requires or demands it. Therefore, Midi Z's films depict not a conflict between different languages, but rather a smooth shift from one to another on different occasions. This is particularly evident in the scene in front of the bus station in *Ice Poison*. The protagonist yells in Burmese for customers to ride on his motorcycle taxi, but he suddenly shifts to Chinese when he recognizes that the female protagonist might be ethnically Han, despite her Burmese appearance. Language, therefore, is immediately able to establish an affinity between the two that helps them reach a quick agreement on the price and later a solid collaboration in the drug-trafficking business.

This affective affinity among the members of the diasporic community is evident not only in Burma, but also when individuals are crossing borders. In Midi Z's films, migrants are always crowded into small spaces—jammed into a truck, a small apartment, or a factory dormitory. There is a spontaneous linkage and sympathy between these migrants, not only because of their undocumented status but also because of their Chinese Burmese diasporic identity. They rely on linguistic and cultural bonds to help them connect to the outside world. Indeed, the extensive network of the diasporic Sinophone community across national borders in Southeast Asia is based on such linguistic, cultural, ethnic, and economic connections.

From this perspective, Midi Z's work provides a poignant example with which to examine contemporary scholarship on the concept of the Sinophone. Shu-mei Shih highlights the divergent characteristics of the Sinophone world in relation to language, ethnicity, and culture (Shih 2013a). In Midi Z's films, the language spoken by the Chinese Burmese is not standard Mandarin, but rather a creole featuring a combination of foreign words and local accents. A similar phenomenon can also be found in the films' presentation of cultural heritage. The genealogical and cultural origin alluded to in *Ice Poison*, for instance, suggests that central China is no longer the sole source of authentic cultural tradition, and in this case the relevant cultural origin is a remote area along China's southwestern frontier. This divergent Sinophone world is further augmented by migration routes, as Chinese Burmese continue to migrate farther away to countries like Thailand, Malaysia, and Taiwan, leaving them with few bonds to the Chinese homeland—either physically or spiritually. Clearly, these migration routes are driven not by a yearning for a homeland, but rather by the will to survive.

David Der-wei Wang, meanwhile, offers another aspect of the Sinophone with the concept of "post-loyalism," which describes a paradoxical sentiment that dislodges the loyalist memory while still attaching itself to the loyalist consciousness (2013, 102). This sentiment seems particularly evident, for example, in the *Anlaoyi* episode in *Ice Poison*, where the burial shroud becomes an empty symbol with no practical use. In general, Midi Z's films present the diasporic Chinese Burmese in Southeast Asia who are neither strongly tied to the Chinese homeland nor particularly engaged with the local environment. Local contact between Chinese Burmese and other ethnic groups is rarely observed in cinema, and in Midi Z's works these Chinese

193

Burmese are the objects of discrimination. They appear as if they have been abandoned by society, living in an interstitial space where their memories and dreams merge and become indiscernible to themselves and others.

This motif is best embodied in the short film *The Palace on the Sea*, which depicts a migrant woman wandering on the streets of Kaohsiung, Taiwan, who yearns to return to Burma. She encounters other migrant women from various countries, including Vietnam and Indonesia, who attempt to persuade her to stay. She finally arrives at a palace by the sea where she meets a young man. They seem to be lovers and begin to dance together. With love songs playing in the background, the entire scene appears to be a flashback of a once memorable romance. When this beautiful and enjoyable moment suddenly ends, however, the woman sobs and announces, "It is time to go home," then adds, "Let me go home." A moment later, a Burmese monk appears and begins a chant to give rest to all beings in the universe. Seeing these surreal and fantastic settings, viewers realize that this wandering woman is actually a ghost who is trapped in a foreign city and unable to return to her homeland even after her death.

This scene reveals the paradoxical nature of Sinophone culture that derives from the term itself. With the prefix *Sino-*, the term *Sinophone* refers to all Sinitic-language cultures as well as their related ethnic communities, and suggests the entirety of the Sinophone diaspora. At the same time, the term connotes multiplicity and hybridity, so that Chineseness loses its absolute unity and solidarity. In the same sense, the Sinophone embraces an in-between or a liminal space beyond any fixed boundaries where constant negotiations between disparate ethnic and cultural identities may take place. Therefore, the term *Sinophone* marks a fundamental element pertaining to this phenomenon and appears suitable for describing the unstable and precarious identities of the Sinophone diaspora.

It is worth noting that, unlike the network of the Sinophone world, which is based on elements like language and culture, the diasporic world that Midi Z depicts in his films is shaped primarily by economic factors. In this regard, Midi Z's work is valuable, as it provides vivid images of a more contemporary Chinese Burmese diaspora. Surrendering themselves to migration, these poor villagers become stowaways, drug traffickers, and sex workers, sometimes at the risk of losing their own lives. They suffer from poverty and destitution, making clearly visible the brutality of social injustice and the violence of global capitalism. Apparently, their primary concern in their diasporic situation is not about their cultural identity, but simply their economic survival.

YU-LIN LEE

Midi Z depicts the Chinese Burmese as minorities in terms of their ethnic and cultural identities as well as their economic status. Marginalized and isolated, their social reality is clearly in evidence in Midi Z's films. On the screen, these characters are often restricted to physically limited spaces. For example, stowaways are trapped in a trunk or a room in a small apartment, and teenagers huddle in a small bedroom, chatting about their migratory dreams or gather in a KTV (karaoke TV) room to give a farewell party for their departing friends. The undocumented migrant workers are crowded into a dormitory, factory workplace, and other venues. These spaces seem isolated and divided. Confined as they are in these small spaces, the migrants appear nervous, frightened, and vulnerable. Further, they seem to be constantly under surveillance, not simply because of their illegal status but also because of the businesses in which they are involved, such as smuggling and drug trafficking. The slow movements of the camera unveil the detailed reality of the daily routines of these migrant workers.[3] Positioning his characters in these separate and fragmented spaces, Midi Z's work visually defines the disparate spaces of the Sinophone diaspora in Southeast Asia.

A Cinematic Semiotics and Its Transformation

The preceding discussion shows that the content of Midi Z's cinema presents a version of the contemporary Sinophone diaspora in Southeast Asia wherein Chinese Burmese are characterized as the poor, subjected to continuous migration across multiple national borders. In Midi Z's diasporic configuration, Chinese cultural features function as thresholds that constitute the Chinese diasporic community beyond ethnic and national boundaries, rather than unifying principles that organize the community as a single entity. This configuration is also illustrated by the expression in Midi Z's films, and specifically the constitution of its cinematic semiotics corresponding to its content.

As is well known, Midi Z was mentored by Hou Hsiao-hsien, so it is useful to examine his cinematic presentation in relation to that of the Taiwan New Cinema. For example, based on the concept of DV realism put forward by Lev Manovich, Wan-jui Wang has proposed a genealogical relationship between Midi Z and Taiwan New Cinema directors such as Tsai Ming-liang and Hou Hsiao-hsien (2017, 154–57). However, identifying such a linkage is not to suggest that the aesthetic principles of Taiwan New Cinema necessarily function as standard rules for Midi Z's cinema. Rather, it is to argue that Midi Z has used Taiwan New Cinema as a model from which to develop his own cinematic semiotics. In this sense, the term *Sinophone* carries additional connotations, suggesting that a semiotic transformation is taking place in cinema that mirrors a broader process occurring across the Sinophone world today.

Generally speaking, the images in Midi Z's films are fragmentary and disconnected, and movements are relatively slow. In terms of his actual filming process, Midi Z initially collects images without a specific purpose, then organizes them into stories after the fact. Sometimes, the same sequences are used repeatedly in different works. This practice is perhaps due to limited funding and scarce resources, but in terms of Midi Z's filming process and image composition, his work does invite an interesting comparison to that of Hou Hsiao-hsien.

In an interview, Midi Z remarked, in relation to his first feature film, *Return to Burma*: "I don't even think that can be called a movie, but rather it is a greeting to my home village and my friends. It is more or less a memorandum or a documentary about that condition" (Midi Z 2012b). Indeed, for Midi Z, delivering "a memorandum or a documentary" about the reality of the Chinese Burmese diaspora is the primary concern of his filmmaking. In addition, his aim to document actual reality compels him to experiment with documentary style, namely, to increase the truthfulness of reality and avoid any interventions that would alter it. This intent is clearly realized by his use of static camera shots, tracking shots, and long takes, among other techniques. The static camera and tracking shots allow the viewer to assess the situation of the characters by watching them and listening to them directly. Similarly, the long takes force the viewer to experience the same duration as that of the scene unfolding on the screen, thereby granting the film a greater sense of verisimilitude.

These cinematic techniques are used extensively by Midi Z, and are exemplified by a few scenes at the beginning of *Ice Poison*. The camera focuses on an old farmer accompanied by his son, as they walk down to the village to visit friends and relatives and ask for financial support. After following the duo down the road, the camera later focuses on their tedious and trivial talk with various characters. These scenes seem fragmented and disconnected, but through them the director provides detailed information about the characters' desperate financial condition. It is notable that the static shots are long takes, of which the actual conversation takes up only a few minutes.[4] The use of static shots and long takes is also a distinctive characteristic of Hou Hsiao-hsien's work. In his static shots, Hou uses the deep focus technique to create a space for the manipulation of the mise-en-scène, while disguising the performance of amateur actors. However, Midi Z uses more medium shots that allow the viewer to feel closer to the actors on the screen.

Despite the similarity in their use of cinematic techniques, one can still observe a significant difference between Hou Hsiao-hsien's and Midi Z's work, which perhaps results from their different understanding of history and their distinctive attitudes toward the presentation of reality. With regard to Hou's aesthetic style and his contemplation on history, James Udden comments on his acclaimed historical film, *City of Sadness*:

> It is important to remind ourselves that this is not style for the sake of style, but style for a particular narrative, lyrical, and consequently historical effect. Every shot is a microcosm of the film as a whole: a wealth of details, but with enough room to offer suggestions of the deeper significance without trumpeting them. History seeps slowly and almost imperceptibly through the quotidian mesh. For all the quietude expressed in seemingly frozen vignettes of everyday life, Hou's film is ultimately about unforeseen, shocking and irreversible change at the most intimate level, those changes which occur beneath the grand and often cruel sweeps of history. (2009, 113–14)

If Hou's cinema, as Udden suggests, tends to provide room for contemplating the transience of history in its presentation of reality, Midi Z requires more immediate contact between the viewer and the destitution of the characters. As a result, Midi Z's films are marked by a deep humanitarian concern, urged on by the pressing problems that he communicates as reality.

With respect to Hou's narrational strategies, Udden, in a discussion of one of Hou's early films, *The Boys from Fengkui*, argues that "while episodic, *The Boys from Fengkui* is not simply a random collection of episodes, but has a deeper structure underlying it" (2009, 62). Compared to the "deeper structure" that underpins Hou's cinema, the narrative line of Midi Z's cinema, which is largely influenced by his documentary style, is more a linear progression. Perhaps Midi Z developed this narrative style with the intention of recording the detailed daily lives of migrant workers. Each shot is connected to the next one, each action producing another, until the end of the sequence. This sort of linear narrative may be observed in works such as *Return to Burma*, *Ice Poison*, and *The Road to Mandalay*. Meanwhile, in *The Poor*, the storyline is disrupted and divided into four separate parts with distinctive stories. However, the narrative line remains largely linear—a spiral

197

progression rather than dialectic montages—as the four parts are related to each other. Combined they make the story complete.

Due to limited resources, a restricted budget, and a hostile environment for film production in Burma, filming, for Midi Z, is a meticulous calculation of time and expense. As a result, he has developed a special method to overcome these challenges, which has resulted in his unique style of shooting and editing. He described the process of filming *Ice Poison* as follows: "I kept writing diaries after I learned about the story; I jotted down some important scenes, as well as characters and symbols related to them. I continued writing and arranged them into approximately thirty plots with a few scenes. But when I began to film, however, I forgot all of them. Instead, I filmed them at random. I think that this randomness can be called impromptu" (Midi Z 2014a).

This impromptu approach means that there are no predetermined principles governing characterization, storyline, image organization, and so forth. Like the migrant workers who have very little knowledge about what they are about to encounter, the filming process is unpredictable. This uncertainty describes the condition of the characters in Midi Z's films and also defines the aesthetic style of his composition. The separated and disconnected images relate to each other in random fashion like the events in the characters' lives.

Indeed, this random way of relating disconnected fragmentary images is one of the most noticeable features of Midi Z's cinematic expression. It should be noted as well that his composition style corresponds to his organization of the content. The images concerning personal trivial matters are scattered in various private and public corners, but they connect as the story develops. However, the development of the storyline is still disorienting and sometimes appears to be almost accidental. Lacking a unifying principle that underpins these episodes, Midi Z's filmmaking becomes a progressive procedure wherein disoriented spaces are connected while yet depicting a world without a firm center. These images, however, can be extended endlessly, creating a network that yields a unique cartography of the Sinophone diaspora in Southeast Asia.

In this regard, the extensive network of disconnected images reflects the continuous migration of the Chinese Burmese in Southeast Asia. Migrants depart from a small village and travel to another place in another city or another country but without a particular destination. Just as the presence of these migration routes suggests the existence of a community, the networking of the images can be extended to suggest the entirety of Sinophone cinema. The constant presence of Sinophone popular music in the films intensifies this effect. Similar to the organization of the Sinitic linguistic family, Sinophone popular music hints at a common platform whereby the Sinophone diaspora is able to communicate shared memories and emotions.

In her study of song narration in Chinese-language films, particularly in the work of Edward Yang, Emilie Yueh-yu Yeh points out the role of popular music in shaping the identity of any marginalized group and revealing the emotional structure of a given history (2000, 155–76). The same can be said of Midi Z's work. Wang Wan-jui argues that the use of popular songs in Midi Z's films is closely associated with the formation of Chinese Burmese identity and a nostalgia for a particular historical period (2017, 147–84). It should also be noted that, in addition to Chinese-language songs, Midi Z uses popular Burmese songs—particularly in *Ice Poison*—not only to express the characters' feelings but also to evoke the shared sentiments of an entire generation. Undoubtedly, this combined use of Sinophone and Burmese popular songs that address both Sinophone and Burmese communities further reinforces their hybrid and ambiguous images of who they are—not only to themselves, but also to the movie viewers.

Regardless of its individual or collective values, Midi Z's cinema is dominated by an autobiographical mode.[5] This particular feature does not simply suggest that the content of Midi Z's films is based on his personal experience, but more significantly that the form of its expression takes a temporal framework pertaining to autobiography. This is best exemplified by the structure of *Return to Burma*. The film surveys the village, as the protagonist returns to his homeland after many years' working in Taiwan. The cinematic presentation gives the impression that the protagonist is reviewing his hometown as a whole, including the villagers and the landscape. These images also appear reflective, as the protagonist continues to compare his homeland village to the outside world. Apparently, this survey, as presented by the camera, is less an exotic exploration intended for the viewer than the protagonist's reflection on the past while envisioning a possible future. The village remains unchanged as it existed in the past, and the structure becomes autobiographical in that all the details are distributed along a temporal framework with the present at one end and the past at the other. The presentation of current reality is clearly embedded with memories of the past and imaginations of the future. 199

More significantly, in Midi Z's films his characters are closely associated with the landscape and tied to the present time. In Taiwan New Cinema and especially in Hou's cinematic work, the characters are sometimes removed from the landscape to produce an empty shot wherein the director can reflect on history and reality. However, such empty shots are rarely seen in Midi Z's cinema. Instead, in his films farmers work in fields, and even the stowaways are visible when they're traveling over the landscape. Apparently, Midi Z's concern with the suffering characters and his obsession with their devastated reality eliminates the possibility of an empty setting. It seems that pressing social and economic problems preclude any possible outside world that could offer alternatives and hope. In comparing his style to the calm and graceful approach to history and life found in Taiwan New Cinema, Midi Z once said that, having grown up in Burma, he knew that the Chinese Burmese, including himself, were driven by the desire for survival and thus lacked the softness and gracefulness specific to people living in Taiwan (Ma 2016, 70). His understanding of the Sinophone diaspora seems to relate to the aesthetic expression of his views in his films.

The Cartography of a Divergent World

As I have argued, Midi Z's autobiographical cinema offers a contemporary version of the Chinese Burmese diaspora in Southeast Asia. These Chinese Burmese are migratory workers victimized by global capitalism that is further intensified by local political turmoil. They are forced to leave their homes and continually migrate across national borders. Unable to return to their homeland, they become "permanent expatriates," alienated from and marginalized by modern society, both physically and psychologically. As they continue to negotiate between the new and the old, however, their already hybrid and ambiguous identity is further complicated by a strong sense of societal precarity.

The Burmese diaspora provides a poignant example of the Sinophone. It appears that their migration is characterized by a centrifugal rather than a centripetal tendency. More precisely, the diasporic movement, instead of directing itself toward the Chinese center, disperses elsewhere to form an alternative Sinophone world that exists across both national and ethnic borders. Hence, the so-called Chineseness loses its authentic value, which presumes an authoritative order, and becomes a series of thresholds whereby a new alternative community is created. In other words, Chineseness becomes less a unifying principle that organizes various linguistic and ethnic groups than a set of common features that allow those groups to connect to each other by creating affinities and a different kind of solidarity.

Yet the mechanism operating within this community is not that of a solid sense of either ethnic or cultural identity; rather, it is the logic of living in an economy that secures their own economic survival. It is Southeast Asian migrants' shared Chinese ethnic and cultural heritage that makes the networking of the Sinophone diasporic community possible; however, this community functions more as an outlet for an escape from poverty than offering a sense of cultural belonging. Clearly, what Midi Z's films demonstrate is by no means a diaspora that requires a decisive choice between the migrants' homeland and their current residence. Rather, it communicates a hesitation between departure and return, and this hesitation leads to constant renegotiation between the two, producing an identity that is marked by precariousness.

Through his work, Midi Z has developed a unique cinematic semiotics corresponding to its content. The form of his filmmaking appears fragmented and disoriented, which mirrors the migratory routes of Chinese Burmese in Southeast Asia. That is to say, his films present a map of divergence wherein China no longer functions as the sole authoritative center. One may also argue that the formal expressive structure of Midi Z's cinema presents precisely his concept of the Sinophone diaspora in Southeast Asia.

It is also worth noting the close relationship between Midi Z's work and Taiwan New Cinema, as Midi Z has adopted many of the techniques commonly used by Taiwan New Cinema directors. This affinity attests to the development of Sinophone cinema wherein Taiwan, replacing China, becomes an alternative resource for inspiration. In this regard, the genre of Sinophone cinema obtains further significance. This by no means indicates a set of aesthetic principles that govern the cinematic presentation, but rather one that shares similar cinematic features but still differentiates itself from the standard rules when confronting very different situations. Just as the condition of the contemporary diaspora continues to change, Midi Z's filmmaking is similarly undergoing a process of transformation. This varying nature of the Sinophone condition, no doubt, is exactly what Midi Z is attempting to portray.

Midi Z's cinematic expression can thus be considered as his "cognitive mapping" of the Sinophone diaspora in Southeast Asia, to borrow Fredric Jameson's words. Jameson provides this concept as a new aesthetic form to describe the process by which the subject situates himself in a vast and incomprehensible social totality (1991, 51–52). This concept is therefore suitable for describing Midi Z's art, in which he provides a convenient framework for revealing the destitution of these migratory workers, including himself, by condensing personal experiences and collective memories into present circumstances.

Midi Z's filmmaking offers a special cartography of the Sinophone diaspora in Southeast Asia—not a map with fixed boundaries, but rather a transformational world that is configured via a particular point of view. These diasporic migratory workers share their memories, suffering, and hopes for the future, and through private and trivial talk, a divergent Sinophone world is then imagined. These migrants are marginalized and confined to small spaces, and these disconnected spaces have a direct bearing on how this fragmented Sinophone space can be configured. In other words, a world of multiplicities is created through the various points of view provided by these marginalized migratory workers.

This world of multiplicities is exactly the Sinophone world that Midi Z presents in his films. His primary purpose is to provide a memorandum on contemporary Chinese Burmese, their desperate poverty and forced destiny of migration. The Sinophone diaspora can be traced back many generations and will continue for various reasons to produce an interwoven history that is interspersed and commingled with ethnic conflicts, political clashes, economic development, and much more. In the history of diaspora, perhaps nothing can be considered as truly original or authentic. This is precisely why the concept of the Sinophone is imperative for Chinese diasporic studies.

Midi Z once indicated that his nostalgia has become permanent. It is impossible for him to return to his original home since he has been so influenced by the cultures of other places (Midi Z 2016a). The world remains fragmentary, but also ever more connected. Because of his concern about the Chinese Burmese diaspora, for Midi Z, filmmaking has become an "event" whereby he can make migration visible and the migrants' suffering sensible. Indeed, this focus is the most significant contribution of Midi Z's filmmaking to the world.

Notes

1 A set of political reforms was put in place by the military regime known as the Union Solidarity and Development Party. Their major political rival, the National League for Democracy led by Aung San Suu Kyi, won the majority of seats in the Assembly of the Union (BBC 2015).

2 The *Anlaoyi* episode was originally a short film, *Anlaoyi*, that Midi Z produced in 2012. This film was combined with other short films by various directors from Southeast Asia, including Tsai Ming-liang, Aditya Assarat, and others, to become *Letters from the South*. All of these short films are concerned with Sinophone diaspora issues. The film *Ice Poison* was actually developed from this short film. See Midi Z 2015, 87–94.

3 This sense of being under surveillance is related to the social atmosphere in Burma and also results from the filming process. Midi Z describes in detail how they filmed the bus station episode in *Ice Poison* by positioning the camera on top of a building in front of the station to avoid any attention from the crowd or interference by the police. See Midi Z's memoir of his filmmaking career, *Ju li bingdu* (2015, 98–106). Midi Z often films images in secret, which may contribute to the particular aesthetic of his work. In addition, due to the political climate in Burma, Melissa Mei-Lin Chan argues that the nature of surveillance should be taken into consideration when analyzing Midi's cinematic works to develop what she regards as an "intermediality" approach (2017, 13).

4 This verisimilitude is of course not the same as "truth." Midi Z himself distinguished between the two in an interview by stating that "art concerns itself with truth rather than reality; the latter is concerned about method and strategies" (Ma 2016, 69).

5 This mode of autobiography is also seen in Taiwan New Cinema and especially in Hou Hsiao-hsien's early works. See, for example, Yeh and Darrell 2005, 146–57.

A Cultural Cartography

WRITING SOUTH

Narratives of Homeland
and Diaspora in Southeast Asia

The Malaysian Chinese author Ng Kim Chew's 2015 short story "Benediction" (Zhufu) opens with a rather curious homecoming scene. The narrator, Xiao Nan, has just arrived in Malaysia with the ashes of her recently deceased father. It turns out that her father—whose full given name is Zaifa, but whom I will refer to here as Ah Fa—was born and grew up in British Malaya, but in the 1950s he was arrested due to his ties to the Malayan Communist Party (MCP) and sent to China. During the midcentury period, the MCP had been an insurrectionist force that challenged British imperial control over Malaya, as a result of which many ethnically Chinese MCP supporters like Ah Fa were often arrested and forced to relocate to mainland China. The narrator notes that her father's relocation was officially described as an act of "repatriation" (qianfan), to which she exclaims, "Heavens, but the South Seas was his birthplace!"

When he was repatriated to China, Ah Fa had to leave his girlfriend, Xiao Lan ("Little Orchid"), behind. Although neither of them realized it at the time, it turned out that Xiao Lan was already pregnant with Ah Fa's child. Consequently, after he was sent away, she married another man, so as not to have to raise the child alone. While he was in China, meanwhile, Ah Fa eventually married another woman and had a daughter—whose name, Xiao

Nan ("Little South"), presumably reflected Ah Fa's continued attachment to the South Seas region he regarded as his true homeland. In fact, over the following decades Ah Fa repeatedly attempted to return home, but was consistently denied a visa by the Malaysian Embassy on account of his previous ties to the MCP. In the end, it was only after his death that Xiao Nan, now an adult, was able to fulfill her father's lifelong dream and return his remains to his homeland.

The story's opening homecoming scene is notable because it challenges a popular narrative that views all "overseas Chinese" as diasporic subjects separated from their Chinese homeland. Instead, "Benediction" revolves around an ethnically Chinese man who regards *China itself* as a diasporic space, and the South Seas region as his true homeland. Taking Ng's story as my starting point, I will consider a set of interwoven narratives of homeland and diaspora, particularly as they relate to Southeast Asian communities of ethnic Chinese. The concept of a diaspora is nominally predicated on the idea of a people's separation from their homeland, though the concept of a homeland itself is often retrospectively constructed based on a set of contemporary imperatives. Accordingly, once the putative homeland comes to be perceived as a diasporic space, it becomes possible to reimagine what might otherwise be viewed as a diasporic space, and instead see it as a new homeland.

Ng's title tropes on the title of Lu Xun's 1924 short story "Benediction" (Zhufu, also translated as "New Year's Sacrifice"), which opens with the narrator's return to the town of Luchen, which he regards as his "homeland" (guxiang)—though he immediately notes that "although I call it my hometown, I already had no home there" (Lu Xun [1981] 2018, 5). During his visit the narrator stays with some distant members of his Lu clan, and happens to run into one of the family's former servants—a woman identified simply as Xiang Lin's wife (Xiang Lin sao). When the narrator encounters her, Xiang Lin's wife has already left the Lu clan, and is now eking out a living as a beggar. By this time, the woman has already been twice widowed and has also lost her young child to wolves. When she runs into the narrator in the street, she immediately asks him whether people turn into ghosts after they die. The narrator is troubled by the fact that he is unable to answer her question and, later, is further disturbed to learn that she had passed away that same day. The remainder of the story offers a retrospective of the woman's tragic life, describing how she repeatedly found herself displaced from one provisional home after another. Mirroring the narrator's disillusioned return to his own "homeland" ("I already had no home there"), Xiang Lin's wife finds herself in a situation where she has no home that she can truly call her own. Although she experiences multiple alienated "homecomings" (returning several times to her in-laws' home and to the Lu clan), the story implies that, in the end, she can only look forward to the afterlife as a true return to her origins.

Ng's "Benediction," meanwhile, opens with a similar homecoming—with a description of the trip Xiao Nan has just taken from China to Malaysia:

> Leaving my snowy and bitter cold hometown, I flew south, covering a distance of more than three thousand *li*.
>
> My purpose was to visit my father's homeland in the tropics, right next to the equator. (Ng 2015b, 18)

This journey from what Xiao Nan calls her hometown (jiaxiang) to her father's homeland (guxiang) captures the key geographic and conceptual gap at the heart of the story since it marks Xiao Nan's first visit to an ancestral "fatherland" from which she appears to feel deeply alienated while at the same time finally permitting her father (in the form of his cremated remains) to return to the homeland to which for decades he had been barred from visiting.

Although Lu Xun's "Zhufu" and Ng Kim Chew's short stories titled "Zhufu" both revolve around moments of alienated homecoming, they diverge from one another in several important respects. Whereas in Lu Xun's story the narrator is returning to a hometown that he remembers well but from which he nevertheless feels deeply alienated, the father and daughter in Ng Kim Chew's story are, technically, not really returning to their homeland at all—for the daughter, Xiao Nan, this is because this is her first time visiting Malaysia, and for her father, whose ashes Xiao Nan has brought with her, this is because he has already died. As a result, the binome *zhufu* in both story titles comes to have a different significance, and even a different meaning.

While the binome *zhufu* could be rendered as "benediction," it could also be translated more literally as "wishing good fortune," with the character *fu* meaning "fortune." The term *zhufu* is thematized at three different points in the story. I will consider each of these discussions in order, together with their broader implications for the relationship between diaspora and the process of localization.

Benediction

The first reference to the term *zhufu* occurs near the beginning of the story, immediately after the opening airport scene. In a flashback, the narrator recalls how, among the things that her father took with him when he was repatriated to China, the only things that were preserved were a book and a letter. The book was a copy of the Western Bible that her father's girlfriend Ah Lan had given him before he left. Inside the Bible she had carved out a hole, into which she had hidden a copy of Mao Zedong's 1938 volume *On Protracted War*. From the latter volume, meanwhile, she had cut out several pages, then carefully sewn in their place a letter she had written "on similar paper, using a similar font, and in a similar handwriting" (Ng 2015b, 19). Xiao Lan then stitched the English word *BIBLE* in large white letters on the front, and in the lower right-hand corner, in red characters, the binome *zhufu*, which in this context could be translated as "wishing [you] good fortune."

In hiding her letter to Ah Fa inside a political volume that would be deemed acceptable within China, and then hiding that volume within a second religious volume that "was the only kind of book that was accepted in British prisons at the time" (Ng 2015b, 19), Xiao Lan was attempting to prepare for any eventuality. More generally, this juxtaposition of references to the Bible and to Mao's *On Protracted War* alludes to two overlapping and mutually contestatory internationalist logics: namely, the logic of British imperialism, on one hand, and of international socialism, on the other. In 1946 Britain established the Malayan Union, which brought together under a single unified administration several different territories that Britain had colonized between the eighteenth and the early twentieth century, including what are now Malaysia and Singapore. The Malayan Union was then replaced by the Malayan Federation in 1948, and secured independence in 1958. In the midcentury period, accordingly, British Malaya was part of Great Britain's broader imperial project, which sought to use the narrative of spreading civilization (which, in turn, was grounded in an underlying logic of Christian evangelism) in order to justify its use of military force to politically subjugate and economically exploit local communities. Conversely, the MCP, challenging British rule in Malaya, saw itself as part of the global movement of international socialism, which worked across national borders to pursue socialist objectives. Although international socialism was not grounded in the sort of military coercion that had been deployed in European imperialism, in the midcentury period international communist organizations such as the MCP were perceived as aiding the expansion of the sphere of influence of Communist states such as the USSR and the PRC, and consequently came to play an important role in the ongoing Cold War conflict. Ultimately, it was out of the overt tension between these two distinct globalizing forces—together with the particular worlding visions on which they were each predicated—that Malaysia emerged as an independent nation.

Returning to "Benediction," Ah Lan's letter itself was neither religious nor particularly political; instead, the passage reproduced in Ng's story contains Xiao Lan's assertion that she will never regret her relationship with Ah Fa, and she adds that if it turns out she is pregnant with his child, she would find another man to marry her and raise the child on his behalf. In the note, in other words, Xiao Lan is affirming her loyalty and devotion to Ah Fa by promising to marry someone else in his place. Moreover, as is revealed later in the story, Xiao Lan's eventual husband's given name was Yongfa, but after he married Xiao Lan, he changed his name to Ah Fu. Xiao Lan subsequently speculates to Xiao Nan that "perhaps he saw that sorrowful '*zhufu*' note that I sent your father" (Ng 2015b, 36). The suggestion, in other words, is that Xiao Lan's new husband, whose name already mirrored that of Ah Fa (Zaifa), deliberately picked a new name that was inspired by her final message to Ah Fa before his departure—thereby underscoring both his status as Ah Fa's replacement, as well as his wife's continued attachment to her former lover. If we consider Lan's attachment to Ah Fa as analogous to a diasporic subject's attachment to an ancestral homeland, then in renaming himself Ah Fu, Yongfa is implicitly positioning himself as a symbol of diasporic nostalgia (Lan's continued yearning for the absent Ah Fa) as well as a process of figurative localization (Lan's decision to establish a new family with Ah Fu, given her inability to be with Ah Fa).

Meanwhile, the second (indirect) reference to the term *zhufu* occurs when Xiao Hong takes Xiao Nan home to meet her family, and Xiao Nan meets Ah Fu for the first time. When she sees him, she is startled to discover that both of his legs have been amputated below the knee. Ah Fu promptly leads Xiao Nan to his study, which is filled with countless different editions of Lu Xun's works and numerous scrolls featuring Lu Xun's distinctive calligraphy:

> The library on the third floor left me truly astonished, and upon stepping inside I couldn't help crying out in surprise, asking how could this be? How could it bear such a resemblance, such that it was as if I had arrived at a Lu Xun memorial museum?

Lu Xun's postmortem portrait was hanging on the wall (the one with whiskers, while in the memorial museum itself there was a photograph of Lu Xun's Japanese instructor Fujino Genkuro), and on the bookshelves next to the wall there was an array of different editions of Lu Xun's works, including a Japanese-language edition of his complete works. On one of the bookshelves there was a volume of *Lu Xun's Handwritten Manuscripts*, and on one of the walls there were several handwritten by Lu Xun himself. (Ng 2015b, 24)

Just as Xiao Nan is wondering how Ah Fu could possibly have obtained so many of the famous author's inscriptions, Ah Fu chortles and says, "Hahaha, that's right. These were all written by me!" (Ng 2015b, 25).

It turns out that after his legs were amputated as a result of a war injury, Ah Fu began to devote himself to studying calligraphy and became particularly interested in imitating Lu Xun's calligraphic writing. The implication is that, for Ah Fu, practicing calligraphy functions as a symbolic compensation for his lost legs, and also perhaps more generally for his lost ties to a Chinese homeland. His own relationship to China, however, is complicated by the fact that the story gives no indication that he ever visited the mainland, and his emotional investment in the region's literature and culture appears to have developed entirely abroad. The ersatz quality of his simulated Lu Xun memorial museum, accordingly, mirrors his presumptive attachment to a Chinese homeland, insofar as they are both virtual simulacra created after the fact. And although "Benediction" (Zhufu) is not among the Lu Xun titles listed in the story's detailed description of Ah Fu's Lu Xun study, its absence could be seen as a virtual presence in its own right—given that this is one of Lu Xun's best-known works. Moreover, the title is the inspiration for Ng Kim Chew's own story.

Finally, the story's third thematization of the term *zhufu* relates not to Ah Fu, but rather to Xiao Nan's father, Ah Fa. In particular, even as it was a set of international Cold War tensions that led to Ah Fa's arrest in Malaysia and his subsequent repatriation to China, his situation remained complicated even after his "return" to China. First, he was sent to a labor reeducation camp in Henan Province during the anti-Rightist movement in the late 1950s. After he was released, however, he decided to remain in Henan—having realized that there he was "in closest proximity to Han culture's excavation site" (Ng 2015b, 31). Ah Fa is referring to the fact that it was in this region that all the oracle bone artifacts had been discovered, and he adds that, while it was

209

unusual to find shells and scapula with actual inscriptions on them, peasants would nevertheless frequently dig up blank Shang dynasty shells and scapula while ploughing their fields. Taking inspiration from the region's historical significance, Ah Fa taught himself oracle bone script and devoted himself to writing in this ancient script.

Initially, Ah Fa focused on rewriting lines from Mao Zedong's poems into oracle bone script. During the Cultural Revolution, however, the Red Guards confiscated both his Bible and these oracle bone inscriptions. The authorities initially assumed that the oracle bone inscriptions were authentic, recently excavated artifacts, but when they sent them to a museum to be examined by experts, the experts discovered that the texts were actually all passages from Mao Zedong's poems. They were, therefore, forwarded to Chairman Mao himself, who initially did not know whether to laugh or cry at the sight of his own poetry in the form of oracle bone inscriptions. When he saw the line "The sky is high, the clouds are pale / We watch the wild geese vanish southward" (tiangao yundan, wangduan nanfei yan), however, Mao smiled and remarked, "A southern man yearns for home, why should we find this strange?" (nanren sixiang, hebi jianguai?).

The lines in question were taken from Mao Zedong's famous 1935 poem, "Mount Liupan" (Liupan shan), which Mao had composed during the Long March to offer encouragement to the Red Army soldiers struggling to make their way north to Yan'an. While the poem's most famous line is the third one, "If we fail to reach the Great Wall, we are not real men" (budao changcheng fei haohan), which explicitly stresses the soldiers' northward march, Ah Fa instead cites the poem's first two lines, which describe the geese's southern migration. Mao Zedong's response to Ah Fa's version of the "Mount Liupan" poem, in turn, acknowledges Ah Fa's reorientation of the poem's original emphasis on northward movement, to an affirmation of Ah Fa's sense of displacement and his yearning for his homeland in the South.

Even as Chairman Mao appeared to validate the sentiment expressed in Ah Fa's inscription, however, he nevertheless found it odd to see lines from his own poems written in oracle bones script, so he encouraged Ah Fa to focus his energies on inscribing text taken from Lu Xun's works instead. Ah Fa agreed to do this, but given that he was uninterested in Lu Xun's old-style poems, and the corpus of Lu Xun's fiction and essays was simply too large to copy in any meaningful fashion, he settled for using oracle bone script to inscribe just *the titles* of Lu Xun's various works. Over time, he found himself returning repeatedly to the two characters *zhufu* that make up the Chinese title of Lu Xun's story "Benediction." Over and over again, Ah Fa wrote this binome in oracle bone script, presumably in response to Xiao Lan's use of the same term in her final message to him (in the cover of the book containing her secret letter). It is these same inscribed artifacts that the narrator brought with her to give to Xiao Lan, whom she addresses as "Auntie Lan," and her father's other Malaysia-based relatives.

Ah Fu's fascination with Lu Xun's calligraphy, meanwhile, is mirrored by Xiao Nan's father's interest in ancient oracle bone inscriptions. Visiting her father's relatives in Malaysia, Xiao Nan gives them a pair of tortoise shells on which he had etched oracle bone–style inscriptions. One of the shells has the traditional oracle bone script version of the characters for the binome *zhufu*, while the other has the simplified oracle bone script version of the same two characters. Xiao Nan observes that the simplified oracle bone script version of the character *zhu* 祝 in *zhufu* lacks the left-hand " 示" radical, leaving only the right-hand 兄 character, which means "elder" brother but is also an honorific term for a man. Therefore, she concludes, the resulting inscription "leav[es] only a man wishing heaven good fortune" (zhi shengxia yige xiangtian zhufu de ren). She notes parenthetically that her father had repeatedly exclaimed, "Look, what a lonely person that is, kneeling on the ground of the fatherland, with nothing to support him, facing the heavens with his mouth wide open." Although Xiao Nan questions the accuracy of her father's etymological analysis, his explanation nevertheless offers a compelling commentary on his own displaced status during the final decades of his life—trapped in his presumptive fatherland, the Chinese mainland, and unable to return to the region that *he* regards as his true homeland: Malaysia.

Near the end of the story, Xiao Nan remarks to Auntie Lan that it is curious that both Ah Fa and Ah Fu (which is to say, both Auntie Lan's original lover and her eventual husband) ended up devoting themselves to copying out text by Lu Xun, to which Auntie Lan replies, "We revolutionary youth were all deeply familiar with Lu Xun's works." She also notes that not only did both men become invested in recopying Lu Xun's text but they also happened to have almost identical names—Ah Fa's full given name being Zaifa 再發 (Prosper again) and Ah Fu's original given name being Yongfa 永發 (Prosper forever). Xiao Lan explains to the narrator that the Chinese people (Huaren) all hope that their children will "prosper" (facai), and therefore they would often give them these sorts of economically aspirational names—which is why revolutionary youth often ended up changing their names to something more politically progressive. Moreover, just as Ah Fa and Ah Fu are positioned in the story as mirror images of one another, the men's respective fascination with oracle bone script and with Lu Xun's calligraphy similarly reflects two inverse understandings of the concepts of diaspora and homeland. While Lu Xun's calligraphy appears to represent the Malaysia-based Ah Fu's nostalgic attachment to a mainland China that he has probably never visited in person, Shang dynasty oracle bone script is used to express the China-based Ah Fa's alienated relationship with his presumptive fatherland and, by extension, his continued attachment to the South Seas region to which he is unable to return.

Textual Traditions

In "Benediction," the attention given to Shang dynasty divination practices and to Lu Xun's calligraphic practices builds on a set of thematic concerns with oracle bone script and May Fourth literature that runs through much of Ng Kim Chew's oeuvre. In fact, these two interwoven themes are introduced as early as Ng's 1990 short story "The Disappearance of M" (M *de shizong*), which Ng wrote near the very beginning of his literary career. The story revolves around the recent publication of a mysterious novel titled *Kristmas*, which one character in the story compares to Joyce's *Ulysses*; another character notes that the work, while written mostly in English, also features an array of other languages "including both modern Malay and a lot of classical Malay—as well as Javanese, Arabic, Bali, German, French"; and a third character further specifies that "two pages of the novel were written in ancient Chinese oracle bone script!"

Although the novel received rave reviews from critics around the world, no one knows for certain who the author is, since the work was published anonymously, under the initial M. Given that there is suggestive circumstantial evidence that the author may be from Malaysia, and more specifically may be a Malaysian Chinese, Malaysia-based authors and critics become excited by the possibility that the nation may have finally produced a literary work capable of entering the ranks of great world literature. A Malaysian journalist, therefore, undertakes a lengthy investigation to discover who the author is, focusing in particular on Malaysian Chinese authors based either in Malaysia or Taiwan. Although the journalist's investigation proves inconclusive, his search ultimately brings him back to Malaysia where, deep in a rubber forest, he investigates reports of the appearance and subsequent disappearance of a mysterious old man who was apparently a writer, and whom the journalist suspects might have been the author of the anonymous *Kristmas*. During his visit to this remote community, the journalist has two parallel reveries, in the first of which he encounters a man who appears to be the famous May Fourth author Yu Dafu, while in the second he sees a giant golden fish with ancient textual markings on its back, some of which bear a distinct resemblance to oracle bone script. Although Ng's story never clarifies whether either of these reveries has any basis in reality, the implication nevertheless is that they may potentially offer some insight into the origins of the novel *Kristmas* and the identity of its author. In other words, the novel may have been written by the May Fourth author Yu Dafu himself, long after he was presumed to have died—or, alternatively, the work may be the product of a delocalized and quasi-autonomous textual practice resembling that of oracle bone divination rituals.

Throughout his career, Ng Kim Chew has repeatedly returned to both of these themes—May Fourth literature and oracle bone inscriptions. In particular, several of his stories revolve around the author Yu Dafu, who was prominently involved in China's May Fourth Movement in the 1920s before fleeing to Singapore in 1937, where he actively supported the establishment of a local tradition of Chinese-language literature. In 1942, following the Japanese invasion of Singapore, Yu Dafu fled to Sumatra, where he lived incognito for three years until he was ultimately seized by Japanese soldiers one night in 1945. It was widely assumed that he was executed, though his body was never found. Ng's primary interest in his own fictional works, however, appears to be neither Yu Dafu's involvement with China's May Fourth Movement nor his subsequent contributions to the establishment of a Chinese-language literary field in Southeast Asia, but rather the possibility that Yu Dafu might somehow have survived his 1945 abduction and continued living out of sight for decades afterward. In several of his stories, Ng explores different variations of this counterfactual scenario, and in each case the primary evidence for Yu Dafu's continued survival is the discovery of a set of texts or textual fragments that appear to have been authored by the famous May Fourth writer long after his presumptive death.

Conversely, many of Ng's stories also prominently feature oracle bone script—either in the form of allusions to the script itself, discussions of how fictional characters attempt to re-create ancient oracle bone inscription techniques in a contemporary context, or by including reproductions of actual oracle bone graphs pasted into the text of his stories. Some of these allusions

213

are surprisingly detailed, such as in the story "Fish Bones" (Yuhai), which opens with several lengthy epigraphs from academic studies of oracle bone inscriptions, while in other works Ng offers detailed etymologies of individual graphs (as he does in "Benediction"). Oracle bone script, one of the earliest known versions of the Chinese writing system, was used in late Shang dynasty divination practices, wherein queries would be inscribed on tortoise shells and ox scapula, the shells and bones would then be heated until they cracked, and the cracks would be examined and deciphered. Knowledge of this practice, and of the corresponding script, subsequently dropped out of the historical record and remained unknown for millennia—until some inscribed artifacts were rediscovered in rural Henan Province at the end of the nineteenth century. In Ng's works, accordingly, oracle bone script typically carries two mutually opposed sets of connotations, in that it symbolized the historical origins of the Chinese script and the cultural formations that have aggregated around it while at the same time representing a node of alterity at the heart of Chinese cultural formation since they are virtually unintelligible to contemporary readers without specialized training.

In his literary deployment of the themes of Yu Dafu's writings and oracle bone inscriptions, meanwhile, Ng Kim Chew emphasizes their dual qualities of familiarity and unfamiliarity—suggesting that they may serve as a locus of shared identity, but also as a kernel of alterity. In both cases, Ng stresses the capacity of these texts and textual fragments to circulate throughout the territory of China and the Chinese diaspora. He appears particularly fascinated by the possibility that the texts might continue to enjoy a productive afterlife long after their presumed extinction (either in the form of Yu Dafu's possibly "posthumous" writings, as well as his multiple descriptions of modern-day individuals carefully re-creating Shang dynasty oracle bone inscription and divination practices).

It is often suggested that Chinese civilization's ability to maintain a coherent identity over a vast geographic and historical expanse is grounded in the relative coherence of the Chinese language. Of course, what is commonly called the Chinese language is actually an assemblage of many different dialects. Moreover, given that many of these dialects are mutually unintelligible, in linguistic terms they are more accurately classified as distinct languages— meaning, in turn, that "Chinese" is more properly classified as a metalanguage. While the argument is often made that the existence of the common written script effectively anchors the language's common identity, this claim sidesteps the fact that different versions of the Chinese written script are sometimes used to render different dialects. While each of these scripts uses Chinese characters, for many common words they use a set of unusual characters that are no longer used in modern Chinese—meaning that a Chinese reader unfamiliar with the dialect or its writing conventions could have considerable difficulty in making sense of the text. To the extent that the Chinese language helps arrest Chinese culture's centripetal tendencies as it moves forward through time and radiates outward through space, accordingly, it does so despite being an inherently heterogeneous assemblage that has its own centripetal tendencies.

Shu-mei Shih has recently considered the relationship between the concept of diaspora and what she calls the Sinophone. In particular, she is interested in the role of language (and specifically Sinitic languages) as a ground for collective identity while also critically interrogating the concept of diaspora (and specifically a Chinese diaspora). Shih contends that the concept of diaspora, particularly as used in a Chinese context, is reductive insofar as it takes what is ostensibly a national concept ("Chinese") and tacitly redeploys it as an ethnoracial concept ("Han Chinese"). Moreover, she argues that the notion of diaspora also has essentialistic tendencies, insofar as it encourages a view of people as defined by their ethnic identity (and presumptive ancestral origins). In place of the concept of a Chinese diaspora, Shih instead promotes the concept of the Sinophone—which she uses to designate those communities outside of China that aggregate around a shared use of Sinitic languages, or "those ethnic communities within China, where Sinitic languages are either forcefully imposed or willfully adopted" (Shih 2013b, 30).

Shih's critique that, in the Chinese case, the concept of diaspora is actually an ethnoracial phenomenon masquerading as a national one is somewhat misleading, however, since this is actually the default understanding of the concept of diaspora itself. No one assumes that the Jewish diaspora or the African diaspora, for instance, are anything but ethnoracial configurations, and the apparent ambiguity that Shih points to in the Chinese case is a result of the fact that, in English, the adjective *Chinese* is polysemous and can be used to refer to an ethnoracially, culturally, or nationally grounded identity. Her proposal to focus more narrowly on Chinese language communities, meanwhile, is indeed useful, and she correctly points out that this linguistic focus sidesteps the presumption of a nostalgic attachment to a homeland that is arguably implicit in the concept of diaspora. Shih observes that while some Sinophone communities use the Chinese language to reinforce their perceived ties to the (Chinese) homeland, others instead use the language to assert their separation and independence from the Chinese mainland.

Even as she advocates the use of the concept of the Sinophone in place of the concept of a Chinese diaspora, however, Shih simultaneously argues that the concepts of diaspora and a linguistic community must have an "end date." In the case of a linguistic community like the Sinophone, Shih argues that "when the descendants of immigrants no longer speak their ancestors' languages, they are no longer part of the Sinophone community" (Shih 2013b, 37). Given that the Sinophone is explicitly defined as a language-based community, it seems perfectly reasonable that once this criterion is no longer present, the community as such would cease to exist. Somewhat more peculiar, however, is Shih's parallel specification that a diaspora (a concept that she is attempting to "debunk") must similarly have an end date, arguing that "when the (im)migrants settle and become localized, many choose to end their state of diaspora by the second or third generation. The so-called 'nostalgia' for the ancestral land is often an indication or displacement of difficulties of localization, voluntary or involuntary. . . . Emphasizing that diaspora has an end date is therefore to insist that cultural and political practice is always place-based. Everyone should be given a chance to become a local" (Shih 2013b, 37). Apart from the fact that it seems odd that Shih, here, is trying to offer a more narrow definition of a concept that she is ostensibly attempting to reject altogether (her article is titled "Against Diaspora"), this specification is also curious on account of its simultaneous emphasis on a kind voluntarism (suggesting that immigrants may "*choose* to end their state of diaspora") as well as on what appears to be a sort of false consciousness (implying that what the immigrants themselves might perceive to be a nostalgia for the ancestral homeland may, in fact, be a product of their "difficulties of localization"). If an immigrant's "choice" to become a local can itself result in a displaced nostalgic identification with the ancestral homeland, then how can one claim that the process of regional identification is fully under the immigrants' voluntary control?

While the argument that a people should not be perpetually defined by the geographic associations of their ethnoracial ancestry is well taken, the break between a diasporic identity and a local one is probably not as clear-cut as Shih implies here. Indeed, it is probably quite common for individuals to have dual investments in both the region where they currently reside (as "locals") *and* the region they identify as their ancestral homeland (as diasporic subjects). Moreover, the fact that the "difficulties of localization" might spur a displaced nostalgia for an ancestral homeland does not make the nostalgic yearning and corresponding diasporic identification any less real.

Indeed, diasporic identities and orientations are often driven by a wide array of factors. In addition to the possibility that diasporic nostalgia may be encouraged by the difficulties of assimilation, it is also possible for this sort of nostalgic identification to be actively encouraged by the country from which the individuals immigrated in the first place. For instance, during the latter half of the twentieth century, the governments of both the PRC, in Beijing, and the ROC, in Taipei, have gone to considerable effort to create and support the diasporic category of "Overseas Chinese," and to encourage expatriate Chinese and their descendants to maintain a meaningful relationship with the Chinese nation.[1] Indeed, Ng Kim Chew's personal trajectory (having gone to Taiwan for college and graduate school, later securing a job there, and having recently become a naturalized Taiwan citizen) was facilitated by the Taiwan government's outreach to ethnic Chinese living abroad, just as Ah Fa's "repatriation," in the story "Benediction," was similarly facilitated by the mainland Chinese government's favorable policies toward overseas Chinese. On the other hand, it was also a set of internal PRC policies that led to Ah Fa's internment in a reeducation camp upon his return. This undoubtedly contributed to his inability to fully assimilate to his adopted nation, with the result being that he became positioned as a diasporic Chinese subject *within China itself*.

In this respect, it would be useful to return to Shih's specification that the concept of the Sinophone, under her formulation, applies both to Chinese-language communities living outside of mainland China as well as to "those ethnic communities within China, where Sinitic languages are either forcefully imposed or willfully adopted." Although in context it is clear that she means "ethnic *minority* communities within China" (since *all* communities, after all, have an ethnic dimension), her formulation here is, nevertheless, quite instructive. In particular, Shih clearly wants to exclude the majority Han Chinese communities in mainland China from her concept of the Sinophone (as opposed to some usages of "world Huawen literature," which may include Chinese-language literature from both inside and outside of China), but it is nevertheless true that at least some Han communities within China could be considered not only Sinophone but also more specifically diasporic. For instance, Ah Fa, in Ng's story, is presumably ethnically Han, but it is nevertheless quite clear that he feels he is a diasporic subject in mainland China and yearns to return to what he views as his homeland: Malaysia.

217

Coda

When Xiao Nan travels to Malaysia to return her father's ashes, her father's relatives decide not to tell his mother (Xiao Nan's grandmother) that her son has died because they did not want to upset her unnecessarily. At the end of the story, accordingly, we find Xiao Nan chatting with her grandmother as though her father were still alive back in China. In particular, Xiao Nan gives her grandmother a giant tortoise shell that her father had completely filled with oracle bone script graphs—including an assortment of "pictographic and associative graphs" (xiangxing huiyi zi), which "resembled a primordial forest before the beginning of civilization" (xiang wenming kaishi zhiqian de yuanshi conglin). The grandmother, however, derives great pleasure from reading this chaotic text, finding that she can recognize and read every graph. Xiao Nan, meanwhile, notes that her father had claimed that this particular shell must have come from a "South Seas tortoise" (nanyang gui) since the northern tortoises found in mainland China did not grow this large. In other stories, Ng similarly remarks on the fact that even some of the original Shang dynasty oracle bone inscriptions were carved on the shells of tortoises that must have come from the South Seas region.[2] The attendant symbolism is poignant, insofar as oracle bone script inscriptions derive from China's heartland (Henan Province is located in the center of what is known as China's Central Plains [zhongyuan] region) while the giant tortoise shells apparently originated from the Nanyang (literally, "South Seas") region on the southern periphery of mainland China.

A fascination with the Nanyang region runs through much of Ng's work, with most of his stories being set either in Malaysia, Singapore, Taiwan, or other South Seas regions. In his 2013 short story collection, *Memorandum of the People's Republic of the South Seas* (*Nanyang renmin gongheguo beiwanglu*) (2013a), Ng explores the counterfactual possibility that the MCP had ultimately succeeded in establishing its own People's Republic in the South Seas territories that were previously British Malaya. In his chapter for this volume, meanwhile, Ng considers a different sort of South Seas republic—a "world republic of southern [Chinese] letters."[3] Troping on Pascale Casanova's notion of a world republic of letters, which she uses to describe a set of authors and literary works that have been vetted by globally recognized literary institutions, and particularly ones based in Paris, London, and New York, Ng suggests that the literary field of the Sinophone South Seas region is one wherein the most relevant center is not Europe but rather China

(Casanova 2007). Ng argues that while it is true that some South Seas authors have been successfully introduced into the mainland Chinese literary market, many instead emphasize their distinctive content, dialect, and style in order to resist assimilation by the hegemonic Chinese mainland and avoid being reduced to the status of figurative vassals of the Chinese state. The result is the precise inverse of Casanova's characterization of authors associated with minor literatures seeking validation by an acknowledged literary center, where authors positioned within a nominally marginal literary field strive instead to maintain their distinctive positionality at the periphery of these globalizing formations.

The Chinese term that Ng uses for "the South," *nanfang* 南方, also has another set of connotations that are relevant to the analysis developed here. In particular, in late imperial China, the term *nanfeng* 南風, or "southern style," was sometimes used as a euphemism for the homophonic term *nanfeng* 男風—which literally means "male style," and was used to refer to male same-sex desire and sexual relations. Although there is no indication that Ng's use of the term *nanfang* was intended to invoke this queer concept of *nanfeng*, his vision of a Sinophone South has distinctly queer characteristics. Apart from the polymorphously perverse erotic subplots that run through many of Ng's works (including sexual practices ranging from onanism to zoophilia), his stories also frequently interrogate conventional assumptions about heredity, foregrounding lines of affinity that are grounded not on biological ancestry but rather on contingent sociality. Ng's stories frequently thematize processes of adoption, surrogacy, and even semen donation—all of which point to the potential divergence between heteronormative assumptions about kinship being grounded on patrilineal lines of descent, and more "queer" configurations of socially grounded family structures.

One of the queerest moments in "Benediction" is a scene that has nothing to do with sexual desire per se, or even with reproduction and kinship, but rather pertains to processes of disassociation and reassociation. In particular, in the lower right-hand corner of each of the tortoise shells carrying the characters *zhufu* 祝福 (benediction) that Ah Fa had prepared for his relatives, he inscribed a tiny "footprint" (jiaoyin)—which is to say, an oracle bone graph for "foot" (*zu* 足). He inscribed this graph in a variety of different orientations, such that the collection of virtual "footprints" resembled a haphazard path. When Auntie Lan sees this trail of virtual footprints, she immediately begins sobbing abjectly—and once she is finally able to recollect herself, she remarks, "The world originally did not have a path, but as

219

people walk through it . . ." (shijian benlai jiu meiyou lu, dan ren zouduole jiu . . .). Here, Auntie Lan is quoting a slightly modified version of a famous line from Lu Xun's story "My Hometown" (Guxiang),[4] and the term used here for "path" is the same one that appears in the short epigraph that opens Ng's story: "*Women cheng zhi wei lu de, qishi buguo shi panghuang.*"

The epigraph in question comes from Kafka's *The Zürau Aphorisms*, which Ng quotes here via George Steiner's essay "Silence and the Poet" (which was published in Steiner's 1967 collection *Language and Silence*). Although Steiner's English translation of Kafka's aphorism ("What we call the way is hesitation")[5] uses the *way* to render the German word *Weg* (with which it shares a common etymological root), a better rendering would arguably be the more concrete *path*,[6] which also happens to be an apt translation of the Chinese word *lu* 路—the term that Ng uses to translate *Weg/way* in the epigraph, and the term that appears in both Lu Xun's original line from "My Hometown" and in Auntie Lan's paraphrase of the line.

The trajectory from the Kafka epigraph at the beginning of the story ("what we call the path, is hesitation") to the citation of Lu Xun's line near the end ("the world originally did not have a path, but as people walk through it . . .) invites a focus on paths as contingent products of movement and as meaningful sites in their own right. To borrow James Clifford's terminology, Ng's story suggests that, over time, empty spaces may develop into routes, which in turn may ultimately develop into new roots. Given that there are preexisting paths to follow, however, prior to the formation of these paths there is merely a space of hesitation.[7] This hesitation, in other words, is the space of diaspora, wherein subjects often find themselves pulled in opposite directions by attachments (real or desired) to both an absent homeland and a present locale.

Notes

1　For a recent discussion of this phenomenon, see Shelly Chan 2018.
2　See, for instance, Ng's story "Fish Bones" (Ng 2016b, 96–120).
3　Ng originally presented this essay as a lecture in 2016. See Ng 2016a. An abbreviated translation of a revised version of this essay appears in this volume.
4　The original version of Lu Xun's line is "shishang ben meiyou lu, zoude ren duole ye jiu chengle lu."
5　The full aphorism is "There is a goal, but no way. What we call the way is hesitation." Kafka's original German is "Es gibt ein Ziel, aber keinen Weg; was wir Weg nennen, ist Zögern."

CARLOS ROJAS

6 Several German-English dictionaries list "path" as the first definition for the German *Weg*. See, for instance, *Collins German-English Dictionary* and the online *Dict.cc German-English Dictionary*.

7 The word that Ng uses to translate Kafka's term *Zögern*, rendered by Steiner as *hesitation*, is *panghuang*, which is the title of Lu Xun's second collection of short stories.

THE CHINESE LITERARY IMAGINARY AND THE GLOBAL SOUTH IN DEEP TIME

This chapter engages with the problematic of China and the Global South by focusing on the ties between China and India within the complex geography of inter-Asian exchange and the long history of Chinese migration to Southeast Asia. As the historian Tansen Sen reminds us, the interactions between China and India took place "among various groups of people, some of whom lived in these two regions and others who operated from intermediary areas and distant parts of the world" (2017, 5). Focusing on Sinophone Malayan literature, this chapter posits Southeast Asia as a mediatory node in this connection and aims to create a dialogue between Sinophone literary studies and the discourse of the Global South.[1] Although these two critical discourses have different disciplinary roots, articulating them could fruitfully enrich and add nuance to our understanding of both China and the developing world—the so-called Global South.

Echoing the editors' emphasis on "the centrality of history, culture, and imaginative processes" in China's engagement with the Global South, this chapter examines two moments in the twentieth century: the first in the early decades and the second in the middle of the twentieth century. Whereas the first moment of China's engagement with the Global South marked a literary and cultural relation based on a worldview of civilizational and humanistic interchange, the second moment was premised on third world internationalism and decolonization that inspired what Prasenjit Duara has called the "convergent comparisons" among China, India, and the newly independent Southeast Asian nations.[2] In both moments, as I will demonstrate, Sinophone culture practiced by ethnic and diasporic Chinese constitutes an important dimension that remains unacknowledged due to the privileged attention given to state-initiated policies and state actors in most discussions of China and the Global South.

The existing scholarship about the ties between China and India tends to present this connection as a civilizational dialogue. This tone was largely set by Rabindranath Tagore, whose travels to China in the 1920s have occupied a central role in many accounts of China-India exchange, particularly those with a focus on the twentieth century (Tsui 2010; Sen 2017; Gvili 2018). Despite some pushback from Chinese cultural radicals such as Chen Duxiu, whom Tagore encountered in his 1924 and 1929 visits to China, Sen has shown that a belief in the civilizational unity between India and China and the idea of "Asia as One" was widespread among intellectuals and revolutionaries regardless of their political orientation or cultural background (Sen 2017, chap. 4). Tagore's culturalist Pan-Asianism materialized in his founding of Visva-Bharati University and Cheena-Bhavana (the Institute for Chinese Language and Culture) in Santiniketan, West Bengal. His Chinese follower and long-term collaborator, Tan Yunshan, a scholar who also served as a political intermediary between the Nationalist government and the Indian National Congress, has gotten as much critical attention as Tagore himself.

This chapter examines the Chinese writer Zeng Shengti, a figure who has hitherto been marginalized in discussions of China-India exchange. Zeng visited Tagore's Santiniketan a few years before Tan and stayed in Gandhi's Satyagraha Ashram for an extended period in 1925. His experience in India provided a good occasion for considering Southeast Asia's important mediatory role in the centuries-old history of China-India exchange. In fact, Zeng had many similarities with Tagore's well-known Chinese collaborator—Tan Yunshan. Both of them worked as teachers in the Chinese schools in Malaya. Tan's first meeting with Tagore took place in British Malaya during Tagore's visit in 1927, when Tagore met several other important figures such as Lim Boon Keng, a Western-educated Chinese community leader well-known for

223

his promotion of Confucianism in Southeast Asia. Tan was a prolific writer of essays and short stories and had edited a literary supplement of the Chinese newspaper *Lat Pau* in Singapore. This means that the China-India connection was far from just a two-way exchange, but involved other places and actors. My study shows that the moral and spiritual power embodied by a charismatic figure like Gandhi inspired Zeng Shengti's empathetic identification with both India and, at a later stage, the coolies in Southeast Asia.

A sustaining preoccupation in Sinophone literature throughout the twentieth century has to do with the "global subaltern"—a dominant figure of the Global South, according to Alfred López.[3] Ethical identification with such a figure facilitates the cultural and political linkage between the earlier twentieth century and the midcentury that witnessed the Non-Aligned Movement and the birth of the so-called third world. At the moment when the supposedly timeless "civilizational dialogue" between China and India gave way to the political alliance between nonaligned nations, Southeast Asia also played a significant mediatory role. I will show, through a close examination of a second Sinophone Malayan writer, Wei Beihua, that Sinophone literature can be viewed as an integral part of what Amir Mufti calls Bandung humanities, which supplements standard accounts of the Bandung Conference in 1955 and the cultural exchanges established thereafter. These accounts generally feature state leaders such as India's prime minister Jawaharlal Nehru or the Chinese premier Zhou Enlai. In fact, the Chinese diaspora's rich supply of nonstate actors and Southeast Asia's geographical position as a node of connection between China and the Global South mediated interstate relations in ways that go beyond official state or international infrastructures.

At the same time, however, when we focus on the Chinese diaspora in the times of decolonization in Southeast Asia, we find that "China" may well be a deterritorialized concept, with its boundaries bleeding into other sovereign states, languages, and cultures. Even the significance of the word *diaspora* is debatable in reference to Chinese communities there. This means that the *China and the Global South* inquiry would yield not just two-way cultural traffic between two countries, but a network of relationality across the Global South. This diffusion, decentralization, and even disappearance of "China" testifies to what Dipesh Chakrabarty has called a "dialogic side of decolonization," which produced "a plural tradition of the humanities" as part of the legacy of Bandung (2010, 64).

SHUANG SHEN

Zeng Shengti was not a native of British Malaya. Born in 1901 in Chaozhou, in China's Guangdong Province, he first went to Singapore in 1922, working there as a teacher in a local Chinese school until his departure for India in 1924. He returned to Singapore in 1927 after a short stay in China and remained there until the end of the Asia-Pacific War. According to the historian Yang Songnian, the period from 1927 to 1933 witnessed a boom of Chinese-language publications in British Malaya, together with the emergence of an active polemical attempt to infuse "*Nanyang* color" (Nanyang secai— "Nanyang" refers to "southern seas," a Chinese term for Southeast Asia) into Chinese literature, with which Zeng Shengti is frequently associated (Yang Songnian 2001, chap. 4). Yet most available discussions of the aesthetics of *Nanyang* color and the broader category of Sinophone Malayan literature follow a diffusion model that prioritizes the influence of May Fourth literature from mainland China. Referring to the spread of Romanticism in the late 1920s, for instance, Yang Songnian states that "the cultural polemics and aesthetic styles [from China] deeply influenced the Malayan literary circles at the time, particularly the romanticist fervor of the Creation Society" (2001, 55). Zeng himself did not deny the impact of May Fourth culture on his worldview, but he presented a more complex trajectory of cultural circulation and transfusion than the dyadic route between the homeland and the diaspora, or from the West to the East.

In a Chinese-language memoir about his Indian experience entitled *Zai Gandi xiansheng zuoyou* (translated into English as *By the Side of Bapu*), published first in Shanghai and then in Singapore in the early 1940s, Zeng explained that his decision to go to India was inspired by the Chinese poet Su Manshu, whom he also credited with introducing the British poet Byron into China. In addition, Zeng claimed that he "had an additional encouragement from the visit to China by the Indian poet, Rabindranath Tagore": "He brought us poems rich in Indian style, such as 'Gitanjali', 'Flying birds' and 'Short stories' he selected himself. His works drowned me in the fanciful imagination of thick jungles, snow-clad mountains, hermits, bushy beards, turbans and buddhas" (1959, 23–24).[4] These statements from Zeng's memoir show that both British Romanticism (Byron, for instance) and Indian poetry (represented by Tagore) influenced the May Fourth Romanticists. In addition, the Chinese writers' expectations of India were informed and mediated as much by orientalist mystification of India as by Asian religions such as

225

Buddhism. Just as Zeng was unclear about what he had set out to look for in India—Byron's Greece or the spiritual home cherished by the poet-turned-Buddhist monk Su Manshu—his stay at Gandhi's ashram in the 1920s was motivated by a combination of political and spiritual reasons.[5]

The moral power of Gandhi was widely commented on by Chinese visitors to India in the early twentieth century, among them Tan Yunshan and Zeng Shengti. In a 1948 issue of the *Sino-Indian Journal* commemorating Mahatma Gandhi, for instance, Tan Yunshan wrote that "to the Chinese Buddhists, Gandhi is the living Ti-Tsang or Ksitigarbha of India to-day, one of the group of the eight Dhyani-Bodhisattvas whose role it is to save all the creatures between the Nirvana of Sakyamuni Buddha and the advent of Maitreya, as described in a Mahayana Buddhist scripture" (1948, 20–21). Viewing Gandhi from a religious perspective, Tan emphasizes "his noble spirit" and "illustrious virtue" and sees the "political movements initiated by him, the success he has achieved and the pacific means he adopted" as secondary. Tan further likens Gandhi's spiritualism to that of the Chinese Confucian sage Mozi [Mo-Tsu], stating, "[Mozi's] doctrine of 'Chine-Ai' or 'Love All', and 'Fei-Kung' or 'Non-Aggression' is exactly like Gandhiji's principle of 'Ahimsa' or 'Non-Violence.' Gandhiji's spirit of self-sacrifice is also exactly like Mo-Tsu's. It was said that Mo-Tsu would grind himself from the top of his head to the bottom of his feet if it would be beneficial to the world" (20–21). Similar comparisons between the teachings of Gandhi and those of Buddha also appear in a eulogy for Gandhi published in the same issue written by Dai Jitao, the Nationalist government official and right-wing ideologue who helped Tan secure funding for the establishment of Cheena-Bhavana.

In contrast with these philosophical and religious intercultural translations of Gandhi, Zeng was more outspoken about the ongoing political struggles in India, which contextualized both his 1920s trip to India and his return trip in 1943. In the preface, he declared that he wrote this memoir to demonstrate his support for the fast that Gandhi was undertaking in order to bring an end to the communal riots at that time. He then provided a detailed account of the political goals and agendas that motivated Gandhi's fasts, but argued that "each time Gandhiji undertook a fast, it had something to do with politics. Yet to argue, as most people do, that fasting was his political strategy is not quite accurate. His fasting is a connotation of the lofty ideals of the human spirit and embodiment of unwavering truths. It is not limited to a spiritual protest in the political dimension" (1959, 6–7). The memoir contains many accounts of the political beliefs and struggles of Gandhi's followers who also resided in the ashram, but Zeng emphasizes in the preface that this book was written not to provide a "factual account" (shilu) about politics, but to "express my feelings" (shuling) (1). For Zeng, as for Gandhi, emotion, interiority, and the self were inseparable from communal ethical values and collective political goals. Thus, he devoted a large portion of the memoir to descriptions of self-cultivation, including taking lessons in Sanskrit, Hindustani, and English, performing manual labor, and observing and practicing the religious rituals at the Satyagraha Ashram, all of which Zeng believed greatly shaped his sense of self.

The memoir can be interpreted as an illustration of what David Der-wei Wang has termed the "poetics and politics of Chinese interiority," although Wang does not go into much detail about the inter-Asia exchange that informed the Chinese lyrical expressions of the twentieth century (D. D. Wang 2015). As we know, Tagore was a major influence on Chinese Romantic writers such as Bing Xin, Xu Zhimo, and Guo Moruo (C. Tan 1998), and as Gal Gvili shrewdly argues, using Bing Xin's poetry as a case study, what Chinese poets and Tagore had in common was their shared interest in religion, specifically how "poetry mediates a religious connection between man and the universe via emotional stimulation" (2018, 199). But besides providing yet another illustration of religion's impact on the conceptualization of the self and emotions, Zeng's exchange with Gandhi further brought out the ethical dimensions of this "poetics and politics of Chinese interiority," underscoring that such practices as the renunciation of material comfort and self-reliance were not solipsistic pursuits, but had a significant social impact and therefore were equivalent to a political agenda.

Although Zeng identified with India's struggles of decolonization and was moved by the moral power of Gandhi, he recognized that there existed vast cultural and social differences between India and China. Thus, the more he came to know India, the more deeply the lyrical speaker of the memoir expressed feelings of "emptiness," "vastness," and "sadness," particularly when he remembered China's wars and struggles:

> At times, I recalled sadly the artillery raging thousands of miles away in my homeland, and immediately, scenes of fleeing, homeless refugees appeared before me. In my homeland, I had my parents, brothers and sisters and good friends. They might now be in the midst of sufferings and miseries. . . .
>
> My loneliness was reflected in my weekly letter to Bapu. In his reply, which came quite soon, he comforted and encouraged me. (1959, 59)

227

Other distractions, such as the desire for Western commodities and modern comfort, also occasionally got in the way of spiritual pursuits. Zeng called these distractions "xin mo"—"the heart's demons"—a phrase that alludes to the protagonists of the classical Chinese novel *Journey to the West*, especially Monkey, whose free-floating mind and carnal desires have to be tamed in order to attain redemption and enlightenment.

Zeng practiced intercultural translation, which allowed him to understand India's anticolonialist struggles through the lens of Chinese history and moral philosophy. For instance, he described the activists at the ashram as "Woxinchangdan de aiguo zhishi" 卧薪尝胆的爱国志士 (hay-sleeping, gall-tasting patriotic warriors), evoking a Chinese metaphor of enduring hardship in order to seek revenge, but emphasizing that they were different from "the Chinese King of Yue Gou Jian" because they "were not seeking after revenge, but to attain their independent free will through non-violent means" (1959, 51). He also rendered the culture at the ashram into more familiar Chinese terms, writing: "To me, the ashram was neither a school nor a revolutionary organization. Nor was it a dull, lonely monastery. It was a harmonious large family with its own set of unwritten rules. This family had integrated itself with the great love of ancient Indian philosophy. When you stayed in the ashram, you only thought it was ordinary. But when you were about to leave, you began to realize the power of its love" (1959, 131). Zeng's description of the ashram as a "harmonious large family," while echoing the Confucian analogy that sees a parallel between the home and the state, also implies the boundedness of this family—for, despite Zeng's own efforts and his friendships with Gandhi and other Indians, India and China were not seamlessly united or integrated into one common political or spiritual universal. As a believer in and follower of Tagore's pan-Asianist ideals, Zeng nevertheless bears witness to the complexity of intercultural exchange where linguistic and cultural difference, the specificities of each local political situation, and different Asian modernities, each with its own blending of East and West, modern and traditional, intersected with their shared political goals of anti-imperialism and nationalism.

Yet it would be simplistic to assume that Zeng's practice of Gandhian self-cultivation had no impact on his life or aesthetics after he left India. Both his Indian memoir and Malayan short stories demonstrate his knack for *shuqing*—lyricism, manifested in terms of his use of emotive language as well as his eschewing of direct depictions of characters' external social conditions in favor of presenting their psychology. The same focus on interiority bridges the memoir about his Indian experience and his literary practices in Malaya, with his immersion in and witnessing of the political and ethical pursuits of the Indian anticolonial activists, adding another ethical dimension to the depictions of coolies in his short stories.

After he returned to Malaya, Zeng Shengti, together with his brothers Zeng Yuyang and Zeng Huading, wrote many stories depicting Chinese coolie laborers and the anti-imperialist struggles of indigenous people in Borneo. In one short story, "Sheng yu zui" (To live and to sin), for instance, Zeng Shengti focuses on a rickshaw coolie who, having just had his cart destroyed by a speeding vehicle, returns home empty-handed to face his pregnant wife and five hungry children. Desperate to feed his family, he leaves the house and decides that he will rob someone to obtain money for food. In his very first attempt, however, he is caught by the police, which is how the story ends. Zeng's lyricism in this story and others exhibits a tension between a highly emotive narratorial voice and the characters who are brought into being by this voice, as if it were an apostrophic address in lyrical poetry. In Jonathan Culler's discussion of lyrical poetry, he explains that apostrophe refers to the practice of using the second person to directly address an absent, dead, or inanimate being, as in the first line of Shelley's poem "Ode to the West Wind": "O wild West Wind, thou breath of Autumn's being." Culler argues that the apostrophic structure captures an ethical dilemma in which the act of calling into being inanimate objects may be akin to "peopling the universe with fragments of the self" or "internaliz[ing] what might have been external," resulting, in other words, in "radical interiorization and solipsism" (2007, 162). Although Zeng's short stories usually adopt a third-person rather than a second-person perspective, given that the language is emotionally charged and has a lyrical quality, the relationship between the narrative voice and the characters is therefore akin to the speaker of lyrical poetry addressing an object constituted through an apostrophic address.

The plot of "To Live and To Sin" is rendered more complex by its language, which comes across as subjective, emotional, and syntactically experimental. It seems as though the language constantly calls attention to itself and becomes a subject of representation rather than a mere medium, as seen, for instance, in the following passage:

> He hesitated, looked around, and caught sight of a cold stove that was mocking him, a pot that seemed to be moaning, hanging upturned on the wall, its round bottom reminding him of the protruding belly of Goujian's

229

mother. [Goujian, "dog-cheap," is the nickname of his son.] He wanted to smash this black thing so badly, but he did not do it.

Five sons are like five terrifying bullets, their mother the gun barrel or the artillery factory. She never stopped working! She's just like a bitch, Goujian's dad thought.

他迟疑着，游目所至，冷灶嘲弄着他，锅子呻吟的被反挂在壁上，凸起的弧形多背影，使他联想起狗贱的妈渐渐凸起的肚子。他很想一拳把那漆黑的事物打碎。不过他没有实行。

五个儿子，好像五颗可怕的子弹，狗贱的妈就是制子弹的枪筒，可恨他同时又是制造火药的兵工厂。她不断地工作！她好像一条母狗，狗贱的爷想。(Zeng 2007, 466)

The metaphor of his children as bullets is repeated several times in the story, as is his wife's question "Where is dinner?" The effect of these repetitions is similar to that of an apostrophe, in that the language takes the story out of its narrative sequence, turning a mimetic representation into a "fictive, discursive event" (Culler 2001, 169) whose temporality resides at the moment of enunciation. Culler states, "To apostrophize is to will the state of affairs, to attempt to call it into being by asking inanimate objects to bend themselves to your desire" (154). The language of Zeng's short story connotes a sense of a strong will and subjectiveness that makes this narrative read almost like a poem.

Approaching the lyricism of the story from the perspective of apostrophe forces us to come to terms with an ethical quandary at the heart of this story: the addressee is not something inanimate, an object or nature, but rather a fellow human being. In fact, calling into being a coolie through an apostrophic address of the lyrical voice might betray an underlying perception that this person is almost inanimate. Dog-cheap's father appears to be a silent, stubborn man who utters little more than a single curse throughout the story. He responds not to the poetic speaker, but only to his wife's plea "Where is dinner?" and his children's needs: "Like five yet-to-explode bullets, they have bored their way into his heart" (Zeng 2007, 470). The tension between the lyrical voice and the voiceless subaltern subject of representation is replicated in the relationship between the husband (Goujian's father) and his wife and children. In the passage quoted above, the speaker compares his wife's bulging belly to a black pot, and her womb to a gun barrel. The protagonist strikes us as cruel and misogynistic even when we empathize with his helplessness and vulnerability.

SHUANG SHEN

Culler also argues that an apostrophic address changes the *now* in a narrative sequence into the *now* of a "fictive, discursive event" (2001, 169). It places characters and their actions at "a time of discourse rather than story" (165). In light of this observation, we notice that, in addition to the narrative sequence that depicts a downward spiral following the coolie's bad fortune, the lyrical voice introduces another temporal dimension into the story, that of fate. The second half of the story depicts the protagonist's encounter with the ghost, suggesting the dominance of cosmic time that flattens the distinctions between nature and humans. "Insects are making music. Are they singing a triumphal song or an elegy for Goujian's father?" The first half of the sentence evokes the pastoral convention common in Chinese lyrical poetry at this time. The second half of the sentence "replaces an irreversible temporal disjunction, the move from life to death, with a dialectical alternation between attitudes of mourning and consolation, evocations of absence and presence" (166). The short story can thus be read as an elegy for a nameless coolie as it turns him into an aesthetic object.

Around the time of the composition of "To Live and To Sin," Zeng Shengti was a vocal proponent of "writing Nanyang." He wrote a number of critical treatises imploring other Sinophone writers to take root in Nanyang and treat Nanyang as fertile ground for aesthetic cultivation. For instance, in the opening issue of the literary supplement *Wenyi zhoukan*, which he edited, Zeng wrote that "this literary supplement assigns itself no other task than to find some locally grown nourishment in this sun-bathed tropical land. We are out there not to search for diamonds and jewels to decorate our marble-covered palaces, but to find kindred spirits so that together we can construct a Nanyang cultural tower, in the shade of palm trees and coconut groves, with our own blood and sweat."[6] Another article attributed to Zeng Shengti proposed two concrete suggestions about how to construct "the Nanyang cultural tower": first, to cover and represent Malay culture; and second, to write about the lives of the Chinese overseas and other races. Yang Songnian's survey of this short-lived literary supplement (six months, forty-one issues in total) suggests that these proposals were implemented during the publication's existence (Yang and Zhou 1980, 35). The translation section, which consisted of Malay myths and stories, Indian epics, and Japanese literature rendered into Chinese, had a rather cosmopolitan outlook, befitting the image of Nanyang not as an intellectual backwater passively receiving literary influence from the homeland, but as a cultural crossroads in inter-Asian and global cultural traffic and exchange. Zeng Shengti and his cohort's efforts to "write Nanyang" are lauded by scholars such as Yang Songnian also for their use of dialect. At the same time, however, Zeng's clarion call of "writing Nanyang" registered a sense of disjunction and disparity that was integral to the emplacement of the cosmopolitan sojourner in the local environs. This was partly because Zeng still approached Nanyang from a position that posited it as the margins of the Chinese cultural world. The titles of several literary supplements he edited for Chinese-language newspapers of that time convey this sense of disjunction rather vividly—*Ku dao* (Barren Island), *Huang dao* (Abandoned Island), *Hong ze* (Marshland), *Huang yuan* (Wasteland), and *Hong huang* (Wilderness), among others. The metaphor of Nanyang color already conveys a sense of exoticism in depictions of local characters and subject matter, suggesting that these characters could serve only to add color to a prefabricated tableau. Zeng's various writings and editorial work reflect the influence of his encounter with India and its anticolonial struggles, and the mediatory role Southeast Asia played in facilitating this civilizational exchange between China and India.

Wei Beihua's Nationalist Internationalism

Unlike those involved in China-India interactions in the 1920s, such as Tagore, Tan Yunshan, and Zeng Shengti, the Malayan Sinophone writer Li Xuemin (1923–1961, aka Lu Baiye, Wei Beihua) was not much interested in the spiritual exchange between the two cultures. In his 1959 travelogue *Impressions of India*, he acknowledged "the historical and cultural traffic between India and Malaya," which proved that "Indian civilization has already been an undisputable constituent of the Malay people" (Lu Baiye 1959, 108), but he put more emphasis on the need for writers to be in tune with the "dynamic momentums of the [contemporary] times." For him, the contemporary moment was a time of decolonization and modernization. In contrast to the pan-Asianist consciousness of Tan Yunshan or Zeng Shengti, Lu's Asian consciousness was premised on the recent constitution of the newly independent nation-state of Malaya. His travelogue reflected the worldview of a citizen of a fellow decolonized nation, which looked up to India as a "big brother" and "the paradise of Asia and pride of Asian people" (Lu Baiye 1959, 4).

Li Xuemin, who wrote nonfictional works under the name Lu Baiye and composed literature as Wei Beihua, was born in Ipoh, Malaya. After a lengthy period of exile in Sumatra and Java, Indonesia, and after joining a guerrilla resistance force there during the Asia-Pacific War, he settled in Singapore and worked as a journalist and legal interpreter in the post–World War II period. Lu Baiye was fluent in several languages, including Chinese, Malay, English, and French. His Sinophone practice exhibits a confluence of multiple trajectories of cultural traffic and exchange in an inter-Asian context.

Lu's visit to India differed from Zeng Shengti's travelogue, which focuses exclusively on the Satyagraha Ashram and shows little contact with ordinary Indians other than the followers of Gandhi or students of Tagore. Lu, by contrast, had a busy itinerary that took him through almost the entirety of India since he visited India as a member of a delegation of Singapore and Malaya journalists. Lu Baiye paid particularly close attention to India's development projects, including the Bhakra Nangal Dam and the nuclear plant in Mumbai and Nehru's Five-Year Plans. For Lu Baiye, India was both a model and a mirror for a fellow Asian nation such as Malaya. His perceptions of India confirm Prasenjit Duara's assessment of the post–World War II conceptualization of Asia. Duara observes that, in this period, "the economic energies of the Asian countries in the two camps were directed more toward the nation and the supraregion than the region itself. The congruence between political and cultural realms also came to be directed toward the two loci" (2010, 974).

Lu's identification with the global vision of the third world project, initiated at the Bandung Conference, is clearly visible in *Impressions of India*, particularly in the chapters depicting Jawaharlal Nehru. Although Lu never mentions Bandung in the book, he praises Nehru's foreign policies of nonalignment and argues that "if Asia has obtained some degree of peace and prosperity, at least half of it has to do with India's efforts" (1959, 112). He endorses the economic and political ties established between India and other nascent nation-states in Asia and Africa. For instance, he mentions with great enthusiasm that India has sent military experts to Malaysia and Ghana to help them build up their air forces (5).

His approach to India was related to his conceptualization of the Malayan nation. We can thus inter-reference this travelogue with his other writings and cultural projects pertaining to nation-building in Malaya. Around the same time that he published *Impressions of India*, Lu wrote a history of Malaya, two books of essays recounting anecdotes from Singapore and Malayan history, and *A Practical Malay-Chinese-English Dictionary*. Together with Abdullah Hussain, he also coedited a monthly publication devoted to Malay language instruction. In the preface, Lu explains the rationale of the trilingual dictionary in the following words:

233

For the past two decades, the younger-generation Asians experienced the same dream and pain, wishing for our nations to gain a speedy rebirth, independence and freedom. For this reason, after our homeland Malaya officially became an independent nation in 1957, not only has our soul shed the oppressive heavy burden of centuries, but the national language—Malay—has gained a new life and is fast growing.

Chinese occupy a large percentage in the national population. Thus, Chinese Malayan cultural workers are obligated to shoulder the task of editing a relatively complete Malay-Chinese dictionary in order to respond to the needs of the new society. Since our country has a large population of English-educated members, the editor has decided to add English interpretations [to each word]. (1959, 1)

The preface situates this project in the context of decolonization and nation-building and clearly indicates the different functions that the three languages had in the new Malayan society, with Malay functioning as the national language, Chinese as an ethnic language, and English as the lingua franca for those with English proficiency. Targeting primarily the Chinese community, itself divided by dialect groups, and showing consideration for those readers without reading competence in Chinese, the dictionary manifests as a project of nation-state–anchored cosmopolitanism. This was not necessarily unique to Lu Baiye, but was widely shared among Chinese intellectuals and writers in Malaya at that time.

Impressions of India endorses a cultural worker's desire to participate in postcolonial nation-building. In one chapter of the book devoted to several Asian and Indian writers' conferences held in India between 1956 and 1957, Lu reflects on the relationship of culture to society as that topic was discussed at one conference:

Someone even said at the conference that when a writer writes with the intention to arouse the people's passion and gain their support for a particular national construction project, the work should not be considered as literary. A poem about the building of a dam cannot be called literature. What kind of nonsense is that? . . . Indian writers are witnessing the dynamic motions of social life all around them, they are hearing the beckoning of an exciting era and feeling the pangs of the birth of a new nation. And they are presenting vivid descriptions of the uplifting atmosphere of national development. Those who accuse these writers for serving as the government's mouthpiece must come from an ivory tower themselves, and that's where they should be sent back and buried. (Lu Baiye 1959, 146–47)

The understanding of the relationship of culture and society conveyed in these statements resembles the position of the socialist realist camp. In the context of the Cold War, Lu Baiye staked out his political position as left leaning by frequently alluding in his writings to Soviet literary works such as Nikolai Ostrovsky's *How the Steel Was Tempered*, Mayakovsky's "A Cloud in Trousers," and Konstantin Fedin's *Cities and Years*. According to Zhang Jingyun, who edited Lu's collected works, Lu Baiye "had some general knowledge about modern and contemporary Soviet literature, [a cultural orientation] that refracted his political leaning, particularly in terms of his attitude toward the Communist government in Mainland China" (Zhang 2016, xlvii). Zhang suggests that Lu most likely gained access to Soviet literature through Chinese translation. I would argue that Lu's interest in Soviet literature extended beyond "general knowledge" or political orientation. Soviet modernist aesthetics influenced Lu Baiye's (or Wei Beihua's) sense of the modern, which was in complex ways also intertwined with Indonesian modernism, particularly the works of Chairil Anwar (1922–1949), the poet who "has become synonymous with the Indonesian Revolution" (Lienau 2011, 13). The circulation of Soviet and Russian literature in Chinese translation in Malaya and Singapore is a fascinating story that demands more complex analysis than space allows for here. For all we know, according to an eyewitness account of the anthropologist Yao Souchou, "translated Russian literature published by the Foreign Languages Press of Beijing that was being sold in the shops in Kuala Lumpur" constituted a healthy dose of progressive literature much desired by Chinese students in the 1950s and 1960s: "So we read, with the same studious devotion as we read Chinese classics, in Chinese, works of Chekhov, Dostoevsky, Tolstoy, Turgenev," along with Western literature by "Mark Twain, Charles Dickens, Jules Verne, Theodore Dreiser, Ibsen, Flaubert, Zola and others" (Yao 1997, 205). This cosmopolitan literary culture in Chinese in Malaya, and probably also Indonesia, nourished the modernist literary sensibilities of Wei Beihua.

I offer one example that gives a sense of what must have been an extended network of Russian/Soviet-Sinophone literary exchange in the middle of the twentieth century. The last in a series of poems by Wei Beihua dedicated to

235

the Deli River in Medan, Indonesia, written in 1948, "Futurists" (weilai pai) opens with a line consisting of the title of a poem by Mayakovsky:

A cloud in pants
Blossoming iron trees
Monks joining the military
Scholars working on the farm
Cold moon spewing enraged fire
All for
The life of the nation

穿起裤子的云
开花的铁树
僧侣在参军
读书人在种田
冷月喷出怒火
全是为了
民族的生命

Mayakovsky's poem is an extended monologue dedicated to the speaker's lover, Maria. In contrast Wei Beihua's poem depicts love for the nation, not romantic love. The central message here is rupture or change. Bold images such as "blossoming iron trees" and "cold moon spewing enraged fire" convey a sense of unexpectedness and contrast. Joined with depictions of "monks joining the military" and "scholars working on the farm," they foreshadow and anticipate the toppling of an old world and the birth of a new one. We can associate this new world with the ongoing Indonesian Revolution. Lu chose the Indonesian Revolution as the subject of the poem because of his unusual experience of being part of a guerrilla force in Indonesia from the final years of the Japanese occupation of Southeast Asia until the beginning of the revolution (Zhang 2016, xxi). The extent to which Lu fought in the battles for Indonesia's independence remains unclear, but he wrote a number of short stories, poems, and essays on this subject, where he delved deeply into the multiple and frequently contradictory facets of this decolonization movement, giving attention not just to the revolution's moral appeal but also to the divided responses it elicited from the Chinese communities, the persecution and scapegoating of Indonesian Chinese by some revolutionaries, and the political intrigues and internal power struggles within the movement.

SHUANG SHEN

Wei Beihua's friendship with and influence by the Indonesian poet Chairil Anwar constitutes another dimension of his modernist practice that could easily be overlooked by conventional approaches to Chinese literature. Anwar inspired some of Wei Beihua's cultural projects, such as compiling the trilingual dictionary, and compelled him to adopt a traditional Malay poetic form called *pantum* for his own Sinophone poetry. In a short story titled "Party," Wei Beihua depicts in semifictional terms a bohemian scene at a meeting of a literary society called Ants in Jakarta, a home for "the educated, writers, poets, scholars, and song writers, as well as those who carry guns" (Zhang 2016, 320). Wei Beihua tells us that the members of Ants were "united by a common goal—to cultivate the wasteland [of Indonesia] and build a city of culture there" (320).

In an essay on Sinophone poetry in Malaya, he writes: "It is human nature to want to be new. . . . What is new today will already be old and outdated tomorrow. . . . That is because the 'future' is ahead of our comprehension" (Zhang 2016, 144). In the same essay, he urges Sinophone poets to "bravely take up the role of the pioneer" in their poetic creations (146). Lu Baiye's fascination with the present and newness mirrors that of Anwar, who defines the modern in terms of "a kind of poetic anarchism, a liberal disorder, more in the sense of the modern as avant-garde" (Lienau 2011, 219). Lu and Anwar, along with Mayakovsky, are linked by their sense of contemporariness— the present as the prime time for literature as well as for politics, for as Lu's description shows, the literary scene of Ants was for writers as well as for "those who carry guns." Lu Baiye's multilingual dictionary project and his openness to Indonesian modernism exemplify the multicultural and multilingual worldliness of Southeast Asia, of which the Sinophone and India were integral components.

Conclusion

In a memorable short story titled "One Man's Mountain," Wei Beihua depicts a young Chinese man's heroic sacrifice for the Indonesian Revolution. In the story's second section, Wei provides a brief ethnographic account of the protagonist Tian Feng's cultural and political position in the context of the social condition of the Chinese community in Indonesia and Indonesian society's racist bias against the Chinese. He tells us that the Chinese community was divided with respect to its support for the Indonesian Revolution: "Most of those who opposed Indonesian independence had incurred material losses

237

in the revolution. They in turn hated not just Indonesians, but also Chinese who empathized with Indonesians, treating them as traitors. Tian Feng was of course among those condemned by them" (Zhang 2016, 231–32). Tian Feng's nationalist identification with Indonesia is depicted from an ecological perspective that emphasizes his connection with the Indonesian land. The story in fact opens with a description of deforestation under Japanese rule, which leaves only two trees standing on the mountain where Tian Feng grew up. The story then concludes with a lengthy description of Tian Feng's slow death, showing how his mind gradually wanders from the pain in his broken limbs to focus on the two trees that survived the Japanese invasion. Tian Feng's attachment to the land of Indonesia turns this story into a nationalist allegory told from the perspective of a minority group.

Wei Beihua's inter-Asian literary practice was influenced by ideologies of decolonization and third worldism, and roughly charts a Bandung trajectory · in terms of its connection with India and Indonesia. Given that he grew up in a multilingual and multiracial place such as Malaysia, however, it is not hard to imagine that his interest in other Asian cultures may have been cultivated long before Bandung. Taking up Southeast Asia as the mediatory node of connections between China and the Global South forces us to embrace all articulations of a decentered, diffused, and disappeared "China," even when the nation-state form has become a historical necessity and reality in the entanglement of decolonization and the Cold War. This chapter can be seen as an attempt to extend the Bandung spirit by backdating pan-Asianist concerns with the global subaltern to the early twentieth century and simultaneously foregrounding the role of the Chinese diaspora in facilitating this exchange.

Notes

1 Sinophone studies refers to some recent critical initiatives in Chinese literary studies that attempt to rethink the Chinese literary landscape by focusing on Chinese languages. These initiatives usefully underscore the heterogeneous and discontinuous nature of the "Chinese" and "Chinese-language." See Shih, Tsai, and Bernards 2013.

2 See Duara's introduction in Duara and Perry 2018. "Convergent comparison" refers to moving away from an exclusive focus on national territoriality, and instead comparing subnational and global circulatory forces.

3 I follow Alfred J. López's definition of the Global South as "global subaltern"—"those who have experienced globalization from the bottom" (López 2007, 5).

For López, editor of the journal *The Global South*, calling attention to "how those on the bottom survive" globalization and its aftermath spells out the agenda of Global South studies (7).

4 Citations from *Zai Gandi Xiansheng Zuoyou* are based on the Chinese original. My translations are adapted from the 1982 English translation entitled *By the Side of Bapu*.

5 The name *Shengti* alone already underscores the spiritual overtone of Zeng's visit of India. As Zeng recalls, Gandhi in a discussion with Shengti about wars and the social turmoil in China said, "China needs unity and peace in order to fight against external threats. Now, I will give you the name 'peace.' In future, we'll call you Shanti which means 'peace' in Sanskrit" (Zeng 2007, 49).

6 Zeng Shengti, quoted in Yang Songnian 1998, 41.

WORKS CITED

Adebayo, Kudus Oluwatoyin, and Femi O. Omololu. 2018. "Moving East: Explaining Aspects of Nigerian Trade to China." *Africology: The Journal of Pan African Studies* 11 (May): 169–85.

Adie, W. A. C. 1964. "Chou En-lai on Safari." *China Quarterly* 18:174–94.

Afonja, Simi. 1981. "Changing Modes of Production and the Sexual Division of Labor among the Yoruba." *Signs* 7, no. 2: 299–313.

Africa Program. "President of South Africa Attended the Ribbon-Cutting Ceremony of Chinese Gateway." *Africa Up Close*, October 17, 2013.

Afro-Asian Writers' Bureau. 1968. *The Struggle between the Two Lines in the Afro-Asian Writers' Movement*. Colombo: Afro-Asian Writers' Bureau.

Aira, César. 2011. *El mármol* [The marble]. Buenos Aires: La Bestia Equilátera.

Akyeampong, Emmanuel, and Liang Xu. 2015. "The Three Phases/Faces of China in Independent Africa: Re-Conceptualizing China-Africa Engagement." In *Oxford Handbook of Africa and Economics*, vol. 2, *Policies and Practices*, edited by Celestin Monga and Justin Yifu Lin, 762–79. Oxford: Oxford University Press.

Aminzade, Ronald. 2013a. *Race, Nation, and Citizenship in Postcolonial Africa: The Case of Tanzania*. Cambridge: Cambridge University Press.

Aminzade, Ronald. 2013b. "The Dialectic of Nation Building in Postcolonial Tanzania." *Sociological Quarterly* 54, no. 3: 335–66.

Anderson, Benedict. 2016. *Imagined Communities*. New York: Verso.

Appadurai, Arjun. 2000. "Grassroots Globalization and the Research Imagination." *Public Culture* 12, no. 1: 1–19.

Barlow, Tani. 1993. "Colonialism's Career in Postwar China Studies." *positions: east asia cultures critique* 1, no. 1: 224–67.

Bauer, Péter Támas. 1963. *West African Trade*. London: Routledge and Kegan Paul.

Bayart, Jean-François, and Stephen Ellis. 2000. "Africa in the World: A History of Extraversion." *African Affairs* 99, no. 395: 217–67.

BBC (British Broadcasting Company). 2015. "Timeline: Reforms in Myanmar." *BBC News*, July 8, 2015. http://www.bbc.com/news/world-asia-16546688.

Bertoncello, Brigette, and Sylvie Bredeloup. 2007. "The Emergence of New African 'Trading Posts' in Hong Kong and Guangzhou." *China Perspectives* 1:94–105.

Blaser, Thomas. 2013. "Africa and the Future." *Africa Is a Country*. November 20. https://africasacountry.com/2013/11/africa-and-the-future-an-interview-with-achille-mbembe/.

Bodomo, Adams. 2010. "The African Trading Community in Guangzhou." *China Quarterly* 203:693–707.

Bodomo, Adams, Dewei Che, and Hongjie Dong. 2020. "Calculator Communication in the Markets of Guangzhou and Beyond." *Journal of Multilingual and Multicultural Development*. https://doi.org/10.1080/01434632.2020.1786575.

Bolinaga, Luciano. 2013. *China y el epicentro económico del Pacífico Norte* [China and the economic epicenter of the Northern Pacific]. Buenos Aires: Editorial Teseo, Colección UAI-Investigación.

Bolinaga, Luciano. 2018. "América Latina en la era del Pacífico: Factores condicionantes para las elites locales que participan de la formulación e implementación de la política exterior y comercial" [Latin America in the age of the Pacific: Conditioning factors for local elites who participate in the formulation and implementation of external and commercial politics]. In *Las relaciones entre Sudamérica y Asia-Pacífico en un mundo incierto: Los casos de Argentina, Chile y Brasil* [The relations between South America and the Asia Pacific in an uncertain world: The cases of Argentina, Chile, and Brazil], edited by María Clelia Guiñazú and Alejandro Pelfini, 115–32. Buenos Aires: Facultad Latinoamericana de Ciencias Sociales FLACSO-CICCUS.

Bolinaga, Luciano, and Ariel Slipak. 2015. "El Consenso de Beijing y la reprimarización productiva de América Latina: El caso argentino" [The Beijing Consensus and the reprimarization of the productive structure of Latin America: The case of Argentina]. *Problemas del Desarrollo* 46, no. 183: 47–48.

Bonacich, Edna. 1973. "A Theory of Middleman Minorities." *American Sociological Review* 38, no. 5: 583–94.

Bongiorni, Sara. 2007. *A Year without "Made in China": One Family's True Life Adventure in the Global Economy*. Hoboken, NJ: John Wiley.

Works Cited

Borensztein, Sebastián, dir. 2011. *Un cuento chino* [A Chinese story]. Film.

Brautigam, Deborah. 2003. "Close Encounters: Chinese Business Networks as Industrial Catalysts in Sub-Saharan Africa." *African Affairs* 102, no. 408: 447–67.

Bremner, Lindsay. 2004. "Bounded Spaces: Demographic Anxieties in Post-Apartheid Johannesburg." *Social Identities* 10, no. 4: 455–68.

Bremner, Lindsay. 2010. *Writing the City into Being: Essays on Johannesburg, 1998–2008*. Johannesburg: Fourth Wall Books.

Brennan, James R. 2012. *Taifa: Making Nation and Race in Urban Tanzania*. Athens: Ohio University Press.

Bullard, Nicola. 2012. "Global South." In *Encyclopedia of Global Studies*, edited by Helmut K. Anheier and Mark Juergensmeyer, 724–27. Seattle: SAGE Publications.

Burton, Eric. 2013. ". . . What Tribe Shall We Call Him?: The Indian Diaspora, the State and the Nation in Tanzania since ca. 1850." *Stichproben-Vienna Journal of African Studies*, no. 25: 1–28.

Butler, Judith. 2009. *Frames of War: When Is Life Grievable?* London: Verso.

Carli-Jones, Dorian, and Melissa Lefkowitz, dirs. 2015. *China Remix*. Film.

Carling, Jørgen, and Heidi Østbø Haugen. 2020. "Circumstantial Migration: How Gambian Journeys to China Enrich Migration Theory." *Journal of Ethnic and Migration Studies*. https://doi.org/10.1080/1369183X.2020.1739385.

Casanova, Pascale. 2007. *The World Republic of Letters*. Cambridge, MA: Harvard University Press.

Castillo, Roberto. 2015. "Landscapes of Aspiration in Guangzhou's African Music Scene." *Journal of Current Chinese Affairs* 44, no. 4: 83–115.

Castoriadis, Cornelius. 1987. *The Imaginary Institution of Society*. Translated by Kathleen Blamey. Cambridge, MA: MIT Press.

CCTV (China Central Television). 2014. "Nanfei Zhonguoren yu Maotan Chang jie'an" 南非中國人遇毛毯廠劫案 [South African Chinese people encounter Maotan Chang robbery]. July 25. http://www.youtube.com/watch?v=KXjh688i5DA.

Chakrabarty, Dipesh. 2010. "The Legacies of Bandung: Decolonization and the Politics of Culture." In *Making World after Empire: The Bandung Moment and Its Political Afterlives*, edited by Christopher J. Lee, 45–68. Athens: Ohio University Press.

Chalfin, Brenda. 2000. "Risky Business." *Development and Change* 31:987–1008.

Chan, Melissa Mei-Lin. 2017. "Mail-Order Brides and Methamphetamines: Chinese-Burmeseness in Midi Z's Burma Trilogy." *Concentric: Literary and Cultural Studies* 43, no. 2: 11–31.

Chan, Shelly. 2018. *Diaspora's Homeland: Modern China in the Age of Global Migration*. Durham, NC: Duke University Press.

Chan, Stephan. 2013. *The Morality of China in Africa*. London: Zed Books.

243

Cheah, Pheng. 2008. "What Is a World? On World Literature as Cosmopolitanism." In "On Cosmopolitanism," edited by James Miller. Special issue, *Daedalus: Journal of the American Academy of Arts and Sciences* 137, no. 3: 26–38.

Chen, Xiaomei. 2002. *Acting the Right Part: Political Theater and Popular Drama in Contemporary China*. Honolulu: University of Hawai'i Press.

Chen, Xiaomei. 2016. "Performing the 'Red Classics': From *The East Is Red* to *The Road to Survival*." In *Red Legacies in China: Cultural Afterlives of the Communist Revolution*, edited by Jie Li and Enhua Zhang, 151–83. Cambridge, MA: Harvard University Asia Center.

Chen, Zhimin. 2008. "Nationalism, Internationalism and Chinese Foreign Policy." *Journal of Contemporary China* 14, no. 42: 35–53.

Cheng, Yinghong. 2011. "From Campus Racism to Cyber Racism: Discourse of Race and Chinese Nationalism." *China Quarterly* 207:561–79.

Chin, Tamara. 2013. "The Invention of the Silk Road, 1877." *Critical Inquiry* 40, no. 1: 194–219.

Chinese Embassy in South Africa. 2015. "Nanfei Huaqiao Huaren anjingshi" 南非華僑華人安警示 [South African overseas Chinese security warning video]. November 20. https://www.youtube.com/watch?v=Q8BTmQA8jQE.

Ching, Victoria Chonn. 2021. "Butting in or Rounding Out? China's Role in Latin America's Investment Diversification." *Global Development Policy Center* GCII Working Paper 016.

Chuku, Gloria Ifeoma. 1999. "From Petty Traders to International Merchants." *African Economic History* 27:1–22.

Clark, Gracia. 2010. *African Market Women*. Bloomington: University of Indiana Press.

Clews, John C. 1964. *Communist Propaganda Techniques*. New York: Praeger.

Clifford, James. 1997. *Routes: Travels and Translation in the Late Twentieth Century*. Cambridge, MA: Harvard University Press.

Clifford, James. 2013. *Returns: Becoming Indigenous in the Twenty-First Century*. Cambridge, MA: Harvard University Press.

Coleman, Simon. 2015. "On Mauss, Masks, and Gifts: Christianities, (In-)dividualities, Modernities." *HAU: Journal of Ethnographic Theory* 5, no. 1: 295–315.

Comaroff, Jean, and John Comaroff, eds. 2000. *Millennial Capitalism and the Culture of Neoliberalism*. Durham, NC: Duke University Press.

Conconi, Alejandra. 2016. "Sombras Chinas" [Chinese shadows]. *Revista Anfibia*. http://revistaanfibia.com/cronica/sombras-chinas/.

Cook, Alexander C. 2019. "Chinese Uhuru: Maoism and the Congo Crisis." *positions: asia critique* 27, no. 4: 569–95.

Corkin, Lucy. 2013. *Uncovering African Agency: Angola's Management of China's Credit Lines*. Surrey, UK: Ashgate.

Crosby, Alfred W. 2004. *Ecological Imperialism: The Biological Expansion of Europe, 900–1900*. Cambridge: Cambridge University Press.

Culler, Jonathan. 2001. "Apostrophe." In Culler, *The Pursuit of Signs*, 149–71. London: Routledge.

Curtin, Philip D. 1984. *Cross-Cultural Trade in World History*. Cambridge: Cambridge University Press.

Dangdai: Primera Revista de Intercambio Cultural Argentina-China. Accessed May 16, 2018. http://dangdai.com.ar/joomla/.

Denardi, Luciana. 2015. "Ser chino en Buenos Aires: Historia, moralidades y cambios en la diáspora china en Argentina" [Being Chinese in Buenos Aires: History, moralities, and changes in the Chinese diaspora in Argentina]. *Horizontes Antropológicos* [Anthropological horizons] 21, no. 43: 79–103.

Derrida, Jacques. 1978. *Writing and Difference*. Translated by Alan Bass. Chicago: University of Chicago Press.

Desai, Gaurav. 2013. *Commerce with the Universe: Africa, India, and the Afrasian Imagination*. New York: Columbia University Press.

Desai, Manisha. 2009. "Women Cross-Border Traders in Africa." *Development* 52, no. 3: 377–86.

Dikötter, Frank. 1992. *The Discourse of Race in Modern China*. Stanford, CA: Stanford University Press.

Dirlik, Arif. 2007. "Global South: Predicament and Promise." *Global South* 1, no. 1: 12–23.

Dirlik, Arif. 2013. "Mao Zedong Thought and the Third World/Global South." *Interventions: International Journal of Postcolonial Studies* 16:233–56.

Donaubauer, Julian, Andrés López, and Daniela Ramos. 2017. "FDI and Trade: Is China Relevant for the Future of Our Environment? The Case of Argentina." In *China and Sustainable Development in Latin America: The Social and Environmental Dimension*, edited by Rebecca Ray, Kevin Gallagher, Andrés López, and Cynthia Sanborn, 33–72. London: Anthem.

Doyle, Christopher. 1997. "Don't Try for Me Argentina." Accessed December 17, 2015. http://www.tonyleung.info/goodies/chris.shtml.

Doyle, Laura. 2014. "Inter-Imperiality: Dialectics in a Postcolonial World History." *Interventions* 16, no. 2: 159–96.

Duara, Prasenjit. 2010. "Asia Redux: Conceptualizing a Region for Our Times." *Journal of Asian Studies* 69, no. 4: 963–83.

Duara, Prasenjit, and Elizabeth J. Perry, eds. 2018. *Beyond Regimes: China and India Compared*. Cambridge, MA: Harvard University Asia Center.

Ellis, R. Evan. 2014. *China on the Ground in Latin America: Challenges for the Chinese and Impacts on the Region*. New York: Palgrave Macmillan.

Ferguson, James. 2006. *Global Shadows: Africa in the Neoliberal World Order*. Durham, NC: Duke University Press.

Ferguson, James. 2015. *Give a Man a Fish: Reflections on the New Politics of Distribution*. Durham, NC: Duke University Press.

245

Fioratta, Susanna. 2019. "A World of Cheapness: Affordability, Shoddiness, and Second-Best Options in Guinea and China." *Economic Anthropology* 6, no. 1: 86–97.

Foreign Languages Press, ed. 1964. *Afro-Asian Solidarity against Imperialism*. Beijing: Foreign Languages Press.

French, Howard W. 2014. *China's Second Continent: How a Million Migrants Are Building a New Empire in Africa*. New York: Alfred A. Knopf.

Friedman, Jeremy Scott. 2011. "Reviving Revolution: The Sino-Soviet Split, the 'Third World,' and the Fate of the Left." PhD diss., Princeton University.

Galeano, Eduardo. 1997. *Open Veins of Latin America: Five Centuries of the Pillage of a Continent*. New York: Monthly Review Press.

Glassman, Jonathan. 1995. *Feasts and Riot: Revelry, Rebellion, and Popular Consciousness on the Swahili Coast, 1856–1888*. Portsmouth, NH: Heinemann.

Goh, Colin, and Y. Y. Woo, eds. 2009. *The Coxford Singlish Dictionary*. Singapore: Forest.

Goldblatt, Howard. 2014. "Ge Haowen: Zhongguo wenxue ruhe zouchuqu" 葛浩文：中國文學如何走出去 [Howard Goldblatt: How can Chinese literature get out?]. *Xinlang wenhua* 新浪文化 [New wave culture], July 7. http://history.sina.com.cn/cul/zl/2014-07-07/113094803.shtml.

Gordillo, Gastón. 2019. "The Metropolis: The Infrastructure of the Anthropocene." In *Infrastructures, Environment, and Life in the Anthropocene*, edited by Kregg Hetherington, 66–94. Durham, NC: Duke University Press.

Graeber, David. 2011. *Debt: The First 5,000 Years*. Brooklyn, NY: Melville House.

Gramsci, Antonio. 1972. *Selections from the Prison Notebooks*. Edited by Quinton Hoare and Geoffrey Nowell-Smith. New York: International Publishers.

Green, Monica H. 2008. *Making Women's Medicine Masculine*. Oxford: Oxford University Press.

Gregory, Robert G. 1993. *South Asians in East Africa: An Economic and Social History, 1890–1980*. Boulder, CO: Westview Press.

Grier, Beverly. 1992. "Pawns, Porters, and Petty Traders." *Signs* 17, no. 2: 304–28.

Guelar, Diego. 2013. *La invasión silenciosa: El desembarco chino en América del Sur*. Buenos Aires: Debate.

Gvili, Gal. 2018. "Pan-Asian Poetics: Tagore and the Interpersonal in May Fourth New Poetry." *Journal of Asian Studies* 77, no. 1: 181–203.

Ha Jin. 2010. "In Defense of Foreignness." In *The Routledge Handbook of World Englishes*, edited by Andy Kirkpatrick, 461–70. New York: Routledge.

Ha Jin 哈金. 2016. "Xiaoshuo jianshi" 小說簡釋 [A brief explanation of fiction]. In *Lianhe wenxue* 聯合文學 (Unitas) 377:34.

Habermas, Jürgen. 1984. *Reason and the Rationalization of Society*. Vol. 1 of *The Theory of Communicative Action*. Translated by T. McCarthy. Boston: Beacon Press.

Habermas, Jürgen. 1985. *Lifeworld and System*. Vol. 2 of *The Theory of Communicative Action*. Translated by T. McCarthy. Boston: Beacon Press.

Hao, Yufan, George Wei, and Lowell Dittmer, eds. 2009. *Challenges to Chinese Foreign Policy: Diplomacy, Globalization, and the Next World Power*. Lexington: University Press of Kentucky.

Harrison, Phillip, Khangelani Moyo, and Yan Yang. 2012. "Strategy and Tactics: Chinese Immigrants and Diasporic Spaces in Johannesburg, South Africa." *Journal of Southern African Studies* 38, no. 4: 899–925.

Hart, Gillian. 2002. *Disabling Globalization: Places of Power in Post-Apartheid South Africa*. Berkeley: University of California Press.

Hasegawa, Tsuyoshi, ed. 2011. *The Cold War in East Asia, 1945–1991*. Washington, DC: Woodrow Wilson Center Press.

Haugen, Heidi Østbø. 2011. "Chinese Exports to Africa." *Forum for Development Studies* 38, no. 2: 157–76.

Haugen, Heidi Østbø. 2012. "Nigerians in China." *International Migration* 50, no. 2: 1–16.

Haugen, Heidi Østbø. 2013. "African Pentecostal Migrants in China: Marginalization and the Alternative Geography of a Mission Theology." *African Studies Review* 56, no. 1: 81–102.

Haugen, Heidi Østbø. 2018. "China-Africa Exports: Governance through Mobility and Sojourning." *Journal of Contemporary Asia*. https://doi.org/10.1080/00472336.2018.1517897.

Haugen, Heidi Østbø, and Jørgen Carling. 2008. "On the Edge of the Diaspora: The Surge of Baihuo Businesses in an African City." *Ethnic and Racial Studies* 28, no. 4: 639–62.

Haynes, Naomi. 2012. "Pentecostalism and the Morality of Money: Prosperity, Inequality, and Religious Sociality on the Zambian Copperbelt." *Journal of the Royal Anthropological Institute* 18, no. 1: 124–39.

Haynes, Naomi. 2013. "On the Potentials and Problems of Pentecostal Exchange." *American Anthropologist* 115, no. 1: 85–95.

Hevi, Emmanuel John. 1963. *An African Student in China*. New York: Praeger.

Ho, Engseng. 2006. *The Graves of Tarim: Genealogy and Mobility across the Indian Ocean*. Berkeley: University of California Press.

Ho, Ufrieda. 2011. *Paper Sons and Daughters: Growing Up Chinese in South Africa*. Athens: Ohio University Press, 2011.

Hood, Johanna. 2013. "Distancing Disease in the Un-Black Han Chinese Politic: Othering Difference in China's HIV/AIDS Media." *Modern China* 39, no. 3: 280–318.

Hoyos, Héctor. 2010. "Three Visions of China in the Contemporary Latin American Novel." In *One World Periphery Reads the Other: Knowing the "Oriental" in the Americas and the Iberian Peninsula*, edited by Ignacio López-Calvo, 150–71. Newcastle upon Tyne, UK: Cambridge Scholars.

247

Hoyos, Héctor. 2015. *Beyond Bolaño: The Global Latin-American Novel*. New York: Columbia University Press.

Huang Handi 黃翰荻. 2015. *Renzhi* 人雉. Taipei: Rye Field.

Huang, Kun. 2020. "'Anti-Blackness' in Chinese Racial-Nationalism: Sex/Gender, Reproduction, and Metaphors of Pathology." Translated by Roy Chan and Shui-yin Sharon Yam. *positions praxis*, June 29. http://positionspolitics.org/kun-huang-anti-blackness-in-chinese-racial-nationalism-sex-gender-reproduction-and-metaphors-of-pathology/.

Huynh, T. Tu, Yoon Jung Park, and Anna Ying Chen. 2010. "Faces of China: New Chinese Migrants in South Africa, 1980s to Present." *African and Asian Studies* 9: 286–306.

Iliffe, John. 1979. *A Modern History of Tanganyika*. Cambridge: Cambridge University Press.

Iovene, Paola. 2014. *Tales of Futures Past: Anticipation and the Ends of Literature*. Stanford, CA: Stanford University Press.

Jameson, Fredric. 1986. "Third-World Literature in an Era of Multinational Capitalism." *Social Text* 15:65–88.

Jameson, Fredric. 1991. *Postmodernism, or The Cultural Logic of Late Capitalism*. Durham, NC: Duke University Press.

Jin Bo-xiong. 2008. *Wo de Feizhou suiyue* 我的非洲岁月 [My years in Africa]. Shanghai: Shanghai Dictionary Publishing.

Karl, Rebecca E. 2002. *Staging the World: Chinese Nationalism at the Turn of the Twentieth Century*. Durham, NC: Duke University Press.

Keenan, Patrick J. 2009. "Curse or Cure? China, Africa, and the Effects of Unconditioned Wealth." *Berkeley Journal of International Law* 27, no. 1: 84–126.

Kelley, Robin D. G., and Betsy Esche. 1999. "Black Like Mao: Red China and Black Revolution." *Souls: Critical Journal of Black Politics and Culture* 1, no. 4: 6–41.

Kissinger, Henry. 2012. *China*. Buenos Aires: Editorial Debate.

Klein, Donald W. 1964. "Peking's Diplomats in Africa." *Current Scene* 2, no. 36: 1–9.

Kuehn, Julia, Kam Louie, and David M. Pomfret. 2014. "China Rising: A View and Review of China's Diasporas since the 1980s." In *Diasporic Chineseness after the Rise of China: Communities and Cultural Production*, edited by Julia Kuehn, Kam Louie, and David M. Pomfret, 1–16. Vancouver: University of British Columbia Press.

Kusimba, Chapurukha M., Tiequan Zhu, and Purity Wakabari Kiura. 2020. *China and East Africa: Ancient Ties, Contemporary Flows*. Lanham, MD: Lexington Books.

Kwa Guan Chong. 2016. "The Maritime Silk Road: History of an Idea." Nalanda-Sriwijaya Centre Working Paper Series No. 23.

Lal, Priya. 2014. "Maoism in Tanzania: Material Connections and Shared Imaginaries." In *Mao's Little Red Book: A Global History*, edited by Alexander C. Cook, 96–116. Cambridge: Cambridge University Press.

Lan, Shanshan. 2017. *Mapping the New African Diaspora in China: Race and the Cultural Politics of Belonging*. New York: Routledge.

Landau, Loren B., and Iriann Stella Marie Haupt. 2007. "Tactical Cosmopolitanism and Idioms of Belonging." Migration Studies Working Paper Series No. 32. Forced Migration Studies Programme, University of the Witwatersrand.

Landsberger, Stefan R., and Marien van der Heijden. 2009. *Chinese Posters: The IISH-Landsberger Collection*. Munich: Prestel.

Lanza, Fabio. 2017. *The End of Concern: Maoist China, Activism, and Asian Studies*. Durham, NC: Duke University Press.

Larkin, Bruce D. 1971. *China and Africa, 1949–1970: The Foreign Policy of the People's Republic of China*. Berkeley: University of California Press.

Le Bail, Hélène. 2009. "Foreign Migration to China's City-Markets." *Asie Visions 19*. Paris: Centre Asie IFRI.

Lee, Ching Kwan. 2018. *The Specter of Global China: Politics, Labor, and Foreign Investment in Africa*. Chicago: University of Chicago Press.

Lee, Christopher J. 2010. "Between a Moment and an Era: The Origins and Afterlives of Bandung." In *Making World after Empire: The Bandung Moment and Its Political Afterlives*, edited by Christopher J. Lee. Athens: Ohio University Press, 1–42.

Lee Kuan Yew 李光耀. 2015. *Li Guanghui huiyilu: Wo yi sheng de tiaozhan Xinjiapo shuangyu zhilu* 李光耀回憶錄：我一生的挑戰 新加坡雙語之路 [Lee Kuan Yew's memoirs: My life-long struggle, Singapore's bilingual road]. Taipei: Shibao chubanshe.

Leguizamón, Amalia. 2016. "Disappearing Nature? Agribusiness, Biotechnology and Distance in Argentine Soybean Production." *Journal of Peasant Studies* 43, no. 2: 313–30.

Lehmann, Angela, and Pauline Leonard. 2018. *Destination China: Immigration to China in the Post-Reform Era*. New York: Palgrave Macmillan.

Li, Jie. 2016. "Introduction: Discerning Red Legacies in China." In *Red Legacies in China: Cultural Afterlives of the Communist Revolution*, edited by Jie Li and Enhua Zhang, 1–22. Cambridge, MA: Harvard University Asia Center.

Li, Zhigang, Michal Lyons, and Alison Brown. 2012. "China's Chocolate City." *African Diaspora* 5, no. 1: 51–72.

Li, Zhigang, Laurence Ma, and Desheng Xue. 2013. "An African Enclave in China." *Eurasian Geography and Economics* 50, no. 6: 699–719.

Lienau, Annette Damayanti. 2011. "Comparative Literature in the Spirit of Bandung: Script Change, Language Choice, and Ideology in African and Asian Literatures (Senegal and Indonesia)." PhD diss., Yale University.

249

Lin Xuezhong 林學忠. 2009. *Cong wanguo dao gongfa waijiao—Wan Qing guojifa de chuanru, quanshi yu yunyong* 從萬國公法到公法外交——晚清國際法的傳入、詮釋與運用 [From public international law to public diplomacy—the introduction, interpretive translation, and use of international law during the late Qing]. Shanghai: Shanghai Guji Press, 2009.

López, Alfred J. 2007. "Introduction: The (Post)Global South." *Global South* 1, no. 1: 1–11.

Lopez, María Alejandra. 2018. "Argentina: Los supermercados chinos suman 20 locales solo en Capital." *América Retail*, August 28. https://www.america-retail.com/argentina/argentina-los-supermercados-chinos-suman-20-locales-solo-en-capital/.

Lowe, Lisa. 2015. *The Intimacies of Four Continents*. Durham, NC: Duke University Press.

Lu Baiye 魯白野. 1959. *Yindu yinxiang* 印度印象 [Impressions of India]. Singapore: Sing Zhou Shijie Shuju.

Lu Xun 魯迅. 2018. "*Zhufu*" 祝福 [Benediction]. In *Lu Xun quanji* 魯迅全集 [Lu Xun's complete works], 2:5–21. Beijing: Renmin chubanshe.

Lu, Yongxiang. 2010. *Science and Technology in China: A Roadmap to 2050*. Beijing: Science Press.

Luhmann, Niklas. 2012. *Theory of Society*. Vol. 1. Translated by Rhodes Barret. Stanford, CA: Stanford University Press.

Lye, Colleen. 2005. *America's Asia: Racial Form and American Literature, 1893–1945*. Princeton, NJ: Princeton University Press.

Ma Ran 馬然. 2016. "*Lun · tan: Guiguguilaibude*" 論 · 談: 歸去歸來不得 [To return or not to return]. *Xiju yu yingshi pinglun* 戲劇與影視評論 [Stage and screen reviews] 4:66–72.

Magnus, Ariel. 2007. *Un chino en bicicleta* [A Chinese on a bicycle]. Bogota: Norma.

Mahajan, Nidhi. 2019. "Dhow Itineraries: The Making of a Shadow Economy in the Western Indian Ocean." *Comparative Studies of South Asia, Africa and the Middle East* 39, no. 3: 407–19.

Masiello, Francine. 2001. *The Art of Transition: Latin American Culture and Neoliberal Crisis*. Durham, NC: Duke University Press.

Mathews, Gordon. 2011. *Ghetto at the Center of the World: Chungking Mansions, Hong Kong*. Chicago: University of Chicago Press.

Mathews, Gordon. 2015. "African Logistics Agents and Middlemen as Cultural Brokers in Guangzhou." *Journal of Current Chinese Affairs* 44, no. 4: 117–44.

Mathews, Gordon. 2017. *The World in Guangzhou*. Chicago: University of Chicago Press.

Mathews, Gordon, Gustavo Lins Ribeiro, and Carlos Alba Vega. 2012. *Globalization from Below*. London: Routledge.

Mathews, Gordon, and Yang Yang. 2012. "How Africans Pursue Low-End Glo-balization in Hong Kong and Mainland China." *Journal of Current Chinese Affairs* 41, no. 2: 95–120.

Mauss, Marcel, and E. E. Evans-Pritchard. 2011. *The Gift: Forms and Functions of Exchange in Archaic Societies*. Translated by Ian Cunnison. Mansfield Centre, CT: Martino Fine Books.

Mawdsley, Emma. 2012. *From Recipients to Donors: Emerging Powers and the Changing Development Landscape*. London: Zed Books.

Mbembe, Achille. 2001. *On the Postcolony*. Berkeley: University of California Press.

McCallum, Stephanie. 2018. "Derailed: Aging Railroad Infrastructure and Precari-ous Mobility in Buenos Aires." PhD diss., University of California, Santa Cruz.

McCann, Gerard. 2013. "From Diaspora to Third Worldism and the United Na-tions: India and the Politics of Decolonizing Africa." *Past and Present* 218, no. 8: 258–80.

McNamee, Terence, Greg Mills, Sebabatso Manoeli, Masana Mulaudzi, Stuart Doran, and Emma Chen. 2012. "Africa in Their Words: A Study of Chinese Traders in South Africa, Lesotho, Botswana, Zambia and Angola." Brent-hurst Foundation. Discussion Paper 2012/03.

Mezzadra, Sandro, and Brett Neilson. 2013. *Border as Method, or, The Multipli-cation of Labor*. Durham, NC: Duke University Press.

Michal, Serge, Michel Beuret, and Paolo Woods. 2012. *Chinafrica*. http://www.instituteartist.com/exhibition-Chinafrica-Paolo-Woods.

Midi Z 趙德胤, dir. 2011. *Guilai de ren* 歸來的人 [Return to Burma]. 2011. Film.

Midi Z 趙德胤, dir. 2012a. *Qiongren liulian mayao touduke* 窮人 · 榴槤 · 麻藥 · 偷渡客 [Poor folk]. Film.

Midi Z 趙德胤. 2012b. "Zai paipian zhi zhong women faxian le yizhong ziyou" 在拍片之中我們發現了一種自由 [We discovered a kind of freedom in filming]. October 1. Interview. http://www.filmcommission.taipei/tw/MessageNotice/NewsDet/2431.

Midi Z 趙德胤. 2014a. "Bie zaihu bieren de dingyi" 別在乎別人的定義 [Don't worry about how other people judge you]. August 18, 2014. Interview. http://opinion.cw.com.tw/blog/profile/202/article/1750.

Midi Z 趙德胤, dir. 2014b. *Bingdu* 冰毒 [Ice poison]. Film.

Midi Z 趙德胤, dir. 2014c. *Haishang huanggong* 海上皇宮 [The palace on the sea]. Film.

Midi Z 趙德胤. 2015. *Ju li bingdu: Zhao Deyin de dianying rensheng jishi* 聚 · 離 · 冰毒：趙德胤的電影人生紀事 [A memoir of my cinema career]. Narrated by Midi Z and transcribed by Zheng Yujong 鄭育容 and Fang Peijing 方沛晶. Taipei: Common Wealth Magazine.

Midi Z 趙德胤. 2016a. "Midi Z: A Film Is Not Just a Film—It Can Be Everything." November 9. Interview. http://www.irrawaddy.com/in-person/midi-z-a-film-is-not-just-a-film-it-can-be-everything.html.

251

Midi Z 趙德胤. 2016b. "Nimen kouzhong de mohuan xieshi, shi women de sheng-huo xianshi" 你們口中的魔幻寫實，是我們的生活現實 [What you call magic realism is our life reality]. November 22. Interview. https://theinitium.com /article/20161123-city-interview-film-director-midi-z/.

Midi Z 趙德胤, dir. 2016c. *Zaijian wacheng* 再見瓦城 [The road to Mandalay]. Film.

Milanovic, Branko. 2006. "La era de las 'desigualdades'" [The age of "inequalities"]. Madrid: Fundación Sistema.

Ministry of Foreign Affairs of the People's Republic of China. 2018. "Full Text of Chinese President's Speech at Plenary Session of BRICS Johannesburg Summit." July 26.

Mintz, Sidney. 1971. "Men, Women, and Trade." *Comparative Studies in Society and History* 13, no. 3: 247–69.

Mohan, Giles, and Ben Lampert. 2013. "Negotiating China: Reinserting African Agency into China-Africa Relations." *African Affairs* 112, no. 446: 92–110.

Mohan, Giles, Ben Lampert, May Tan-Mullins, and Daphne Chang. 2014. *Chinese Migrants and Africa's Development: New Imperialists or Agents of Change?* London: Zed.

Mohan, Giles, and May Tan-Mullins. 2009. "Chinese Migrants in Africa as New Agents of Development? An Analytical Framework." *European Journal of Development Research* 21, no. 4: 588–605.

Monson, Jamie. 2008. "Liberating Labour? Constructing Anti-Hegemony on the TAZARA Railway in Tanzania, 1965–76." In *China Returns to Africa: A Rising Power and a Continent Embrace*, edited by Chris Alden, Daniel Large, and Ricardo Soares de Oliveira, 197–220. London: C. Hurst.

Monson, Jamie. 2009. *Africa's Freedom Railway: How a Chinese Development Project Changed Lives and Livelihoods in Tanzania*. Bloomington: Indiana University Press.

Moore, Sally Falk, and Paul Puritt. 1977. *The Chagga and Meru of Tanzania*. London: International African Institute.

Morrel, Robert. 1998. "Of Boys and Men." *Journal of Southern African Studies* 24, no. 4: 605–30.

Murray, Martin J. 2011. *City of Extremes: The Spatial Politics of Johannesburg*. Durham, NC: Duke University Press.

Muthu, Sankar. 2003. *Enlightenment against Empire*. Princeton, NJ: Princeton University Press.

Needham, Joseph. 1971. *Science and Civilization in China*. Vol. 4, Part 3, *Civil Engineering and Nautics*. Cambridge: Cambridge University Press.

Neuhauser, Charles. 1968. *Third World Politics: China and the Afro-Asian People's Solidarity Organization, 1957–1967*. Cambridge, MA: Harvard University East Asian Research Center.

Ng Kim Chew 黃錦樹. 1996. "Zai 'shijie' zhi nei de huawen yu 'shijie' zhiwai de huaren" 在"世界"之内的華文與"世界"之外的華人 [*Huawen* located inside the "world" and Chinese people located outside the "world"]. In Ng Kim Chew, *Mahua wenxue: neizai Zhongguo, yuyan yu wenxueshi* 馬華文學: 内在中國、語言與文學史 [*Mahua* literature: And the China, language, and literary history that it contains]. Kuala Lumpur: Huashe ziliao zhongxin chubanshe.

Ng Kim Chew 黃錦樹. 1998. "Huawen/Zhongwen: 'Shiyu de nanfang' yu yuyan zaizao" 華文/中文:「失語的南方」與語言再造 [Sinophone/Chinese: The South where language is lost and reinvented]. In Ng, *Mahua wenxue yu Zhongguoxing* 馬華文學與中國性 [Malaysian Chinese literature and Chineseness]. Taipei: Yuan Zun Culture Enterprise.

Ng Kim Chew 黃錦樹. 2001. "Zhongwen xiandai zhuyi? Yi ge mole de jihua" 中文現代主義? 一個未了的計畫 [Chinese modernism? An unfinished project]. In Ng, *Huangyan yu zhenlii de jiyi: Dangdai Zhongwen xiaoshuo lunji* 謊言與真理的技藝: 當代中文小說論集 [Techniques of truth and lies: Collection of writings on contemporary Chinese fiction]. Taipei: Rye Field.

Ng Kim Chew 黃錦樹. 2013a. *Nanyang renmin gongheguo beiwanglu* 南洋人民共和國備忘錄 [Memorandum of the People's Republic of the South Seas]. Taipei: Linking Books.

Ng Kim Chew 黃錦樹. 2013b. "Sinophone/Chinese: The South Where Language Is Lost and Reinvented," translated by Brian Bernards. In Shih, Tsai, and Bernards, *Sinophone Studies*, 74–92.

Ng Kim Chew 黃錦樹. 2015a. "Huawen ke" 華文課 [Huawen class]. In Ng, *Huo xiao le* 火笑了 [The fire smiled]. Taipei: Rye Field.

Ng Kim Chew 黃錦樹. 2015b. "Zhufu" 祝福 [Benediction]. In Ng, *Yu* 魚 [Fish], 15–39. Taipei: Ink.

Ng Kim Chew 黃錦樹. 2016a. "Nanfang wenxue gongheguo" 南方文學世界共和國 [The world republic of southern letters]. Keynote address at a conference, "Sinophone Studies: New Directions," held at Harvard University on October 14–15. An abbreviated English translation of a revised version of this essay is included in this volume.

Ng Kim Chew 黃錦樹. 2016b. *Slow Boat to China and Other Stories*. Translated and edited by Carlos Rojas. New York: Columbia University Press.

Ng Kim Chew. 2016c. "Xingma Huawen wenxue yitilun" 星馬華文文學一體論 [A unified theory of Singapore-Malaysian literature], Lianhe zaobao 聯合早報, May 6.

Nkrumah, Kwame. 1965. *Neo-Colonialism: The Last Stage of Imperialism*. London: Thomas Nelson and Sons.

Nyerere, Julius Kambarage. 2011. *Freedom, Non-Alignment, and South-South Cooperation: A Selection from Speeches, 1974–1999*. Oxford: Oxford University Press.

Nyíri, Pál. 2005. "Global Modernisers or Local Subalterns? Parallel Perceptions of Chinese Transnationals in Hungary." *Journal of Ethnic and Migration Studies* 31, no. 4: 659–74.

Obadare, Ebenezer. 2016. "Raising Righteous Billionaires: The Prosperity Gospel Reconsidered." *HTS Teologiese Studies/Theological Studies* 72, no. 4, a3571. http://dx.doi.org/10.4102/hts.v72i4.3571.

Ogunsangwo, Alaba. 1974. *China's Policy in Africa, 1958–71*. Cambridge: Cambridge University Press.

Overå, Ragnhild. 2007. "When Men Do Women's Work." *Journal of Modern African Studies* 45:539–63.

Oviedo, Eduardo. 2005. "China en expansión" [An expanding China]. Buenos Aires: Editorial Dunken, Colección Thesys UCC.

Oviedo, Eduardo. 2006. "China: Visión y práctica de sus llamadas 'relaciones estratégicas'" [China: The vision and practice of its so-called strategic relationships]. *Estudios de Asia y África* (Colegio de México) 41 (September/December): 385–404.

Parello-Plesner, Jonas, and Mathieu Duchâtel. 2015. *China's Strong Arm: Protecting Citizens and Assets Abroad*. London: London International Institute for Strategic Studies.

Park, Yoon Jung. 2009. *A Matter of Honour: Being Chinese in South Africa*. Lanham, MD: Lexington Books.

People's Republic of China. 2006. "Documento sobre la Política de China hacia América Latina y el Caribe" [A document on China's politics toward Latin America and the Caribbean: Diary of a village]. White paper published in *Diario del Pueblo*, November 11. https://www.fmprc.gov.cn/esp/wjdt/wjzc/201611/t20161124_895012.html.

People's Republic of China, Consejo de Estado. 2016. "*China's Policy Paper on Latin America and the Caribbean*." White paper, November 24. http://english.www.gov.cn/archive/white_paper/2016/11/24/content_281475499069158.htm.

Perdue, Peter C. 2015. "The Tenacious Tributary System." *Journal of Contemporary China* 24, no. 96: 1002–14.

Perry, Donna. 2005. "Wolof Women, Economic Liberalization, and the Crisis of Masculinity in Rural Senegal." *Ethnology* 44, no. 3: 207–26.

Pfafman, Tessa M., Christopher J. Carpenter, and Yong Tang. 2015. "The Politics of Racism: Constructions of African Immigrants in China on ChinaSMACK." *Communication, Culture and Critique* 8, no. 4: 540–556.

Pietila, Tuulikki. 2007. *Gossip, Markets, and Gender*. Madison: University of Wisconsin Press.

Pollack, Shoshana, and Amy Rossiter. 2010. "Neoliberalism and the Entrepreneurial Subject." *Canadian Social Work Review* 27, no. 2: 155–69.

Portes, Alejandro. 1997. *Globalization from Below: The Rise of Transnational Communities*. Oxford: University of Oxford Press.

Pratt, Mary Louise. 1992. *Imperial Eyes: Travel Writing and Transculturation*. London: Routledge.

Prestholdt, Jeremy. 2008. *Domesticating the World: African Consumerism and the Genealogies of Globalization*. Berkeley: University of California Press.

Qiu Kewei 邱克威. 2012. "Lun 'Huayu' yu Malaixiya Huayu yanjiu" 論「華語」與馬來西亞華語研究 [On "Huayu" and Malaysia *Huayu* studies]. *Malaixiya huaren yanjiu xuekan* 馬來西亞華人研究學刊 [Journal of Malaysian Chinese] 15:1–24.

Qiu Ping 裘萍, and Feng Zhoufeng 馮宙鋒. 2014. "Guangzhou fushizhang Xie Xiaodan" 廣州市副市長謝曉丹 [Deputy mayor of Guangzhou City Xie Xiaodan]. *Nanfang dushi bao* 南方都市報 [Nanfang Daily]. 11 月 01 日. http://epaper .nandu.com/epaper/A/html/2014-11/01/content_3337053.htm?div=-1.

Read, Jason. 2009. "A Genealogy of Homo-Economicus." *Foucault Studies* 6:25–36.

Reuters. 2015. "China Will Not Take Path of 'Western Colonists' in Africa— Foreign Minister." January 12. http://www.reuters.com/article/china-africa -idUSL3N0UR1J920150112.

Roberts, Jayde Lin. 2016. *Mapping Chinese Rangoon*. Seattle: University of Washington Press.

Robertson, Clare. 1974. "Economic Woman in Africa." *Journal of Modern African Studies* 12, no. 4: 657–64.

Robertson, Clare. 1984. "Formal or Nonformal Education? Entrepreneurial Women in Ghana." *Comparative Education Review* 28, no. 4: 639–58.

Rofel, Lisa, and Sylvia Yanagisako. 2019. *Fabricating Transnational Capitalism: A Collaborative Ethnography of Italian-Chinese Global Fashion*. Durham, NC: Duke University Press.

Sassen, Saskia. 2003. "Strategic Instantiations of Gendering in the Global Economy." In *Gender and U.S. Immigration*, edited by Pierrette Hondagneu-Sotelo, 43–60. Berkeley: University of California Press.

Sautman, Barry. 1994. "Anti-Black Racism in Post-Mao China." *China Quarterly* 138:413–37.

Schroeder, Richard A. 2012. *Africa after Apartheid: South Africa, Race, and Nation in Tanzania*. Bloomington: Indiana University Press.

Sedgwick, Eve Kosofsky. 1985. *Between Men: English Literature and Male Homosocial Desire*. New York: Columbia University Press.

"Seminar Sponsored by the Afro-Asian Writers' Bureau to Commemorate the 25th Anniversary of Chairman Mao's 'Talks.'" 1967. *Chinese Literature* 9:48–56.

Sen, Tansen. 2017. *India, China, and the World: A Connected History*. London: Rowman and Littlefield.

Sheriff, Abdul. 1987. *Slaves, Spices and Ivory in Zanzibar: Economic Integration of East Africa into the World Economy*. London: James Currey.

Sheriff, Abdul. 2010. *Dhow Culture of the Indian Ocean: Cosmopolitanism, Commerce and Islam*. New York: Columbia University Press.

Shih, Shu-mei. 2001. *The Lure of the Modern: Writing Modernism in Semicolonial China, 1917–1937*. Berkeley: University of California Press.

Shih, Shu-mei. 2013a. "What Is Sinophone Studies?" In Shih, Tsai, and Bernards, *Sinophone Studies*, 1–16.

Shih, Shu-mei. 2013b. "Against Diaspora: The Sinophone as Places of Cultural Production." In Shih, Tsai, and Bernards, *Sinophone Studies*, 25–42.

Shih, Shu-mei. 2013c. "Race and Revolution: Blackness in China's Long Twentieth Century." *PMLA* 128, no. 1: 156–62.

Shih, Shu-mei. 2013d. "Comparison as Relation." In *Comparison: Theories, Approaches, Uses*, edited by Rita Felski and Susan Friedman, 79–98. Baltimore: Johns Hopkins University Press.

Shih, Shu-mei. 2016. "Race and Relation: The Global Sixties in the South of the South." *Comparative Literature* 68, no. 2: 141–54.

Shih, Shu-mei, Chien-hsin Tsai, and Brian Bernards, eds. 2013. *Sinophone Studies: A Critical Reader*. New York: Columbia University Press.

Sigalla, Huruma Luhuvilo. 2014. "Changing Trends in the Tanzania-China Relationship: A Sociological Inquiry into the Mixed Perceptions of the Tanzania-China Relationship on the Eve of Globalization." *Österreichische Zeitschrift für Soziologie* 39, no. 1: 61–78.

Slipak, Ariel. 2013. "¿De qué hablamos cuando hablamos de reprimarización? Un aporte al debate sobre la discusión del modelo de desarrollo" [What are we talking about when we talk about reprimarization?: A contribution to the debate over the discussion of the development model]. VI *Jornadas de Economía Crítica*. Facultad de Ciencias Económicas de la Universidad Nacional de Cuyo, August 29, 30, and 31, Mendoza, Argentina.

Snow, Philip. 1994. "China and Africa: Consensus and Camouflage." In *Chinese Foreign Policy: Theory and Practice*, edited by Thomas W. Robinson and David Shambaugh, 283–321. Oxford: Clarendon Press.

Stoler, Ann Laura. 2008. "Imperial Debris: Reflections on Ruins and Rumination." *Cultural Anthropology* 23, no. 2 (May): 191–219.

Su Shangyao 蘇尚堯, ed. 1993. *Zhonghua renmin gongheguo zhongyang zhengfu jigou* 中華人民共和國中央政府機構 [Central government organs of the People's Republic of China]. Beijing: Jingji kexue chubanshe.

Sun, Yun. 2014. "China's Aid to Africa: Monster or Messiah?" Brookings East Asia Commentary, February 7. https://www.brookings.edu/opinions/chinas -aid-to-africa-monster-or-messiah/.

Suryadinata, Leo. 1997. "Ethnic Chinese in Southeast Asia: Overseas Chinese, Chinese Overseas or Southeast Asians?" In *Ethnic Chinese as Southeast*

Asians, edited by Leo Suryadinata, 1–32. Singapore: Institute of Southeast Asian Studies.

Svampa, Maristella. 2013. "'Consenso de los Commodities' y lenguajes de valoración en América Latina" ["Commodities Consensus" and languages of valorization in Latin America]. *Nueva Sociedad* 244 (March–April): 30–46.

Svampa, Maristella. 2015. "Commodities Consensus: Neoextractivism and Enclosure of the Commons in Latin America." *South Atlantic Quarterly* 114, no. 1: 65–82.

Svampa, Maristella, and Ariel Slipak. 2015. "China en América Latina: Del Consenso de los Commodities al Consenso de Beijing" [China in Latin America: From the Commodities Consensus to the Beijing Consensus]. *Revista Ensambles* 2, no. 3: 34–63.

Sylvanus, Nina. 2016. *Patterns in Circulation*. Chicago: University of Chicago Press.

Tan, Chung. 1998. *Across the Himalayan Gap: An Indian Quest for Understanding China*. New Delhi: Gyan, 1998.

Tan, Yunshan. 1948. "Gandhi and China." *Sino-Indian Journal*. "Gandhi Memorial Number," vol. 1, pt. 2 (December): 20–21.

Than, Mya. 1997. "The Ethnic Chinese in Myanmar and Their Identity." In *Ethnic Chinese as Southeast Asians*, ed. Leo Suryadinata, 113–46. Singapore: Institute of Southeast Asian Studies.

Tinajero, Araceli. 2004. *Orientalismo en el modernism hispanoamericano* [Orientalism in Hispanic modernism]. West Lafayette, IN: Purdue University Press.

Tsui, Brian. 2010. "The Plea for Asia—Tan Yunshan, Pan-Asianism and Sino-Indian Relations." *China Report* 46, no. 4: 353–70.

Udden, James. 2009. *No Man an Island: The Cinema of Hou Hsiao-hsien*. Hong Kong: Hong Kong University Press.

UNCTAD (United Nations Committee on Trade and Development). 2011–14. *World Investment Report*, 2011–2014. https://unctad.org/publications -search?f[0]=product%3A397.

Urdinez, Francisco, Jan Knoerich, and Pedro Feliú Ribeiro. 2018. "Don't Cry for Me 'Argenchina': Unraveling Political Views of China through Legislative Debates in Argentina." *Journal of Chinese Political Science* 23, no. 2: 235–56.

Van Dijk, Rijk. 2009. "Social Catapulting and the Spirit of Entrepreneurialism: Migrants, Private Initiative, and the Pentecostal Ethic in Botswana." In *Traveling Spirits: Migrants, Markets and Mobilities*, edited by Gertrud Hüwelmeier and Kristine Krause, 107–17. New York: Routledge.

Volland, Nicolai. 2008. "Translating the Socialist State: Cultural Exchange, National Identity, and the Socialist World in the Early PRC." *Twentieth-Century China* 33, no. 2: 51–72.

257

Volland, Nicolai. 2017. *Socialist Cosmopolitanism: The Chinese Literary Universe, 1945–1965*. New York: Columbia University Press.

Wang Anyi 王安憶. 1996. "Piaobo de yuyan" 漂泊的語言 [Drifting language]. In Wang Anyi, *Piaobo de yuyan* 漂泊的語言 [Drifting language], 214–28. Beijing: Zuojia chubanshe.

Wang, Ban, ed. 2017. *Chinese Visions of World Order: Tianxia, Culture, and World Politics*. Durham, NC: Duke University Press.

Wang Chen-ho 王禎和. 1996. *Jiazhuang—niuche* 嫁妝一牛車 [An oxcart for dowry]. Taipei: Hongfan.

Wang Dajun 王大鈞, ed. 1979. *Zhongguo dangdai wenxue yanjiu ziliao: Yang Shuo zhuanji* 中國當代文學研究資料：楊朔專集 [Research materials on contemporary Chinese literature: Special collection on Yang Shuo]. Xuzhou: Xuzhou shifan xueyuan Zhongwenxi.

Wang, David Der-wei. 2013. "Post-Loyalism." In Shih, Tsai, and Bernards, *Sinophone Studies*, 93–116.

Wang, David Der-wei. 2015. *The Lyrical in Epic Times: Modern Chinese Intellectuals and Artists through the 1949 Crisis*. New York: Columbia University Press.

Wang Hui 汪暉. 2004. *Xiandai Zhongguo sixiang shi qiyuan* 現代中國思想之起源 [The origins of Chinese thought]. Vol. 1. Beijing: Sanlian chubanshe.

Wang Wan-jui 王萬睿. 2017. "Shaowukegui: Shuwei xieshizhuyi, liuxing gequ yu Zhao Deyin de 'Guixiang sanbuqu'" 少無可歸：數位寫實主義、流行歌曲與趙德胤的「歸鄉三部曲」 [No country for young Men: DV realism, popular songs and Midi Z's 'Homecoming Trilogy']. *Zhongwei wenxue* 中外文學 [*Chung Wai Literary Quarterly*] 46, no. 1: 147–84.

Weber, Max. 2002. *The Protestant Ethic and the Spirit of Capitalism*. New York: Routledge.

Weinstein, Warren, ed. 1975. *Chinese and Soviet Aid to Africa*. New York: Praeger.

Westad, Odd Arne. 2005. *The Global Cold War: Third World Interventions and the Making of Our Times*. Cambridge: Cambridge University Press.

Wilcox, Emily. 2017. "Performing Bandung: China's Dance Diplomacy with India, Indonesia, and Burma, 1953–1962." *Inter-Asia Cultural Studies* 18, no. 4: 518–39.

Williamson, John. 1999. "La democracia y el 'Consenso de Washington'" [Democracy and the "Washington Consensus"]. In *La cultura de la estabilidad y el consenso de Washington*, edited by Manuel Giutián and Joaquín Muns, 118–38. Barcelona: La Caixa.

Williamson, John. 2003. "No hay consenso en el significado: Reseña sobre el Consenso de Washington y sugerencias sobre los pasos a dar" [There is no consensus in the meaning: Review of the Washington Consensus and suggestions on what steps to take]. *Finanzas y desarrollo: Publicación trimestral del Fondo Monetario Internacional y del Banco Mundial* 40, no. 3: 10–13.

Wong Bik-Wan 黃碧雲. 1999. *Lienü zhuan* 烈女傳 [Portraits of martyred women]. Taipei: Datian chubanshe.

Wong Kar-wai 王家衛, dir. 1997. *Chunguang zhaxie* 春光乍洩 [Happy Together]. Film.

Wu He 舞鶴. 1995. *Shi gu* 拾骨 [The bone collector]. Kaohsiung: Chunhui chubanshe.

Xiang, Biao. 2017. "Hundreds of Millions in Suspension." *Transitions: Journal of Transient Migration* 1, no. 1: 3–5.

Yang Songnian 楊松年. 1998. *Xinma zaoqi zuojia yanjiu (1927–1930)* 新馬早期作家研究 (1927–1930) [Research on writers from Singapore and Malaya in the early decades, 1927–1930]. Hong Kong: Sanlian Shudian.

Yang Songnian 楊松年. 2001. *Zhanqian Xinma wenxue gentu yishi de xingcheng he fazhan* 戰前新馬文學本土意識的形成和發展 [On the formation and development of local consciousness in pre–World War II literature of Singapore and Malaya]. Singapore: Xinjiapo Guoli Daxue Zhongwenxi.

Yang Songnian 楊松年, and Zhou Weijie 周維介, eds. 1980. *Xinjiapo zaoqi Huawen baozhang wenyi fukan yanjiu, 1927–1930* 新加坡早期華文報章文藝副刊研究, 1927–1930 [Research on the literary supplements of Chinese-language newspapers in the early decades, 1927–1930]. Singapore: Jiaoyu chubanshe.

Yang, Yang. 2011. "A New Silk Road: African Traders in South China." *China Monitor* 61:4–7.

Yao, Souchou. 1997. "Books from Heaven: Literary Pleasure, Chinese Cultural Text and the 'Struggle against Forgetting.'" *Australian Journal of Anthropology* 8, no. 2: 190–209.

Yap, Melanie, and Dianne Leong Man. 1996. *Colour, Confusion and Concessions: The History of the Chinese in South Africa*. Hong Kong: Hong Kong University Press.

Yeh, Emily T., and Elizabeth Wharton. 2006. "Going West and Going Out: Discourses, Migrants, and Models in Chinese Development." *Eurasian Geography and Economics* 57, no. 3: 286–315.

Yeh, Emilie Yueh-yu 葉月瑜. 2000. *Gesheng meiying: Gequ xushi yu Zhongwen dianying* 歌聲魅影: 歌曲敘事與中文電影 [Phantom of the music: Song narration and Chinese-language cinema]. Taipei: Yuanliu.

Yeh, Emilie Yueh-yu, and William Darrell. 2005. *Taiwan Film Directors: A Treasure Island*. New York: Columbia University Press.

Yoon, Duncan. 2015. "'Our Forces Have Redoubled': World Literature, Postcolonialism, and the Afro-Asian Writers' Bureau." *Cambridge Journal of Postcolonial Literary Inquiry* 2, no. 2: 233–52.

Yoon, Duncan. 2018. "Bandung Nostalgia and the Global South." In *The Global South and Literature*, edited by Russell West-Pavlov, 23–33. Cambridge: Cambridge University Press.

Works Cited

Yu, George T. 1975. *China's African Policy: A Study of Tanzania*. New York: Praeger.

Zeng Shengti 曾聖提. 1959. *Zai Gandi xiansheng zuoyou* 在甘地先生左右. Singapore: Qingnian Shuju. [English version: *By the Side of Bapu* (Rajghat, Varanasi, India: Sarva Seva Sangh Prakashan, 1982)].

Zhan, Mei. 2009. *Other-Worldly: Making Chinese Medicine through Transnational Frames*. Durham, NC: Duke University Press.

Zhang Jingyun 張景雲, ed. 2016. *Wei Beihua wenyi chuangzuo ji* 威北華文藝創作集 [Wei Beihua's literary works, a collection]. Kuala Lumpur, Malaysia: Novum Organum.

Zheng Jiancheng 鄭建成, and Long Xiangyang 龍向陽. 2011. "1949–1964 nian Zhongguo waijiaobu she-Fei diqu si de san ci tiaozheng" 1949–1964 年中國外交部涉非地區司的三次調整 [Three adjustments in the Chinese Ministry of Foreign Affairs' department in charge of the African region, 1949–1964]. *Dangdai Zhongguo shi yanjiu* [Studies in contemporary Chinese history] 5:82–85.

Zheng, Yangwen, Hong Liu, and Michael Szonyi, eds. 2010. *The Cold War in Asia: The Battle for Hearts and Minds*. Leiden: Brill.

Zhongguo jiaoyu nianjian bianjibu 中國教育年鑑編輯部, ed. 1984. *Zhongguo jiaoyu nianjian, 1949–1981* 中國教育年鑑, *1949–1981* [Chinese education yearbook, 1949–1981]. Beijing: Zhongguo da baike quanshu chubanshe.

Zhonghua renmin gongheguo waijiaobu 中華人民共和國外交部, ed. 1958. *Zhonghua renmin gongheguo tiaoyue ji: Di wu ji* 中華人民共和國條約集：第五集 [People's Republic of China international treaties: Fifth collection]. Beijing: Falü chubanshe.

Zhonghua renmin gongheguo waijiaobu 中華人民共和國外交部, Duiwai wenhua lianluoju 對外文化聯絡局, eds. 1993. *Zhongguo duiwai wenhua jiaoliu gailan, 1949–1991* 中國對外文化交流概覽, *1949–1991* [Chinese cultural exchanges with foreign countries: An overview]. Beijing: Guangming ribao chubanshe.

CONTRIBUTORS

ANDREA BACHNER is professor of comparative literature at Cornell University. Her research explores comparative intersections between Sinophone, Latin American, and European cultural productions in dialogue with theories of interculturality, sexuality, and mediality. She is the author of *Beyond Sinology: Chinese Writing and the Scripts of Cultures* (2014) and *The Mark of Theory: Inscriptive Figures, Poststructuralist Prehistories* (2017), as well as the coeditor (with Carlos Rojas) of the *Oxford Handbook of Modern Chinese Literatures* (2016).

LUCIANO DAMIÁN BOLINAGA is associate professor, senior researcher, and director of the Center for Legal, Political and Economic Studies of Asia at the Austral University School of Government in Argentina. He is an expert in international relations with a focus on studies in Asia and the Pacific. His areas of interest are the processes of productive relocation, the phases of the rise and fall of great powers, and the processes of economic modernization. One of his most important publications is *China y el epicentro económico del Pacífico Norte* [China and the Economic Epicenter of the North Pacific] (2013).

NELLIE CHU is assistant professor of cultural anthropology at Duke Kunshan University. She has published on the topics of migrant entrepreneurship, transnational capitalism, global supply chains, migrant labor, and China's urban villages. Her publications include "Jiagongchang Household Workshops as Marginal Hubs of Women's Subcontracted Labour in Guangzhou, China," in *Modern Asian Studies*, as well as "Paradoxes of Creativity in the Age of Fast Fashion in South China," in *Culture, Theory, and Critique*.

RACHEL CYPHER is a PhD candidate at the University of California, Santa Cruz. She is interested in environmental anthropology and gender, as well as coming up with new ways to write ethnography. She is currently finishing her dissertation on the soy and cattle worlds of the Argentine pampas.

MINGWEI HUANG is assistant professor of women's, gender, and sexuality studies. Her research ethnographically explores contemporary Chinese migration to Johannesburg, South Africa, and the reconfiguration of race, capitalism, and empire underway in the twenty-first "Chinese century." Her work has been published in *Scholar and Feminist Online*, *Radical History Review*, *Public Culture*, and *Anxious Joburg: The Inner Lives of a Global South City* (2020).

T. TU HUYNH is associate research professor at Jinan University in Guangzhou, China. Her research interests include studies of Chineseness, racialization, diaspora, historical sociology, culture and political economy, as well as the socialization of contemporary Africa-China relations. Her recent publications include, among others, "'Dear Friends': From People's Cultural Exchange to People's Cultural Production," in *African and Asian Studies* (2020), and "Reflections on the Role of Race in China-Africa Relations," in *New Directions in Africa-China Studies* (2019).

YU-LIN LEE is research fellow at the Institute of Chinese Literature and Philosophy at Academia Sinica, Taiwan. His research interests include literary theory, modern Taiwan literature and cinema, translation studies, environmental studies, and Deleuze studies. His recent publications include *Liminality of Translation: Subjectivity, Ethics, and Aesthetics* (2009) and *The Fabulation of a New Earth* (2015).

NG KIM CHEW is professor of Chinese literature at National Chi Nan University in Taiwan. Much of his academic work focuses on issues relating to Chinese-language literature in Malaysia and Southeast Asia, and he is also a prize-winning creative author. His latest monograph is *Youling de wenzi* [Spectral text] (2019), and some of his fiction is available in English translation in *Slow Boat to China and Other Stories* (edited and translated by Carlos Rojas).

LISA ROFEL is professor emerita, Department of Anthropology, University of California, Santa Cruz. Her academic interests include the intersections of political economy, gender, sexuality, desire, and postcolonial and neocolonial geopolitics. Her current research focuses on China's rising presence in the Global South. Her latest publication, with coauthor Sylvia Yanagisako, is *Fabricating Transnational Capitalism: A Collaborative Ethnography of Italian-Chinese Fashion* (Duke University Press, 2019).

CARLOS ROJAS is professor of Chinese cultural studies at Duke University. His interests include gender and sexuality, visuality and corporeality, and nationalism and diaspora. His recent publications include the monograph *Homesickness: Culture, Contagion, and National Transformation in Modern China* (2015), the collection (coedited with Meihwa Sung) *Reading China against the Grain: Imagining Communities* (2020), and a translation of Yan Lianke's novel *Hard Like Water* (2021).

SHUANG SHEN is associate professor of comparative literature and Asian studies at Pennsylvania State University. Her research interests include Sinophone literature, Asian American and Asian diaspora literatures, Cold War studies, Hong Kong studies, and Southeast Asia studies. She is the author of *Cosmopolitan Publics: Anglophone Print Culture in Semicolonial Shanghai* (2009) and coeditor of a special issue of *Social Text*, "China and the Human" (2011 and 2012).

DEREK SHERIDAN is an assistant research fellow at the Institute of Ethnology, Academia Sinica. He studies China-Africa relations, migration, and the ethics/politics of global inequality. His first book, currently in preparation, is an ethnography of how Chinese migrants and ordinary Tanzanians have come to depend on each other for their livelihoods within an uneven and hierarchical global political economy.

NICOLAI VOLLAND is associate professor of Asian studies and comparative literature at Pennsylvania State University. His research focuses on modern Chinese literature in its transnational dimensions. He is the author of *Socialist Cosmopolitanism: The Chinese Literary Universe, 1945–1965* (2017).

263

debt, 41–42, 44, 99, 104, 114, 116–17, 120, 127, 129–30, 134, 137; concept of, 136–37

Deng Xiaoping, 12

dependency theory, 11

Derrida, Jacques, 6

diaspora, 17, 68, 187, 201–2, 205–6, 212, 215–16, 220, 224–25; Chinese, 174, 214–16, 224, 238; Chinese in Argentina, 151–53, 163–64; Chinese in South Africa, 163, 171; Sinophone, 188–189, 191–92, 194–195, 199–200, 202; Sinophone in Southeast Asia, 188, 190, 195, 198, 201

diplomacy, 26, 39, 70, 173; bilateral, 46, 170; cultural, 15, 21–22, 24, 30, 33; global, 26

displacement, 8, 17, 116–17, 152, 157, 159–60, 162, 164–65, 167, 210, 216

Doyle, Laura, 7

Ecuador, 2, 47, 50, 53, 133

European Union, 1

foreign, 56

Forum on China-Africa Cooperation, 2, 169

free trade agreement(s), 50, 51, 52, 53

French, Howard, 73, 170

Galton, Francis, 65, 74

Gandhi, Mahatma, 67, 224, 226–28, 233, 239

gendered labor, 97–98, 100–101, 110–11, 132

globalization, 61, 65, 77, 96, 149, 152, 156–57, 163, 165, 189, 191; from below, 16–17, 96–97, 111, 238; grassroots, 110, 147; low-end, 64, 96, 106, 109–11

Global North, 4, 21–37

Global South, 1–4, 6–9, 13–15, 17–18, 22–27, 29–30, 32–35, 64–65, 70, 120, 131–33, 174–75, 177, 184–85, 222–24

Goldblatt, Howard, 78

Gorbachev, Mikhail, 3

Graeber, David, 136–37, 148

Gramsci, Antonio, 8

Habermas, Jürgen, 6

Hong Kong, 81–91, 101, 103–5, 151, 154, 163–64, 172, 250, 257, 259

Huawen, 80–82, 86–87, 89, 91, 217, 253

imperialism, 146, 246, 253; anti-, 9, 23, 34, 228; British, 207; Chinese neo-, 70; ecological, 132–33, 144, 146; European, 9, 58, 61–62, 207; infrastructural, 139, 141; socialist, 22; US, 22; Western, 63

India, 18, 26, 36, 43, 68, 222–23, 225–26, 229, 231, 234, 237–38

Indonesia, 10, 26, 36, 82, 104, 194, 232, 235–38

interimperiality, 7

International Monetary Fund, 41–42, 56, 99, 120, 137

Jameson, Fredric, 78, 190, 201, 248

Jiang Zemin, 2

Keynesian Consensus, 43

labor, 70, 72, 93, 120, 137, 157, 163, 165; Chinese, 149, 152; distribution of, 156; division of, 76, 108; gendered, 97, 110, 132; as identity, 160; racialized, 66; reproductive, 97; transnational, 70

laborscapes, 153, 157, 161, 164–65

Lee Kuan Yew, 82–85

literary geography, 29–30, 76

literature, 17; African, 31–32; Chinese, 77, 80–81, 90, 225, 237; Chinese world, 90; Huawen, 80, 87, 90; modern Chinese, 77–78, 81; Soviet, 30, 32, 235; Taiwan, 81–82, 90; third world, 75, 78; world, 15, 30, 75–78, 212

Luhmann, Niklas, 1, 5–7

Malaya, 81, 86, 90, 204, 207, 223, 229, 232–35, 237

Malaysia, 81–82, 84, 86–87, 90–91, 189, 191–93, 204, 206–9, 211–12, 217–18, 233, 238

Mao Zedong, 22, 28, 207, 210
May Fourth Movement, 213
Mbembe, Achille, 74, 170
Mexico, 2, 44, 47, 50, 53, 151
Midi Z, 17, 187–203, 243, 251–52, 258
modernism, 90; Chinese, 90; Indonesian, 235, 237; modernismo, 166
monster or messiah, 3, 14

Nanyang, 218, 225, 231–32
nationalism, 9, 11, 67, 69, 81
neocolonialism, 11, 59
neoliberal, 4, 41, 43, 68, 71–72, 96, 106, 120, 131, 134, 157
new world order, 3–4, 7, 14
new world orderings, 14, 98
Non-Aligned: Movement, 224; nations, 3

One Belt One Road (Belt and Road) Initiative, 2, 13, 34, 41, 60–62
One China Policy, 45
Overseas Chinese, 68, 173, 178, 187, 205, 217

Peaceful Rise Doctrine, 48
periphery, 10, 30, 35, 39–41, 45, 54, 76, 82, 89, 176, 219
Peru, 2, 47, 50, 54, 151
poetics, 227
postcolonial, 22, 25, 63, 66, 68, 70, 262; Africa, 26, 59, 97, 99; Asia, 26; nation-building, 234; nations, 12; studies, 22
Pratt, Mary, 8, 67
premodern, 5–6, 60, 64–65, 76
prosperity doctrine, 115–17, 119–23, 127, 129–30
Protestant Ethic, 115, 120

racism, 109, 116, 129, 133, 144, 182, 184; anti-Black, 67
realism, 30, 195
revolution: Chinese, 70; Cuba, 44; Cultural Revolution, 10, 21, 25, 29, 33, 210; Indonesian Revolution, 235–37; world, 13, 22, 33; Xinhai, 84
revolutionaries, 22, 223, 228

security: crime, 178, 181; international, 3; United Nations Security Council, 39
Silk Road, 34, 60, 65, 71
Singapore, 12, 18, 81–85, 87, 90–91, 207, 213, 218, 224–25, 233, 235
Sinophone, 81, 89, 187, 189, 193–94, 196, 198–200, 202, 215–17, 222, 237; cinema, 190, 198, 201; literature, 224, 263; studies, 238; world, 190, 192, 194, 196, 200, 202
socialism, 9–10, 67; international, 10, 69, 207
Socialisme ou Barbarie, 5
socialist internationalism, 7, 13, 172
solidarity, 21–24, 29, 31, 33–34, 157–58, 194, 200; international, 3, 21; Soviet Committee for, 27
Southeast Asia, 1, 59, 64, 67, 187, 193, 195, 198, 205, 213, 223
sovereignty, 9, 11, 46, 56, 70, 120, 139
Soviet Union, 10, 12, 22, 24, 27, 29–30, 32–33, 35, 40, 47, 56
system, international, 35, 38–39

Taiwan, 13, 17, 44–45, 50, 81–82, 84–87, 89–91, 135, 138, 188–94, 199–201, 217–18, 262; New Cinema, 17, 188–90, 195, 199–201, 203
Tanzania, 60, 63–64, 69–73, 100
Thailand, 31, 82, 102, 130, 189–93
third world, 4, 10–12, 22–23, 25, 31–32, 37, 224; literatures, 76, 78
third world nation, 3, 12, 27, 29, 76, 138
tianxia, 9–10, 12, 14–15
traditional Chinese medicine, 8

United Nations, 23, 26, 39, 45, 50
United States, 35, 40–41, 44, 46, 77–78, 102, 105, 131, 133, 137, 147–48, 150
Uruguay, 2, 50, 53, 147

Venezuela, 2, 47, 50–51, 53–54, 57, 137, 176
Vietnam, 31, 80, 194

267

CPSIA information can be obtained
at www.ICGtesting.com
Printed in the USA
BVHW071024030223
657823BV00022B/139